Never Trust a Teacher
Fight to Make Things Right!

Let One Family's Journey Through Public School Show You How

An Empowering, One-of-a-Kind Guide For
Parents & Students of All Ages

Flip Book Over For
Twenty-Two Timeless Tips
To Trump the System

Susan Fay Ryan
Doctor of Education

authorHOUSE®

AuthorHouse™
1663 Liberty Drive
Bloomington, IN 47403
www.authorhouse.com
Phone: 1 (800) 839-8640

Published by AuthorHouse 11/27/2017

ISBN: 978-1-5246-9882-9 (sc)
ISBN: 978-1-5246-9880-5 (hc)
ISBN: 978-1-5246-9881-2 (e)

Library of Congress Control Number: 2017910510

Print information available on the last page.

Front cover designed with stock imagery ©Thinkstock.

This book is printed on acid-free paper.

Detailed credits for illustrator, Ray Russotto, can be found on p. v.

Author's photo by Christopher Bridge, North Palm Beach, Florida

Layout of book by author along with artwork for
cover of Twenty-Two Timeless Tips

Susan Fay Ryan, Ed.D.

Dr. Ryan speaks as a parent of five children who attended public school and a teacher with thirty-six years of experience in the classroom. Even though she believes that the good teachers do undoubtedly outnumber the bad, she concentrates in this book on warning caregivers about teachers of low caliber, with little conscience, who wield power and influence over their children.

Author's Background: 36 Years as an Educator

Born Susan Fay in Boston, Massachusetts
Grew up in Milton, Massachusetts
Married Joseph Ryan, Captain, U. S. Merchant Marine
Resident of Cohasset, Massachusetts - 11 years
Resident of Palm Beach County, Florida - since 1974
Mother of 5 children; Grandmother of 8 children

Education
Milton High School
Newton College of the Sacred Heart - Now Boston College
Mount Holyoke College - **Bachelor of Arts Degree**,
Political Science
Boston University - **Master of Science Degree**, Journalism
Suffolk University - Education classes
Nova Southeastern University - **Educational
Specialist Degree**, Gifted Child Education
Nova Southeastern University - **Doctor of
Education Degree,** Early & Middle Childhood
Florida State University - **Master of Science Degree,**
Library & Information Studies

Publications Dissertations/Theses – Practicum Papers
Eric Document: *Nurturing children's literacy through
the establishment of a community-funded preschool
lending library.* Eric Document: *Advocating cultural
literacy and creative play for youngsters.*
University of Illinois, Urbana-Champaign

Outstanding Educational Improvement Projects:
*Increasing language & literature appreciation in
a gifted class.* Nova Southeastern University

English Language Studies
University of London; University of Oxford: Exeter College

Teacher of the Year Program*:* One of twenty-one
Palm Beach County District Finalists - 1994

Author's Background (continued)

**Certification: National Board for
Professional Teaching Standards - 2004**

**Spanish Language Studies
Ongoing, part time since 2002:**
Palm Beach State College;
University of Santiago de Compostela, Galicia, Spain;
Florida Atlantic University; Academia de Profesores
Privados de Español: Antigua, Guatemala

25 years as a Classroom Teacher
Language arts students of varying levels

11 years as a School Library Media Specialist/Teacher
Critical Thinking; Video Production

**12 Years as President of Board of Directors:
Thelma B. Pittman Jupiter Preschool** in Jupiter, Florida

Illustrator's Background
Ray Russotto, creator of the caricatures, is a freelance
illustrator living in Deerfield Beach, Florida. His cartoon
strip, *It's the Humidity* ran weekly for several years in
the opinion page of the *Sun-Sentinel*. His work has also
appeared in the *Miami Herald,* the *Boca Raton News, Jazziz*
magazine, and *Mutual Funds* magazine. A collection of his
editorial cartoons for the *Boca Raton News* was published
as a limited edition in a book entitled *BocaRatoons*.
Find Ray at his website: **ray@cartoonsbyray.com**

Song: *I'm a PRO! Preschooler Reading Often*
Brett Dupuis of Jupiter, Florida, wrote the musical score,
played the guitar, and sang the solo selections of the song.
Brett attended Jupiter High School and the
University of Florida. He studied music extensively
for many years and performed in a number of
innovative bands. **Susan Fay Ryan** wrote the lyrics.
Singing the chorus were preschool students,
T. Parchment, J. Ross, and **C. Scott.**

Dedicated

To

Good Teachers Everywhere

And to

My Beloved Family

In Whom

I am Well Pleased.

Our Exceptional Journey Continues.

Eternal Thanks

To

Captain Joe Ryan

Who made it all possible,

My Daughter Fay Ryan

*Who read the first draft and offered
detailed, constructive criticism,
giving me confidence to persevere;*

All of My Children

Who encouraged me unconditionally.

With Warm Wishes

To

My only sibling, my brother

Philip Fay
Whom I love very much;

With Affectionate Memories of
Our Parents, Philip Fay & Elinore Burns Fay;

Our Grandparents:
John J. Burns & Lilian Wholey Burns,
Peter A. Fay & Louise A. Fay;

My Eight Grandchildren,
Our Hope for the Future:

RHR, ARC, ERC, PHR,
AMR, SSR, PJR, NAR;

My Extended Family of
Curtins, Fays,
Hannas, & Ryans.

Special Appreciation

To

My Loyal, Steadfast Friend

Dorothy M. Roberts

Who remained with me throughout the long haul,
reading and rereading every word with her precise, critical eye,
providing suggestions and communicating with me daily
until the journey was complete;

All my Lifelong Friends who are very dear to me,
notably: Ann P. K., Carole M. W., Carole S. M.,
Cornelia S., Ellen G. L., Faith E. M., Ginny O'H. B.,
Josephine K. C., Leah C. M., Mary Jane E. E., Marta M.,
Nancy W. D., JoAnn M., Joanne L.O., Lynn O'T. D.,
Muriel K. R., Kathy W. K., Kay W. F.,
Patty Hall K., Rosemary S. D.,
& Coleman Leo H.,
Dynamic Family Colleague
From Days of Yore;

Mis Amigas Especiales Leniyems y Yanelaika de Cuba,
Miami, y North Palm Beach, FL; Escritora Elssie Cano
de Ecuador quien me dio inspiracion para escribir,
Mis Amigos de Colombia, Constanza y Joe;
Mi Amigo Lino, de Mexico,
Con Quien Puedo Hablar Español;
Mis Amigas Ada de Cuba y Adriana
de Argentina, Muy Buena Gente;

Mis profesores extraordinarios de Antigua,
Guatemala: *Norma Moreno, Vinicio Gomez,*
Fernando B.; Mis Amables Anfitriones Aura, Rogelio,
y Los Novios R. & P.

Fond Remembrance

of

Two Angelic Friends:

Beth Goudey
Who cheered me on each day

&

Her Boston College Classmate
Beth Sullivan,

aka

Sister Thérèse of the Child Jesus

Whose prayers gave me strength.

Muchísimas Gracias

al

Intérprete Internacional

José José
José Rómulo Sosa Ortiz

El Príncipe de la Canción

Ciudadano de México y de los Estados Unidos

Quien, sin saberlo, me acompañó por
cinco años mientras yo escribía este libro.
Su voz incomparable, su estilo único,
sus interpretaciones magníficas del corazón y
del alma, su sensibilidad, la dedicación a su trabajo,
su sabiduría, su coraje frente a la adversidad,
y su precioso sentido del humor
me ayudaron a seguir adelante,
y también a mejorar mi español.

Gracias por todo, Maestro,
y gracias por tu llamada personal,
el 9 de enero, 2016 @ 2:17 P.M.
Un Día Inolvidable!

También aprecio a tu amada esposa,
Sarita Salazar Sosa,
Tu verdadero Ángel de la Guarda
y el Gran Amor de tu Vida.
Gracias, Sara, por tu Cariño.

Translation of previous page

With great thanks to International singing star
José José, The Prince of Song, Citizen of Mexico & the
United States who, ***without knowing it,*** accompanied me
for five years while I wrote this book. His incomparable
voice, his unique style, his magnificent interpretations
sung from his heart and from his soul, his sensitivity,
his dedication to his work, his wisdom & courage during
Great Adversity, along with his precious sense of humor,
helped me continue onward while improving my Spanish.

Thank you for everything, **Maestro**, and
gracias for your personal phone call on
January 9, 2016 @ 2:17 PM.
An Unforgettable Day!

I also appreciate your beloved wife**,**
Sara Salazar Sosa,
your true
Guardian Angel and
Great Love of your Life.
Gracias, Sara, for your Kindness.

CONTENTS

Page

Preface 1

Introduction 6

Chapter

1   Wise, Wonderful Wendy & Wanda.................. 11

2   Florida, Here We Come................................ 15

3   Deadbeat, Derelict Dave............................ 21

4   Milton, Massachusetts
     Grammar School Revisited 25

5   Zero Options: Back to Florida 33

6   *Sesame Street* Sadie: Shameless Shirker 41

7   Unintelligent Intelligence #1:
     Superficial Screener Sal.............................. 51

8   Bugsy the Befuddled Bug Man...................... 57

9   Lessons from Bugsy and the Bad Brad.......... 65

10   Dishonorable Honor Society Advisor #1:
     Do-Little-or-Nothing Debbie 75

11   Secret Slacker Sam & Others 83

12   Broken-Promise Buddy................................ 93

Chapter		Page

13	Year-Round School: Randall the Retaliator.... 99
14	Paula the Perfect Pro 117
15	Manual-Bound Manny 123
16	Reign of Terror Tess 133
17	Dishonorable Honor Society Advisor #2: Malicious, Malevolent Max..........................149
18	Illiterate Liza & the Literati........................159
19	Wretched Retread Reeba 169
20	Working the System: Reaching for the Stars 181
21	Unintelligent Intelligence #2: Rigid Robot Rob...189
22	Loans 'R Us.. 205
23	¡Ay Caramba! #1: Middle School and High School Learners of Spanish 217
24	¡Ay Caramba! #2: Older Adult Learners of Spanish & More 227

Conclusion 233
South of the Border 237
Family photo 246
Citations & Reference Notes 247

Preface

Although I earned a doctorate in Early and Middle Childhood Education and became more enlightened in the field as a result, I did not complete the requirements of the degree until my children were in college or graduate school. Like Swiss developmental psychologist, Jean Piaget, however, I was a keen observer of my children from their infancy onward.

Piaget's detailed studies of his three children were a significant component of his research, and the education of all children became of great importance to him, ***"Only education is capable of saving our societies from possible collapse, whether violent, or gradual."*** [1]

As a mother, a teacher, and a lifelong student, education has represented a high priority for me. In one respect, I outdid Piaget in that I had five children to observe. Like most mothers, I too, believe that my observations and interactions with my children carry weight.

Not working outside of the home until my oldest child was thirteen, I was absorbed with each stage of my children's physical and intellectual development. I took considerable care to see that my children were prepared to experience success within a public school setting. Even if my family's finances had made it possible to send five children to private schools, my husband and I believed in the public school system.

Contrary to the convictions of many experts who note that there are differences between the sexes in their modalities of learning, I never observed that to be the case with my children. In their early-age literacy development, my three sons learned in the same way and within the same time frame as my two daughters.

When they entered school, they all worked hard, studied the same subjects, and did well. They were admitted to excellent universities and went on to complete their coursework in graduate school. Four of my children became attorneys. My youngest child immersed himself passionately in the field of Latin American & Caribbean Studies.

Nevertheless, there had been obstacles. On several occasions, I found myself locking horns with their public school teachers or school administrators in order to right a wrong that had made my child a victim of incompetence. From these personal, first-hand experiences and from being on the front line as a classroom teacher for thirty six years, I figured out how to maneuver my way through the public school system.

I learned how to fight for my children when necessary. Guy Strickland in his book, **Bad Teachers,** cautions parents about the dangers of placing too much trust in teachers,

"Most teachers are nurturing, self-sacrificing, and inspiring, but it would be naïve to pretend that they all are. Some are indifferent, some are incompetent, and a few are downright destructive." [2]

Through exposure to program deficiencies and a number of unconcerned, undistinguished teachers, I became proficient at recognizing bad academic practices. As a young mother, I had not foreseen becoming a constant vigilante for my children's fair treatment in the classroom.

All but one of those unfortunate experiences with teachers occurred many years ago under the aegis of The School District of Palm Beach County. Parents, however, need to be mindful that they may run into bad teachers anywhere, in any time period, who may be guilty of the same sins:

A. SINS OF OMISSION

- **everlasting avoidance: doing nothing to rectify a longstanding, student-related problem**

- **refusal to change an ineffective, harmful teaching method**

B. SINS OF COMMISSION

- **calculated retribution toward a student for a teacher's bruised ego**

The bulk of this book covers the higher grades and is designed primarily for parents of public school students. It is not intended for those parents who can afford elite, private preparatory schools. Yet, it is within the realm of possibility that bad teachers may lurk in the hallowed halls of ivy. The last chapter of the book focuses on older adult learners who seek a degree after an extended absence from school.

Even though I have found many weak links in public schools, I remain a firm advocate for public education. My expertise lies with students placed on traditional academic tracks designated as, basic, regular, advanced or gifted.

Other than being certified to teach gifted children, I have no training in teaching children who qualify for the various special needs classes covered by the *Individuals with Disabilities Education Improvement Act* (IDEIA)—although in some states, gifted education falls under this act.

There were times when students with *Specific Learning Disabilities (SLD)* had been *mainstreamed* into my class, but they were, nonetheless, directly under the supervision of a trained SLD expert with whom I could consult if necessary. As a teacher in The School District of Palm Beach County, I learned that public schools can be well equipped to teach students with learning disabilities. I worked for ten years in one middle school and twelve years in another where special education coordinators supervised teams of certified SLD teachers.

Those teachers held ample caseloads of learning disabled students. All of the teachers had undergone extensive training in order to become certified, including holding a graduate certificate or a master's degree, as required in many states.

The basic guidelines or parental **Tips** offered on the **Flip** side of this book entitled, **Literacy and Love Go Hand in Hand: Twenty-Two Timeless Tips to Trump the System,** may or may not apply to students with learning disabilities. Their parents or teachers can make that decision.

I formulated them originally for my own children, first with newborns and preschoolers in mind and later for students in kindergarten through grade twelve, for whom I became qualified to teach. These *Tips* were designed to prepare children for a happy, successful life at school.

In spite of the fact that this book's title sends a harsh warning to parents and students, I believe that the majority of public school teachers are dedicated to their profession. They work tirelessly to teach their academic discipline in an effort to produce informed, confident, and successful students.

Throughout my tenure, I was fortunate to work with a number of outstanding colleagues. My own children and grandchildren have benefited from the expertise of some of the best instructors in the country. I taught my children to hold their teachers in high regard.

Notwithstanding, it is imperative for parents to know that they must be *ever vigilant*—always on the lookout for teachers at every level who cheat their students out of a proper education while managing to remain above scrutiny by school administrators and parents.

A strong supporter of teachers unions, I was a union member for thirty-three years, from 1977 through 2010, until my retirement. From my observations, if poor teachers remain rooted in schools, it is not the fault of the union but the fault of inattentive school administrators who continue to apply the following lax methods of oversight:

- **being ignorant of how and what their teachers teach**

- **failing to address bad attitudes on the part of their teachers**

- **neglecting to mandate training opportunities targeted to their teachers' deficiencies**

Of necessity then, in defense of their children, parents and caregivers must be the watch dogs, the **whistle blowers**, and the prime movers for bringing about meaningful change.

In her book, ***Battle Hymn of the Tiger Mother,*** Amy Chua has set forth seven driving principals by which she governed her children. Her fifth rule is

". . . (5) if your child ever disagrees with a teacher or coach, you must always take the side of the teacher or coach;" . . .[3]

My advice states the contrary, and I offer convincing, concrete examples as to why you should ...

Never Trust a Teacher!

Introduction

During my thirty-six years in the education field, I attended more than one thousand conferences with fellow teachers, administrators, parents, and students. In so doing, I met with and observed the behaviors of outstanding educators, mediocre educators, and out-and-out worthless educators.

Throughout my tenure, I took advantage of a myriad of training programs that gave me further insight into the teaching profession. The following offerings via The School District of Palm Beach County prepared me to assist developing teachers in their performance:

- **Florida Performance Measurement System—trained as a State Certified Observer**

- **Project T.E.A.C.H.—trained in Teacher Effectiveness And Classroom Handling**

- **Educator Support Program—trained in Clinical Education**

Based on these additional credentials, my principals would, when necessary, ask me to observe teachers as part of their formal evaluations. During the observations, I could identify those teachers who knew how to teach their subject matter and those who did not. I could observe those teachers who knew how to help their students and those teachers who served only to confuse them.

Human nature dictates that from time to time, even the best of teachers may make mistakes. When they are made aware of such aberrations, *good teachers* will recognize and repair them. They will, at a moment's notice, set things right with their students.

Bad teachers will refuse to acknowledge blunders and will engage in cover ups. Parents and caregivers must realize that teacher missteps will occur. On behalf of the children in their

6

care, parents need to pay close attention to test grades and homework assignments and learn how to resolve a variety of problems with all types of teachers.

In birth order, averaging two years apart, my children are Joy, Nick, Tony, Fay, and Thad. My first child began public school in 1966, and my fifth child finished public school in 1989. School records would reveal that the five Ryan children were socially adjusted, high-achieving students with excellent attendance and no discipline problems.

They interacted with friends of similar interests and abilities. Generally well liked by their teachers, they experienced collectively at least two hundred, harmonious teacher-student matchups from the start of kindergarten through twelfth grade.

Still, as one of my children advised me for this book, *"Don't make us sound perfect. We were not."* And so be it; there was neither a Valedictorian nor an Olympian among them. All things considered, though, they excelled in their academics, and they were strong competitors in sports. Some were involved in band, and some were elected as class officers.

Without a doubt, their personalities are decidedly distinct from one another, but as in many families, my children have several interests in common. For this book, I focus on a shared character trait—that of wanting to earn top grades in their school work and always striving to do their personal best in their athletic endeavors.

Because my children attended the same local schools with little teacher turnover, they had many of the same teachers at each level of attendance: elementary, middle, and high school. For the majority of those twenty-three years, school-related matters progressed extremely well for all of them.

If they felt uncertain about the subject being taught or had questions as to how a teacher had graded their work, they would have been comfortable in talking with that teacher on their own to obtain answers. They had enough confidence to advocate for themselves. There was no need for my assistance.

Regrettably, however, there were some extreme cases where I had no choice but to initiate a dialogue with incompetent or unfair teachers in order to protect my children from an academic injustice.

Circumstances forced me to experience **thirteen critical showdowns** with such teachers. At no time, did I engage in ad hominem attacks against teachers—either at the school in their presence—or when referring to them at home in front of my children.

Along with my memory of events, I describe our unpleasant scenarios from detailed file notes and other documentation that I maintained for each incident.

Sometimes, I was unsuccessful in effecting changes that were needed. In others, I emerged victorious but not without battle scars, in terms of the emotional toll exacted by each situation—along with the extra time and effort required to mount my children's defense.

Within a personal narrative, I present those confrontations as they occurred chronologically. Parents and caregivers of school-age children can benefit from looking carefully at these stressful, yet revealing interventions. Undeniably, there are inadequate teachers, guidance counselors, and administrators working in schools today.

I find **vivid reminders** of them time and again with educators responsible for the seven of my eight grandchildren, currently of public school age. Inside these pages, parents will be alerted to behaviors and practices of bad teachers and learn what they can do to insulate and protect their children who fall prey to academic **malfeasance** in the classroom.

Descriptions of my children's bad teachers have been altered herein to some extent, but the unerring facts of each encounter remain unchanged. Portrayed with pseudonyms and illustrated with non-identifying caricatures at the beginning of each chapter, those real-life teachers have long since retired. Some are deceased.

In Chapter 13, one good teacher is referred to as Teacher Y in order to conceal identity. In some chapters, I refer to a discipline as *Academic Subject X* in order not to identify the class or its teacher.

With the passage of time, students or other faculty members of that era would be unable to recognize those negligent teachers with any degree of certainty. Furthermore, what took place in our private conversations behind closed doors was known by those persons in attendance—and by no one else.

Only two of the chapters highlight good teachers, but indeed, the **good** did predominantly outnumber the **bad.** Even so, I focus here on the inferior teachers as a warning to all student caregivers that what happened to my children **then** could happen to their children **now,** or in the **future,** while teachers of low caliber with little conscience still remain firmly entrenched in classrooms, wielding power and influence over students.

Below the caricature of each teacher, I have indicated the names of family members featured in that chapter. If, in reading this book, teachers or administrators should happen to recognize themselves from one of our scholastic skirmishes, their identity will continue to remain our little secret.

Chapter 1
Wise, Wonderful Wendy & Wanda

**They were knowledgeable, enthusiastic,
and lovingly responsive to children's needs.**

Family members: Joy, Nick, Tony, Fay

In 1965, my two oldest children got off to a superb start in a nurturing preschool in the town of Cohasset, Massachusetts. Although the town is known for its affluent residents and seaside mansions, we were a family of slightly above average income, living in a remodeled gardener's cottage, once part of a large estate.

We were enamored with the town primarily for its proximity to the ocean, for its beautiful craggy coastline, and for its historic New England common in the center of the village.

Back then, one of the highest status symbols for Cohasset families with young children was sending a child to preschool at the Cohasset Community Center. Then known as a *nursery school,* it offered separate programs for three and four-year olds. The fees were reasonable. Admission criteria was simple: *First come; first served.*

Never an early riser, I made a great sacrifice for my children. When registration time came, I arrived at the center at six-thirty in the morning with two children in tow. Triumphantly, I sat down outside on the stone stoop, first in line, to wait for the nine o'clock opening.

I excitedly enrolled Joy and Nick in the corresponding age group programs. When my next two children were of preschool age, I followed the same procedure with the same results.

Ms. Wendy and Ms. Wanda had worked at the school for many years and were acclaimed by parents throughout the town. *They were knowledgeable, enthusiastic, and lovingly responsive to children's needs.* It was fascinating to witness the mutual admiration between teachers and students.

Learning and singing songs was a big part of the day along with creative play, dramatizations, role playing, and a variety of pre-reading and socialization activities that contributed emphatically to the children's early childhood development.

When looking back and ascribing reasons for my children's academic success, I always point to that first formal learning experience with those remarkable teachers where it all began.

Advisory: Choose a quality preschool with teachers who truly care about children.

Chapter 2
Florida, Here We Come

**Accordingly, we were a large family
with little money and no jobs in sight,
headed south to parts unknown.**

Song: *Floridays*
Singer, Songwriter: Jimmy Buffet

Ryan family

After their nursery school experience, Joy, Nick, Tony and Fay moved over to the Cohasset public schools. The two older children attended Joseph Osgood Elementary School and Deer Hill Middle School. Joy attended Cohasset Junior High School for two years.

All things educational went smoothly for each of them. I was a stay-at-home mom basking in the freedom that a distinguished school system with top-notch teachers could provide. My husband, Joe Ryan, the sole breadwinner, was a United States Merchant Marine ship master of ocean-going vessels that traveled all over the globe.

In late summer of 1970, Captain Joe retired from his job in an effort to find work close to home and lead a more traditional family life. This decision, although sudden when it occurred, had been under consideration for a few years. Still we had not managed to accumulate any substantial savings. As a result of this change that we both wanted, our finances plummeted, but our bills remained constant.

A realtor located a family to rent our house for eight months so that we could do a trial run in Florida. We believed we could live more economically in the warmer climate. Because we had been fortunate to obtain a substantial rental fee, money remained for other expenses after we made our monthly mortgage payment.

The tenant was delighted with our unusual, five-bedroom home with an ocean view from the third level. General Dynamics had brought him and his family to the Northeast on a temporary assignment and had provided all expenses for the relocation, including a housing allowance. By a stroke of luck, his time frame coincided closely with the extent of our planned absence from home.

That September, in the middle of packing for the trip, I learned that our fifth child would be joining us in the spring. As usual, I was happy about the upcoming arrival, but since my husband was by nature a worrier, I decided to defer revealing this news to him until after we reached our destination.

For the moment, Captain Joe had enough stress. *Accordingly, we were a large family with little money and no jobs in sight, headed south to parts unknown.* Had he been fully updated, I was certain that Captain Joe would have canceled our move without hesitation. We both knew that returning to a guaranteed income on the high seas was always an option.

Some might say that my decision seemed whimsical, but I believed it was important to explore a permanent lifestyle change in Florida. It was good for the children to have their father at home.

Fortunately, our immediate plans had fallen into place with relative ease. In all truth, I did enjoy the unconventionality of it all. Being an optimist, I had great faith that things would work out for us. The children were good travelers. They read much of the time and played games.

On our first journey south as a family, Captain Joe initiated a search for *South of the Border* signs, luring drivers and their passengers to *Pedro's* tacky tourist trap in South Carolina just south of the North Carolina border. Travelers of this route are familiar with the hundreds of billboards that line Interstate 95 for about one hundred fifty miles in either direction, north and south.

Deplorably, I realize now that we were unthinking and insensitive to Mexican stereotypes, portrayed in the advertisements which indicate nothing about the enormous diversity of people and cultures within Mexico. Finding the signs was simply a way of keeping the children amused and occupied on the long, monotonous drive.

By assuming the persona of *Pedro,* the American, non-Latino owner, gave unsolicited assistance to travelers through his signs, *"Pedro's Weather Forecast: Chili today, hot tamale!"* [4]

Being naturally competitive, the children decided to award points. The winner was the person who called the most signs. I kept score. To earn a point, a player had to yell out, *"South of the Border!"* before anyone else. The trick was not to be deceived by a competitor's signs that contained the same vivid colors: orange, yellow, red, green and black.

Each sign was set back from the highway, often partially obscured from view by trees and other foliage—until just the right moment when it loomed large. If someone called out the sign for **Thunderbird Motor Inn** by mistake, that offender incurred a penalty. Players needed to exercise extreme caution. The children played this game for years whenever we drove back and forth to Massachusetts.

Usually, but not always, the older children got the better of the younger ones. Occasionally Captain Joe wedged himself into the act, deliberately distracting the children by pointing to phantom landmarks on the opposite side of the highway. At other times, he became a full-fledged, fierce competitor himself.

After the big buildup, we usually stopped briefly for gas at **South of the Border,** took a quick look around, used the clean rest rooms, and then went on our way. This ritual broke up the trip, provided comic relief, and was great fun for the kids.

Another travel tradition, born at the same time, was stopping at the **Days Inn - Oasis Motel** on Interstate 95, outside of Savannah, Georgia. Not in the caliber of the Ritz, to say the least, this well-maintained motel, nevertheless, seemed to be far ahead of its time with regard to its supersized, curvaceous swimming pool surrounded by lush plantings.

The focal point of the pool was an impressive waterslide with a small tunnel crafted of realistic, artificial rock in the middle of the slide. The children found it exhilarating. It was not a modern-day water park by any means. Yet, it had great appeal for my youngsters, and even today, their frolicking and cavorting at the **Oasis** conjures up colorful memories of their happy-go-lucky youth.

Shortly after our arrival in South Florida, we rented a custom-built, one-story house in Pompano Beach, directly across from the intracoastal waterway, one block from the ocean. An enormous banyan tree shaded the expansive corner lot from the scorching Florida sun. All of the rooms in the two-bedroom house were oversized.

High ceilings added dimension to the living room and adjoining family room. An attractive, light-colored brick fireplace was on one wall of the living room, floor to ceiling. With an unusually warm winter that year, however, we had no occasion to light a fire. Two children slept in one bedroom, and two children slept in the family room.

On the opposite side of the living room was a large screened patio with a separate entrance at the far side of the house. Adjoining the patio was an extra twin-sized bedroom and full bath. To our great advantage, the owners of the dwelling allowed us to rent out that section of the house to two middle-aged sisters from Michigan who, like us, were happy to spend the winter on Riverside Drive.

Our new tenants were good-natured, responsible, and independent. The layout of the porch offered privacy for both families. Conveniently for all, they kept to themselves, preoccupied with their own pursuits. Their rent was an unanticipated, most welcomed financial gain.

Captain Joe looked into operating a small sightseeing boat on the intracoastal waterway, but no opportunity opened up for that enterprise. In the nick of time, he began receiving his union retirement pension from the *International Organization of Masters, Mates & Pilots* (IOMMP).

After spending twenty-five years as a ship's officer, he had recently become eligible for that benefit. Having been a young retiree, he received that allotment for almost thirty years thereafter.

A little money here, and a little money there, kept us out of the poor house. When Joy and Nick were at school, Tony,

Fay and I enjoyed carefree trips to the beach—while Captain Joe studied for the Massachusetts real estate exam.

A casual visit to the Pompano Beach municipal swimming pool unexpectedly initiated Joy and Nick into the world of competitive swimming under the guidance of their very first swim coach: twenty-five year old, patient and encouraging *Coach Jim*. The three other Ryan children would eventually take up that sport, and all of them stayed with it through high school. *Thanks, Gentleman, Jim!* Now my grandchildren are competitive swimmers.

Joy, Tony, and Fay competed on college varsity swim teams. Captain Joe became an avid fan of the activity and soon adopted Doc Counsilman's book, *The Science of Swimming,*[5] as his bible. Studying and reading kept his mind off additional responsibilities and expenses to be incurred in the spring.

Chapter 3
Deadbeat, Derelict Dave

How long, did he suppose, that this
arrangement of neglect could continue?

Family members: Joy & Nick

Immediately after settling into our new surroundings in early October of 1970, we enrolled Joy and Nick in a Pompano Beach elementary school. Typical of area schools at the time, all classrooms were designed with one door that opened to an outside corridor and a courtyard with an array of Florida palm trees. This was a novel concept to us accustomed to the closed-in schools of New England.

Additionally, we learned that unlike the schools of Massachusetts and the school districts of many other smaller states, Florida's schools are regulated by **counties,** and **not** by cities or towns. Our beloved Cohasset was a self-contained school district all to itself, and in those days, the town had one elementary school, one middle school, one junior high school, and one high school,

In sharp contrast, Pompano Beach was just one of many cities that made up the School District of Broward County. Today, according to its website, this district with headquarters in Fort Lauderdale, is the **sixth** largest in the United States in terms of population.

It was in that system that I began my first of several clashes with an *inferior teacher.* That school was and still is an excellent school, but that one teacher forced me to realize that my role as a mother had expanded.

I needed to be not only the overall architect of my children's education, but the daily field operations manager as well. Up until then, I had naively thought that I could rely on my children's teachers to bear full responsibility for their instruction.

Although my education and that of my brother had been of primary importance to my parents, they had, without any qualms, delegated that responsibility to our teachers. They did not get involved with school assignments.

All of those educators had been competent, hardworking, and principled. But, for my children, it was a different story. From that moment on, I was forced to acknowledge that I could not place *blind trust* in my children's teachers.

In the middle of the third week in her new fourth-grade class, Joy came home to tell me that she had finished her assigned school work each day in less than two hours.

Her teacher allowed her to read a library book for the remainder of the day. She hadn't mentioned it earlier because she thought that the teacher was getting to know her ability and that this routine would soon change.

Besides, she loved reading independently. A fast reader, Joy had read several books in that short time, and she had made some new friends with whom to enjoy recess on the playground. School was all fun and games in sunny, southeastern Florida.

The next morning, after a night of worry with little sleep, I met Joy's teacher, Deadbeat Derelict Dave, as he stood by the classroom door waiting for his students to arrive. My husband accompanied me. We spoke to him with regard to Joy's daily activities in his class, and he confirmed her report of the previous afternoon.

He told us that Joy was a *"gifted"* child and that he was unable to provide the curriculum she needed. Whether she was officially labeled gifted would remain to be seen.

The reality was that her teachers in Cohasset had prepared her well—so well that she was far ahead of the fourth-grade Florida class she had entered. What bothered me most was that Deadbeat Dave had not been conscientious enough to notify us of this dilemma.

How long, did he suppose, that this arrangement of neglect could continue?

Heedlessly, he had made no effort to provide for his new student, nor alert her parents to details of the vast wasteland that was his class. He had chosen the path of least resistance.

After Captain Joe and I determined that Dave's class was no longer an option for Joy, we met with Dave, the guidance counselor, and the school's principal. The meeting was very cordial.

Dave was not the only fourth grade teacher. The guidance counselor could have recommended a transfer to another teacher at the same level, but after talking with Joy and carefully reviewing her records, she decided that the better choice would be to move her up to fifth grade.

Without a hitch, Joy had no difficulty keeping up with the new curriculum while it simultaneously demanded that she work to the best of her ability. She remained comfortable in that class for the duration of our time in Florida. Once she had moved beyond Derelict Dave's unresponsiveness, Joy spent several academically rewarding months at that Pompano Beach school.

Nick's case was different. In spite of being the top second-grade student, according to his teacher, his assignments still challenged him. Nick and his parents were pleased to learn that he earned the highest grade in his Florida history test in a subject completely new to him.

He also took the lead in a Thanksgiving performance that his class presented to the entire school. In his Massachusetts accent and wearing an extra tall, black Pilgrim hat, he delivered from memory a speech by Captain Myles Standish, the controversial defender of the Plymouth Colony. Indeed, Nick had represented his native state honorably in the pageant.

Some years later, I was advised that Florida was significantly ahead of the rest of the country in offering classes for gifted students, but there had been nothing available for my children at that time.

Moreover, up until then, I had not heard the word *gifted* used in the context of students in a public school classroom. Being evaluated for a gifted program would bring about another hurdle for Joy and Nick in the near future.

Advisory: Act quickly to protect your child from a negligent teacher.

Chapter 4
Milton, Massachusetts
Grammar School Revisited

**To put it more bluntly, the Milton school
system had kicked my children out of school.**

**Song: *You've Got a Friend*
Singer, Songwriter: Carole King**

Family members: Joy & Nick

When we arrived back North near the end of April, we brought home with us our healthy, new family member, our fifth child and third son, Thaddeus, who was born in Broward General Hospital in Fort Lauderdale, on April 19, 1971.

The three-day drive lulled him to sleep throughout the trip. As a permanent reminder of our sojourn to the South, we gave him the middle name of Broward in honor of the hospital and the county in which he was born.

Although we had enjoyed our seven-month stay away from home, we had no plans to return to Florida fulltime. Primarily, we were attached to our families and to our roots in and around the suburbs of Boston.

Thaddeus enjoyed being different from his siblings. Despite the fact that his four grandparents of Irish descent were somewhat taken aback by his uncommon name, Thaddeus Broward Ryan was proud of it.

Upon researching his predecessor much later, he learned that Napoleon Bonaparte Broward was a daring, Florida river pilot who had also, like Captain Joe, worked on ships along the New England coast.

Ultimately, N. B. Broward became governor of Florida. Along with the distinction of being the only Ryan born in Florida, Thad also reveled in the fact that he had arrived in this world on **Patriot's Day,** an important holiday for the people of Massachusetts. From his point of view, he personified the best of both worlds.

Rather than remain in Florida until the end of the school year, we returned to Massachusetts shortly after Thad was born. Not only were our families anxious to see the new baby, but Captain Joe had a summer business to run.

A year earlier, he had purchased a *party boat* to accommodate fishing enthusiasts a few miles outside of Boston Harbor. To make the most of the season, he put the *Toby Two* in the water on the first of May. During the week, he operated the boat by himself, but his brother Phil, an engineer, offered much-needed assistance for weekend excursions.

Since the Cohasset tenants would remain in our house through the end of May, we divided up our family between the homes of grandparents. Joe and I and the three youngest children went to live with his parents on Fossdale Road in Dorchester, a quiet tree-lined street tucked away behind Ashmont Station, not far from the Milton line.

Joy and Nick moved in with my parents who continued to live in the Milton house where I grew up at 32 Sias Lane. My parents' backyard abutted the soccer field of Milton Academy, the world renowned private, preparatory school.

A historic, **tossed** stone wall, then and now, separates the two properties. Just up the street from my childhood home was, and still is, the Milton Public Library. As I frequently did in my youth, my children enjoyed taking the short walk to the library as a form of entertainment.

Before Captain Joe retired from the big ships, and I was attending graduate school at Boston University, we lived in the back section of that house when Joy and Nick were very young.

My parents had remodeled the house just for us with a separate entrance, galley kitchen, great room, spectacular fireplace, full bathroom, and an extra staircase leading to two existing bedrooms on the second floor.

An oversized picture window on the first level offered a panoramic view of Milton Academy's soccer field, always a marvelous place for children to run and play when official games or practices were not in session.

After we moved to Cohasset, my parents decided to move into our apartment. They rented out the main section of their house to two teachers retired from Boston Latin School. Understandably, Joy and Nick felt completely at ease in my parents' house. It had been their first home before our family welcomed new members.

Both sets of grandparents were happy to be close to the children once again. Traveling from one house to another took only ten minutes.

With seven weeks of school remaining, I enrolled Joy and Nick in the Vose Elementary School that I attended as a child. They were comfortable with that arrangement. Endowed with a sense of adventure, they did not mind being new students once again or attending three different schools in one year. They had started out in Cohasset immediately after Labor Day before our move to Florida in late September.

I was extremely surprised but especially pleased that both Joy and Nick found themselves in classes taught by two of my former teachers. Twenty-four years earlier, when I was a student at Vose School, I had thought of those teachers as elderly, but they were still proceeding full speed ahead.

Another bonus for being in Milton was that Leah and Jack, two of my childhood friends, lived a few houses away from my parents. Their five children were the same ages as mine, and with the exception of the babies, they had been friends for years, often visiting, sometimes sleeping over at one another's house.

Our family activities were moving forward and on target until a week later, when I received a startling phone call from the office of Milton's Superintendent of Schools. An assistant to the superintendent ordered me to keep my children home the next day—and every day thereafter. **To put it more bluntly, the Milton school system had kicked my children out of school.**

During Joy and Nick's registration process, I listed both the Milton and Dorchester addresses as part of their contact information. It seems that a low-level administrator had taken a closer look at the information I provided and incorrectly surmised that my husband and I were permanent residents

28

of Dorchester—audaciously trying to enroll our out-of-town children in the highly-ranked Milton public schools.

There had been a number of precedents for this scam, and the school system was attempting to crack down on any and all *school crashers*.

Luckily, I knew a results-oriented liaison person who resolved the dilemma for us. My dentist, also a friend, was a member of the Town of Milton School Board. After I explained the situation to him, he immediately placed a phone call to the superintendent.

To enhance my profile, he not only emphasized that I had been raised in Milton and attended Milton public schools, but that I had been elected to two, three-year terms as a Milton Town Meeting Member shortly after I graduated from Mount Holyoke College.[6] That was true, although it had nothing to do with the matter at hand. Yet as long as his tactic benefited my children, I was thankful.

Without delay, the superintendent called me personally to apologize, and all was well from then on. Joy and Nick did not miss a day of school. Academically, they kept up with their classmates and earned outstanding grades on their final report cards of the year.

When I spoke with the superintendent, I mentioned that I had been a student in his *hygiene class* twenty-one years earlier as an eighth grader. Even though I knew there was no chance he would remember me, that fact gave us an opportunity to talk comfortably with one another, recollecting a bit of Milton history and discussing changes to the educational system.

What I did not disclose, was that several of my classmates and I had been so impressed by the youthful good looks of Coach Harry that we were often distracted from the lesson at hand. Having been a talented and handsome football player when he was at Milton High School, he had become his alma mater's Head Football Coach at the same time he was our teacher.

In fact, that job was his first teaching position after serving in World War II and later earning a master's degree in education. To his credit, he always conducted himself with the utmost of professionalism. Students came away with a solid understanding of the lessons he had prepared for them.

Before the concept of **middle school** had taken hold, Milton had two junior high schools which encompassed grades seven through nine. One of them, the Mary A. Cunningham Junior High School, was a free-standing building in East Milton, on the opposite side of town from Milton High School. My school, known as Central Junior High School, was located near the center of town where I lived.

Not a free-standing building, Central was housed in the very same building as Milton High School. My friends and I thought that we were quite cool to be studying in proximity to the high school students, and in some instances, walking to and from school, we pretended that we *were* high school students. Perhaps we fooled no one, but we enjoyed the occasional pretense.

With a few exceptions, Central Junior High School students attended seventh through ninth grades on the **first floor** of the two-story building, while Milton High School students attended tenth through twelfth grades on the **second floor** of the building. Some faculty members, like the future superintendent, taught both levels of students.

When they entered tenth grade, Central students made new friends on their move up to the **second floor**. At that time, Cunningham students joined us on the upper level. From that point on, we were **united** as **one class** for our three years together at Milton High School.

In any event, in 1971, it was gratifying to know that our former mesmerizing hygiene teacher from Central Junior High School had worked his way up the system to the position of

Superintendent of Schools. And according to reliable sources, he enjoyed the reputation as an outstanding administrator. Both the Town of Milton and Milton High School had good reason to be proud of their native son.

Chapter 5
Zero Options: Back to Florida

The vagabonds were on the run once more.

Song: *On the Road Again*
Singer, Songwriter: Willie Nelson

Ryan Family

Not long after our return to Cohasset, we decided to put our home on the market. Our monetary situation was continuing to spiral downward, but we thought we would be in good shape if we could sell our house and buy another one nearby that came with built-in income property.

There were then, and still are, many large, older homes in Cohasset, similar to that of my parents' home in Milton, having one or more apartments within the main house, each with a separate entrance.

Regular income from a tenant in one such apartment could have provided enough extra income to make a substantial difference for us, just as the steady rent from our Florida tenants had been able to fortify us when we needed that extra boost.

Captain Joe, in the meantime, tried his hand at real estate. In 1972, I finished my thesis to earn a Master of Science degree in Journalism at Boston University's School of Public Communication.

I had begun the program twelve years earlier, shortly after I was married. Procrastinating after completing my coursework, I had let my motherly duties take precedence over the thesis, but the fear of forfeiting my credits was always on my mind.

My professor, noted author and scholar in mass communications, Dr. David Manning White, generously allowed me to return to my thesis and waived any deadline that could have been imposed. I continue to hold unending appreciation for his acceptance and understanding.

Next, I began to take education classes at Suffolk University in Boston, so that I could soon pursue a teaching career and help out with our finances. As part of earning a Massachusetts educator's certificate, I completed a three-month student internship at Cohasset High School.

Captain Joe and I had analyzed the numbers, and we were confident that our financial plan could succeed. Nevertheless, the depressed economy of the times worked against us.

My husband's venture into the real estate profession coincided with the recession of the 1970's. He was a hardworking, honest broker, who made some excellent sales of South Shore properties but not enough to keep pace with our demanding monetary needs.

In this period of *"economic stagnation,"* [7] the volume of home sales was low, the selling price of a home was low, and the resulting commission on a sale was even lower.

Our own house at 7 Haystack Lane took three full years to sell. Just off scenic Jerusalem Road, it had been moderately priced, but the unusual home did not appeal to traditional buyers.

With the small equity remaining after the sale, we were in no position to buy another home for several years. Furthermore, we had learned from our time spent in Florida, that it would be less expensive to live there with our large family of growing children. Realistically, we saw only one option.

We sold or gave away almost all of our possessions and headed back to the *Sunshine State* to start over as permanent residents. Most profoundly, we knew that we would miss our families and friends and the outstanding Cohasset schools, but I vowed that my children's education would not suffer. I convinced myself that I could deal with any bad teachers we might encounter. *The vagabonds were on the run once more.*

Traveling in a crowded station wagon pulling a *U-Haul-It,* we were a family of seven along with our docile Golden Retriever, Becky and our hyperactive Irish Setter, Bridget. We left the Boston area on the weekend of July Fourth 1974, *Independence Day!*

Thaddeus was too young for the fast-paced **South of the Border** competition, but on the next vacation trip heading north, he was fully indoctrinated. [At the end of the book, readers will find **Thad's version** of that trip which he recounted for a graduate writing class at Hamline University in Minnesota.]

As we made our way south for the second time, **Pedro's** vivid sign, reached out and spoke to me with his wisdom of the ages, **"Take it easy on the road of life."** [8]

This time, upon the recommendation of my husband's friend, Franklyn, a fellow ship's officer from Massachusetts, we settled farther north in Palm Beach County in Tequesta, where we remained for thirty years, long after our children had grown and moved on.

His friend had purchased land in the nearby Jupiter Inlet Colony for an investment. The inlet colony, by the ocean, is adjacent to Tequesta, but it is a separate municipality all to itself.

Jupiter and Tequesta are in essence interlocking towns, referred to as the Jupiter/Tequesta area. Jupiter is known for its historic Jupiter Lighthouse which has protected mariners since 1860. Captain Joe had made countless sea voyages guided by its beacon.

Both towns offer ocean access. Several unincorporated areas adjoin the village of Tequesta. Winding through each of these coastal towns is the Loxahatchee River, officially designated by the Federal Government in 1985 as a *National Wild and Scenic River.*

Aside from its tropical, rainforest climate and its luxuriant vegetation, Tequesta, to us, resembled a small New England town. At that time, about four thousand residents lived in the actual Village of Tequesta.

Captain Joe and I had an affinity for the ocean. Throughout most of our lives, we lived only a few miles from the water. In

1974, the majority of homes in Tequesta were less than fifteen years old, built to accommodate the influx of Pratt Whitney employees who had moved to Florida from Connecticut in the 1960's.

Coming from historic New England, I found it odd to be living amongst such newness. My parents' home in Massachusetts was a Victorian farmhouse. When we arrived, townspeople made us aware of celebrities in the Jupiter area: Perry Como, Burt Reynolds, and Tammy Wynette, all of whom owned houses there at the time, and none of whom we ever met. Tequesta boasted of National League pitching legend, Bob Shaw, and later New York Jets superstar, Joe Namath.

We spent four weeks trying to find a house to rent in Tequesta but could find no landlord willing to rent to a family with five children and two medium-sized dogs. Who could disagree with any of them? Strangely enough, an apartment complex manager willingly accepted us.

Accordingly, just before school began, we settled into a two-bedroom Tequesta apartment. It was a far cry from the spacious home we had left, but it was the best we could do. The neighborhood was quiet and convenient to shopping.

We put up two sets of bunk beds in one bedroom for four children, and Joy slept on a day bed in the living room. It sounds cramped, but we were not at home often, and we spent a most agreeable ten months there.

The weather was perfect all winter, and on many weekends, we had barbecues or picnics at the beach. We joined the North Palm Beach Country Club, ten miles to the south of us, via a swim membership, so that Joy, Nick and Tony could continue their competitive swimming each day after school.

In the spring of that year, all swim team members at the club were invited to participate in a swim meet in the Bahamas and stay as guests in private homes. Although the trip had been well chaperoned, it was especially exciting for my children because they were out of the country—and without their parents.

Of particular interest to Captain Joe and me were the following facts about Tequesta, still true to this day.

- Tequesta has a well-supplied branch library, part of the greater Palm Beach County Library System. (Our family checked out books often.)

- There have never been public schools in Tequesta.

- The southern part of Tequesta lies in Palm Beach County; the northern part of Tequesta lies in Martin County.

- Public school students living in the southern part of Tequesta attend nearby Jupiter schools which fall under the supervision of The School District of Palm Beach County. (The Ryans lived in this area.)

- Public school students living in the northern part of Tequesta attend schools farther north which fall under the supervision of The School District of Martin County.

- Some parents living in the northern end of Tequesta prefer to send their children to private schools in Palm Beach County, rather than have them travel north to Martin County schools.

Once we were settled, I set out to find my first teaching job. Surprisingly, the Superintendent of Schools of Palm Beach County had, not long before we arrived, issued a mandate to all principals *prohibiting* them from hiring any teacher with a master's degree.

I was, therefore, automatically excluded from applying for a public school teaching position—ironically penalized for having earned my long overdue Boston University diploma. It was a hard-and-fast rule based upon limited state revenue allotted for education.

Having no choice, I took an alternate route. In August of 1974, I launched my teaching career with a low-paying position at a private school in the neighboring town of Palm Beach Gardens. From that day forward until my retirement, my free-flowing way of living completely vanished.

Being a stay-at-home mother of five children was ever so much easier for me than being a classroom teacher. In spite of the fact that teaching brings about untold rewards every day, I found it to be—and still believe it to be—one of the most difficult of professions. At the end of that year, my school went bankrupt. I continued to teach for two more years in different private schools, still with meager wages.

My transition to public school came in 1977, when I began teaching in Martin County in rural Indiantown about thirty miles northwest of Tequesta. With that change, my salary increased, and I took advantage of the affordable, family health insurance offered.

In 1979, after the hiring ban was lifted, I accepted a position with The School District of Palm Beach County. That move made me feel as if I had jumped up to the major leagues. I remained there teaching for thirty-one more years. Benefits were better, and I was able to work much closer to home. While there, I earned three more advanced degrees without taking time away from my job.

About seven years before retirement, I decided to work toward certification through the National Board for Professional Teaching Standards (NBPTS). This was an arduous task of self-reflection and analysis that incorporated along with it a lengthy writing component and a number of student-centered projects.

Aimed at making excellent teachers even better, certification procedures required continued use of tried and true **Best Practices**, while encouraging flexibility of style and a willingness to adopt new modalities of teaching and learning.

I was fortunate to work in cooperation with an uncommonly, competent colleague who taught gifted students. He cheerfully and patiently offered me invaluable assistance throughout the lengthy process. After I earned that certification, I returned to my recent and ever-evolving passion of studying the Spanish language.

In my youth, I never for a moment imagined that I would become a teacher, let alone be a student for almost all of my life.

It is not an exaggeration, though, to say that my extended time in the classroom, both as a **teacher** and as a **student,** along with my wide-ranging associations with teachers—as a **parent** of my own children—has given me a distinct advantage at observing and recognizing *good* and *bad* teachers.

Chapter 6
Sesame Street Sadie:
Shameless Shirker

**She looked at her with a disapproving scowl and
scolded abruptly, "Stop raising your hand.
Don't answer any more questions."**

Family members: Tony & Fay

Not without some trepidation on my part, our children started school in Palm Beach County, Florida, in August of 1974. Joy entered ninth grade, her first year of high school, and Nick entered sixth grade, his first year of middle school. Both took their classes at the high school on a system of **double sessions**. Joy attended school in the morning whereas Nick attended school in the afternoon.

Thaddeus joined a class for three-year olds at a Lutheran preschool in Tequesta, two afternoons per week. He spent the remaining time at his father's new business, **The Captain's Chair**, which featured unfinished furniture along with a line of quality paints and wood stains.

Thad was proud of having his very own wooden toy box for storing his books and playthings. Between customers, Joe and he read books together, played games, and made twice-daily trips to the ice cream shop a few doors away.

Mindful of the earlier, unproductive experience in Broward County with Joy and Deadbeat Dave, I decided to change things up with regard to our son Tony.

Instead of enrolling him with a normal progression into third grade, I submitted his cumulative folder from Cohasset and declared him to be a fourth grader on the day of registration.

What might have been considered an underhanded, risky move, went off seamlessly with nary a glitch. Tony was tall for his age, and no one noticed the discrepancy between grade levels from one year to the next. Looking back on it now, if I had been questioned, I could have justified my action, but there was no need to do so.

Tony's energetic teacher, *Clever Cathy*, enjoyed his upbeat but mild-mannered disposition. He excelled at his teacher's well-planned lessons, and he had a happy year. To top it all off, Cathy arranged the unprecedented number of eleven field trips—never to be equaled in any of my children's classes before or after.

All in all, it was a splendid introduction to Florida schools and a way for Tony to become acquainted with a variety of Palm Beach County's worthwhile attractions.

During the second term, I confessed the truth to Cathy about Tony's semi-clandestine jump to a higher grade. She was surprised but not one bit concerned. Tony had blended in all along with the rest of her fourth-grade class.

As it turned out, I never knew what teacher Tony would have had if he had entered third grade. I knew only that I was satisfied with my decision, and that I had made the right choice for my child. Tony sailed along without a care for the remainder of elementary and middle school. Each school offered him intellectual challenges and much fun.

That recipe was a sound one. Tony enjoyed his teachers, and he had a diverse group of friends. In fact, he had no problems whatsoever until *seven years* later.

Then, as a junior in high school, he came up against two power-hungry teachers who, to the detriment of their students, wanted to preserve their **egos** and the *status quo*— no matter what the cost (Chapters 13 & 16).

For her first school year in Florida, Fay was headed for first grade. In her case, unlike that of Tony, I chose *not* to bump her up to a higher level after we arrived. I mistakenly held the belief that first grade would be essential to her educational growth. I was *dead wrong*. In that class, Fay became subjected to the nonteaching practices of *Sesame Street* Sadie who designed her morning curriculum as follows:

- Students watched *Sesame Street* until recess.

- Students watched *Sesame Street* upon their return.

- Students went to lunch.

Fay has no recollection of doing math with her so-called teacher. It seems that there was a small segment on *Sesame Street* that Sadie—in her mind's eye—designated as a math lesson. Otherwise, *Sesame Street* Sadie felt no compunction to prepare follow-up lessons on that subject.

In the afternoon, students engaged in a low-level reading activity. Every day, without fail, Sadie held up several, individual 5" x 8" index cards—one at a time—each displaying one three-letter word which she asked the children to identify. Upon seeing them, Fay was able to read each word instantly.

While the other students were trying to decipher the words, Fay raised her hand repeatedly, and with permission, broke the silence to offer the correct response.

After a while, *Sesame Street* Sadie became increasingly annoyed with Fay. **She looked at her with a disapproving scowl and scolded abruptly, "Stop raising your hand. Don't answer any more questions."**

Fay could not see much point in remaining in that class. She had been reading well above grade level back in Cohasset by the end of kindergarten.

Cohasset teachers had pioneered a new system wherein a select group of kindergarteners moved up to first grade for the last two weeks of school to work with their next year's teachers. Fay's kindergarten class met in the morning, and for the remainder of the year, she spent the afternoon in first grade concentrating on reading.

It was a thrilling experience for the children, and what made it even more special was that Fay had been assigned to the class of *Fabulous Faith,* a family friend from my youth.

Faith's mother and my mother had met before they were married when they worked as librarians at the Boston Public Library, North End Branch. Faith was an outstanding teacher who lit up the classroom with her natural caring manner, her expertise in early childhood, and her spontaneous sense of humor. Fortunately for Tony, she had been his first-grade teacher for an entire year.

I've long recognized the value of *Sesame Street* and the role it played in all of my children's preschool upbringing. Using it, however, as a substitute for first-grade curriculum was insupportable. I was panicked once again and thought, *"What have we done to our child?"*

Fay's new school scenario was intolerable. *Sesame Street* Sadie's teaching style was even worse than that of Deadbeat Derelict Dave. At least he had allowed Joy to check out library books for her reading enrichment.

Within a few weeks of starting school, Captain Joe and I met with school administrators and the guidance counselor to discuss our daughter's unhappy plight. It was the counselor who made the final placement decision.

In a case, very similar to Joy's, the counselor saw no benefit in having Fay make a lateral move to another first grade teacher. She was too advanced for that level. There was no alternative but to move Fay up to second grade where fortunately, she found herself with hard-working, *Personable but Particular Patricia,* who wanted the best for her students.

Fay kept up with the rest of the class without a problem. As circumstances would have it, Fay unexpectedly became the **third Ryan** to skip a grade. Thankfully, for the remainder of elementary school and most of middle school, Fay learned from excellent teachers and had no further incidents.

One remarkable third-grade teacher named *Goldie* truly symbolized her name in terms of the quality of education she provided. It was not until **several years later** that Fay experienced a problem with the grading system of a middle school teacher (Chapter 11).

Over time, I have observed that even some very respectable teachers employ questionable tricks of the trade that they manage to conceal from supervisors, students, and parents.

When we moved to the area, the schools of Jupiter were not the high-ranking schools they are today. Jupiter was noticeably more of a country town at the far northern end of the county. Later, there was a building boom and along with it came many demanding parents with education uppermost on their minds.

In the early days, the teachers in Florida seemed to have had more freedom in planning their curriculum. This can be an advantage or a disadvantage for students, depending upon the work ethic, intelligence, and creativity of the teacher.

Undoubtedly, there were many conscientious teachers in that era, but without uniform standards, there was plenty of room for **shirkers.** *Sesame Street* Sadie was indeed a **shirker** of the highest order.

In the late 1970's, after Fay's incident with Sadie, the School District of Palm Beach County, under the guidance of the state of Florida—and not without controversy—adopted a *Unified Curriculum.* It was long before the polemical *Florida Comprehensive Achievement Test* (FCAT) was embraced in 1998.

Many states, including Florida, began to adopt *Common Core Standards* in 2010. Phasing them in gradually, Florida later renamed them the *Florida Standards.* Full implementation was planned for 2014-2015. These standards have precipitated heated debate between supporters and detractors. Along with those standards came *End of Course Assessments.*

In my years with the School District of Palm Beach County, I have witnessed many programs come and go. No matter what the title or the intention, in the end, it all comes down to the ability of and the flexibility of the individual teacher in the classroom to teach the lesson properly.

With regard to planning, good teachers will go to great lengths to design a thought-provoking curriculum within the required framework of grade-level objectives to be covered.

Poor teachers will do the minimum amount of work. For me, as a new teacher, there was much to learn. I had enjoyed every minute of the thirteen years spent at home with my children. Adjusting to being in a classroom was difficult. There were painful moments.

For the greater part of my teaching career I taught English, a subject that later came to be known as language arts. There was no doubt that I knew my subject matter. I was raised with a solid foundation in English grammar.

Both sides of my family from Lowell, Massachusetts, were well educated and had a strong command of the English language. The following is an overview of my family's educational background:

1. My Father's Side of the Family

- My paternal grandfather passed the Bar Exam in Massachusetts after attending Harvard Law School.

- His two sisters, my father's aunts, became public school teachers after graduating from a Massachusetts *normal school*.

- Having originated in France, *normal schools* were the precursors of teachers colleges, designed to teach students by establishing standards or *norms*.

- One of those sisters had been secretly married for a short time, defying the rule of that era that female teachers must remain single. Both of these women had been friends of my maternal grandmother, also a teacher.

- My father attended Boston College and earned a law degree from Northeastern University in Boston.

- My father's three sisters were teachers, all graduates of four-year teachers college programs, who later earned master's degrees as well.

2. My Mother's Side of the Family

- My maternal grandfather passed the Massachusetts Bar Exam with an eighth-grade education.

- My maternal grandmother, a Massachusetts *normal school* graduate, had been a teacher and a principal of an elementary school before she married. She enjoyed her job immensely but was forced to relinquish it once she chose marriage.

- Massachusetts state law decreed that female teachers could not be married. The basis for that legislation originated in English common law. As a carryover of that law, all of my *female* public school teachers were unmarried.

- My mother, in 1921, had been accepted for admission to Radcliffe College—which gradually became integrated into Harvard University in the 1960's and became completely absorbed by Harvard University in 1999.[9] But because of her sheltered religious background, my mother was too timid to venture forth to a secular institution.

- Instead, she selected the College of Saint Elizabeth in Convent Station, New Jersey, one of the first Catholic colleges in the United States to confer degrees upon women.

- There, in 1925, she earned a Bachelor of Arts degree in English Literature.

- She went on to earn a Master of Arts degree in English Literature from Boston University in 1929, the same year she was married.

- My mother, having been a librarian before marriage, returned to work after I began school. For a married woman living in the Massachusetts suburbs in the 1950's, it was not commonplace to have a career.

- When I was growing up, all but one of my friends' mothers were deemed to be traditional *homemakers* who remained at home raising their families.

- My mother's college roommate Alice, who became my godmother and a close family member, earned a Master of Arts degree in literature at Columbia University. She too became a career librarian.

I didn't realize until many years later, that the majority of women of my mother's generation did not go on to higher education. Growing up, I took it for granted that after high school, both men and women automatically went on to college and graduated.

I knew that my brother and I would do the same. All the while I was attending Milton High School, I was conscious of the school's strong reputation for nurturing and producing college grads.

It was almost second nature for my brother and me to use correct grammar at an early age. That doesn't mean that we always spoke flawlessly, but if we made mistakes, we were quickly corrected by our parents or even by our aunts, when in their presence.

An important component of my upbringing was that I received my formal education from outstanding public school teachers at every grade level. They and my university professors taught me well.

In spite of that solid educational background, I had no idea how to design curriculum, or how to discipline a class of young teens. With time, I learned that at the heart of good discipline was a dynamic lesson plan.

That aspect of teaching along with the pacing of a lesson eventually became my strength. Above all, I did not want to become bored by the material that I was required to teach. I *spiced it up.*

A major resource for my students and me was the school district's **textbook depository**, one section of which housed books no longer on adoption by the school system. Those books were offered free to teachers. To my students' advantage, the *off-adoption* reading anthologies were often far more entertaining, better designed, more colorful, and more comprehensive than the *newly-adopted* material.

My class bookshelves were filled with complete sets of high quality, appropriate, grade-level literature that I shared with my students. They had no down time. I surrounded them with a print-rich environment and immersed them in literacy, concentrating on reading and writing.

My manner of teaching evolved over the years to keep up with the times and with students' changing needs. As all principled teachers do, I continually sought to create and implement a lesson that would capture and hold students' attention while teaching the objectives of the day.

Not only is that the best course of action for students, it is a matter of teacher survival in the classroom. *Sesame Street* Sadie, on the other hand, preferred to delegate, abdicate, and relegate her teaching duties to a television monitor.

Advisory: Give serious thought to your children's complaints about their teachers.

Chapter 7
Identifying Gifted Students
Unintelligent Intelligence #1:
Superficial Screener Sal

"Don't feel bad," she consoled,
"your children can still do well in college."

Family members: Joy & Nick

While Tony and Fay were settling in to elementary school, Joy and Nick were adjusting to their new school. Not long after classes began, Joy became friendly with a girl named Lianne who lived nearby. Lianne was a tenth grader in the gifted program. She described her richly diverse experiences in the program and hoped that Joy could participate as well.

The classes were not limited to students in one grade. For example, some students in ninth grade might be in the same class as other students in the tenth grade. In more advanced classes, some eleventh graders might be in the same class with twelfth graders.

When I found out that a gifted program existed, I contacted the school's guidance department to inquire about specifics and how my children might be admitted to it. I learned that the program was part time.

One teacher certified in gifted child education and in language arts would be responsible for teaching gifted students in grades six through twelve. In light of the school's configuration for a system of double sessions (Chapter 6), she arranged her schedule to teach high school students in the morning and middle school students in the afternoon.

Without delay, I arranged an evaluation for Joy and Nick. After the assessment took place, I received a note from the school's guidance department advising me that my children did not qualify for the program.

Following up on the matter, I was referred to Superficial Screener Sal, the teacher in charge of the gifted program. She advised me that she, herself, had administered a brief screening test to both Joy and Nick. Neither of them had earned the score required for entrance.

"Don't feel bad," she consoled, "your children can still do well in college."

I did not take her remark lightly. Superficial Screener Sal may have meant well, but her tone struck me as condescending.

From there, I investigated my options and learned that I had the right to request an evaluation through psychological services at school district headquarters in West Palm Beach.

Within a week, a psychologist arrived to see Joy and Nick at the school. Today, with the backlog of testing and parent conferences, it would take several months before an evaluation could be scheduled.

To each of the children, individually, the psychologist administered an extensive battery of written and verbal tests. Afterwards, he phoned me at work to report that both of them unequivocally qualified for admission to the gifted program, and he supervised their immediate placement. He was particularly impressed by Nick's poetry which he happened upon serendipitously by engaging Nick in a medley of topics.

To her credit, Superficial Screener Sal welcomed Joy and Nick to her program and apologized to me for the initial fiasco which had surprisingly, but rightfully, brought to her attention the fallibility of the district's screening instrument.

Joy and Nick enjoyed many productive and enriching experiences in Sal's classes for two and one half years before Sal returned to her home state after the Christmas holidays with one semester remaining. Concentrating on her speciality of language arts, she engaged them in both expository and creative writing.

The academics worked out for Joy and Nick in the end, but the above narrative illustrates the point that Sal, a respected teacher at the school, originally used a superficial screening tool to block my children from a program for which they were legitimately qualified.

Had I not taken the matter further, they would have been permanently excluded. That procedure occurred in 1974. Unfortunately, there are similar, unreliable and unjust screening mechanisms still in existence today (Chapter 21).

In my conversation with the school psychologist, I told him about my experiences with Deadbeat Derelict Dave, *Sesame Street* Sadie, and Superficial Screener Sal. It was logical for me to express my anxiety.

Having moved away from an excellent school system and having experienced three significant brushes with **bad teaching practices** within a short time span, I held valid reasons for being skeptical and duly concerned about the proper education for my children. When the psychologist learned that I had two children at the elementary school, he set up appointments to evaluate Tony and Fay.

Shortly thereafter, they, too, attained the required score for gifted placement. But by that time, I was appeased because the children were doing well with their regular teachers. I did not want to make any further changes.

The following year, Tony and Fay joined a part-time gifted program. With the advent of CONCEPT 6 (Chapter 13), many gifted students at the elementary school were short changed as to their hours of participation in classes for the gifted.

Two teachers came after Sal to fill her position. Both of them had excellent academic credentials, but they arrived straight from their universities. Unwisely, they allowed students to dictate the nature of assignments, and they offered them no structure.

These inexperienced teachers were not able to address the needs of gifted students in a consistent, comprehensive manner. Both with cheerful, affable personas, they tried to please, but students perceived this as a weakness and dominated them. After that school year, the gifted program ended permanently at the high school. Demanding, advanced classes began to become the norm.

As time went on, I was satisfied overall that the classes for my children were sufficiently challenging for their abilities. I realized that the majority of their teachers—**both in and out** *of the gifted program*—were excellent teachers.

**Advisory: Say, "No!" to thoughtless,
negative labels affixed to your child.**

Chapter 8
Bugsy the Befuddled Bug Man

**The D remained a permanent stain
on her otherwise impeccable record
throughout high school.**

Family member: Joy

Toward the end of Joy's first year of high school in 1975, her regular science teacher suddenly left school, and his young, inexperienced intern took over the class. He required all students to submit a bug collection of twenty bugs. Along with general **verbal** instructions, he gave students a list of common, Florida bugs from which to choose.

There could be no duplication of bugs. All bugs had to be attached to some type of backing via a straight pin and clearly labeled as to common name, family name, genus, and species. Bugsy gave no other specific instructions. One woefully unforgettable example from Joy's collection is the following specimen and its nomenclature whose acquaintance we were forced to make upon moving to Florida.

Common name: Florida Wood Cockroach (Palmetto Bug)

Family Name:	**Blattidae**
Genus:	**Eurycotis**
Species	**Eurycotis floridana**

Joy rarely sought my assistance with her schoolwork and never with science because it was not my strong point. Nevertheless, when it came time to assemble the project, she insisted that I help her collect samples because she was squeamish about bugs. She had not been looking forward to the assignment, but she knew there was no way to avoid it.

Since we were busy after school and on weekends, we did much of our sleuthing at night. We found some bugs in the grass, close at hand, guided by a light attached to our apartment building. Across the street, we located several bugs in marshy reeds illuminated by a lamppost.

In spite of our instructions to catch the critters, we wanted to exterminate them rather humanely and still preserve their shape as much as possible. We were rank amateurs at the job, but we managed to obtain the required number of twenty specimens.

Placing the project horizontally on our dining room table, we attached the bugs neatly in four rows of five onto a piece of 2" x 15" x 10" foam. I had bought some straight pins with tiny colored balls at the tip. We were glad that the grunt work had been satisfied and that we had filled the required quota.

Joy conscientiously labeled the bugs with precision and submitted the project on time. I must admit I took some pride in the project myself. Although neither of us had been thrilled with the assignment, we felt we had done it justice, and that it was certainly worthy of the A, that Joy had consistently earned on school projects.

About two weeks later, on the **second last** day of the school year, Bugsy the Bug Man gave students their grades verbally. He did not return the projects. I could understand this because the bugs were probably in an advanced state of decay by that time, and we had not been planning to give the project a place of honor in our home. Bugsy told Joy that she earned a grade of C. Never having earned grades that low, she was naturally surprised and disappointed.

When Joy inquired as to the reason for the low grade, Bugsy told her that she would have earned an A in the project if she had not used colored pins.

After class, Joy reminded Bugsy that she had used **straight** pins as per his instructions, and that those were the only straight pins available at our neighborhood store.

She emphasized that the tiny colored tip on the pins did not prevent the labels from being read. Nor did they diminish the integrity of the project in any way. Remaining steadfast in his decision, Bugsy refused to change the grade.

When I tried to get in touch with the Bug Man, he had left for summer vacation. Deciding to make the best of a bad situation, Joy and I had calculated that she could live with the low grade if necessary, and it would not make too much of a dent in her science grade for the term, nor in her overall grade point average.

Consequently, we resigned ourselves to it for the time being, but I planned to talk to Bugsy upon his return in another attempt to raise Joy's grade.

As our family's first, full school year in Florida came to a close, Tony and Fay received excellent final grade reports from the elementary school. Instead of grades reports, however, Joy and Nick brought home a notice advising parents that grades for middle school and high school students would be mailed to families during the summer. I was anxious to review them.

Immediately after the close of school, we moved to a three-bedroom rental home, still in Tequesta. With a spacious yard, the house offered us a comfortable step up from apartment living. I waited in vain for report cards to arrive.

When I went to the school to obtain Joy and Nick's reports, I found out that there had been a mix-up with the mail. In spite of the fact that I had notified the local post office of our new address, the grade reports had been sent to the old address and returned to the school labeled, *no longer in residence; no known forwarding address.*

When we at last reviewed the reports, we quickly noted that Nick had an all-A report card. The big shock came when we noticed that Joy received a D for the fourth quarter in science even though she had earned excellent grades in all assignments except for the bug collection.

Upon looking into it, an administrator checked Bugsy's grade book and learned that Befuddled Bugsy had written,

"Zero = F "
For Joy's bug report grade along with a note,
"No Project Submitted."

Evidently, the Bug Man had disposed of the project without recording Joy's grade, **recalled nothing** about their discussion of the colored pins, and never gave it another thought.

To make matters worse, Bugsy the Befuddled Bug Man decided to exercise his option to count the bug collection as an exam grade instead of giving students an actual exam. Consequently, the zero exam grade was heavily weighted and resulted in Joy's receiving a D for the entire term.

Joy and I were shocked and angry at this turn of events. Granted, we had not been happy with the grade of C that Bugsy had affixed to the project, but we would gladly have accepted it in lieu of a **failure.**

In August, when the new academic year began, I was ready to greet Bugsy on his first day of work. Ironically, Bugsy the Befuddled Bug Man had terminated his employment with the school, or vice versa. School personnel told me that they could not get in touch with him, that he was **no longer in residence; no known forwarding address.** There was no way for me to reach him.

Through Bugsy's incompetence, Joy had not only been treated unfairly, but she had been put at a significant scholastic disadvantage. The principal took the word of the missing teacher and did not change her grade.

In the academic world, this episode in its entirety had resulted in a travesty of justice for a young student who had worked hard to earn the best grades possible in all of her classes. This incident occurred at the close of her first year in high school. Up until that point, she had experienced an excellent year. She had earned honors grades in all of her other classes, and she was a strong athlete. She participated in swimming year round for the **Amateur Athletic Union (AAU),** and she qualified to participate in the state meet at the end of the high school swim season.

My efforts to help Joy were ineffective. I felt powerless. At that time in my life, I did not know how to work the system.

I did not know enough to appeal Joy's case to a district supervisor.

The D remained a permanent stain on her otherwise impeccable record throughout high school.

Early on, Joy had been in line for class Valedictorian but was bumped down by this irreversible error. She could never make it up. Well aware of that fact, long in advance of graduation, she was resigned to it by the time senior year rolled around.

There were, of course, other bright students in her class, all competitive to within one tenth of a percent when it came to calculating Grade Point Averages (GPA's) for the Number One slot.

We did not know for certain if Joy could have earned the top slot without the bug report incident, but we knew that she had been demonstrably close. This predicament substantiates all too clearly how much one teacher's ineptitude can distort a student's true academic achievement.

In spite of her bad experience with the Bug Man, Joy was fortunate to have studied under several excellent teachers who prepared her well for college. On a much more positive note, Joy earned high honors via an alternative route at graduation by earning a **National Merit Scholarship:**

"Scholarship winners represent fewer than 1% of the initial pool of student entrants, based on official statistics released by the National Merit Scholarship Corporation." [10]

She applied this monetary award to her expenses at Brown University in Rhode Island.

Her extra-curricular reading activities since childhood, her excellent grades throughout the four years, her qualifying scores on the Preliminary Scholastic Aptitude Test (PSAT), taken in her junior year, and her high scores on the Scholastic

Aptitude Test (SAT), taken in her senior year, had made that possible.

When Joy was a brand new student in high school, she and I had talked to the principal about her going to college in the Northeast. The principal was cordial but replied with conviction that many students think the same as Joy when they first arrive in the **Sunshine State.** She added that they soon change their minds and want to remain in Florida for college.

All I could think of was the land of the
"Lotus Eaters" [11]
from *The Odyssey* where those eating the
lotus plant never wish to leave.

But Joy was determined to go North after high school. Through her diligence, she had done exceptionally well, gained admission to the college of her choice, and returned to New England where she had spent her early childhood.

In 1978, a school administrator remarked to me that to her knowledge Joy was the third person in the history of the school to attend an Ivy League college.

A 1977 female graduate was admitted to Brown University, and in the same year, a male student was admitted to Cornell University. Decades later, that statistic has changed, with a much larger representation of the school's graduates at elite universities.

Advisory: Seek help from a higher authority if you cannot right a wrong with the school's principal.

Chapter 9
Lessons Learned from Bugsy and the Bad Brad

The Bad Brad had no idea what he had been doing wrong.

Family: Susan & Grandchildren

Still feeling the sting from the bug project, I reflected upon the fact that Bugsy had been a new teacher. Major weaknesses were 1) his inadequate communication skills, 2) his poor record keeping, and 3) his lack of empathy for students.

- As to the first point, he gave **insufficient** guidelines for projects by not setting up objective grading criteria in writing. Moreover, he could not remember Joy's expressed disappointment with her grade, nor the follow-up conference with her after class.

- Secondly, he had a poor system of recording students' grades and of handling their projects as evidenced by losing Joy's work.

- Thirdly, he felt no remorse for giving Joy a zero for the project.

Assigning a **zero** for an exam grade is a big deal, and it should have given Befuddled Bugsy great pause before he finalized that grade in his official grade book.

It would have been far better to have taken a more rational approach, asking himself, *"Why would a student with an A average in science up until this point suddenly decide not to submit an important assignment? This is out of the ordinary."*

Bugsy should have called me at work or at home to ask why Joy had not submitted the project, and then he would have been reminded of their conversation about the colored pins. All of my supervisors had repeatedly emphasized the importance of contacting parents for reasons such as the following:

- **to clarify misunderstandings**

- **to offer students the benefit of the doubt**

- **to notify parents about their children's missing work.**

This intervention strategy had been drummed into me throughout my teaching career. I spent countless hours on the phone with parents, and usually a phone call resolved the problem.

Another factor in connection with Bugsy was that he had recently taken over the class in midstream. He did not have a feel for the class as a whole, not knowing which students were reliable and which were more lax about completing assignments. In any case, that was not an excuse for his negligence.

Even a cursory look at his predecessor's gradebook would have provided that information. Evidently, he was anxious to finish up the year and head back to his home in northern Florida.

Some students had reported that he intended to leave teaching and get into another field. From my perspective, that would have been a wise decision.

Fortunately for my other children, none of their teachers ever lost one of their time-consuming projects. There was one time, though, early in my teaching career and after Joy's bug collection disaster, when I could not find a student's work.

It was an important research paper of an eleventh-grade student who had made a habit of not submitting assignments. He was the only student who had not conferenced with me beforehand to determine if his thesis statement was workable.

After I graded and returned all of the papers I had received, I spoke to him about the missing paper. He was the epitome of cool, and he confidently attempted to assure me that he had left his research paper on my desk. I told him that I would get back to him the next day.

Again, with no luck, I searched my classroom, my briefcase, my office, my home, and my car. I was almost positive that he had not done the assignment, and that furthermore, he would have had the nerve to lie about it.

Still, there was an element of uncertainty that it could have landed on the floor and been thrown away by a nighttime custodian.

On one occasion, some brand new posters I had planned to hang up in my classroom had suffered such a fate. In that event, I could not give this student a failing grade.

The next day, I advised the student that I had assigned an A to the paper. He was not at all concerned about allegedly losing the only copy of his work as other, more serious students might have been in those pre-computer days.

Undeniably, he was thrilled to receive the A, and that was the end of the matter for him. I, on the other hand, have never forgotten the incident.

First, there was my ego problem thinking that the student had probably gotten the better of me. But if he had submitted the work and it was missing, there was the issue of whether I had taken enough care to avoid this situation.

My decision to give him the A was loosely akin to Blackstone's Formulation, **"Better that ten guilty persons escape than that one innocent suffer."** [12]

From then on, I established rigid procedures for collecting students' work. I forbid students from leaving work on my desk. Instead, I went directly to the students, walking up and down rows, picking up individual assignments in a shallow bin and checking off student names in my grade book as I went along.

If students did not have their work, I could address the issue right then and there in class and notify parents of the delinquency in a timely manner.

Many teachers instruct their students to place their work in color-coded bins as they leave the classroom, but that system is questionable if a student's work is missing.

All of these procedures may appear mundane; but well planned safeguards, as described above, must be in place for protection of both the student and the teacher.

Regrettably, the Befuddled Bugsys of the world are still out there in different forms. The Bad Brad, one of my university teachers, had a similar, lackadaisical method of assigning and grading projects as did Bugsy.

I met Brad six years after I had earned my doctorate when I was enrolled in a Master of Science in Library and Information Studies degree from Florida State University (FSU).

Although FSU is located in Tallahassee, a six hour-drive from my house in Tequesta, the university had set up a satellite program at the eight-story Broward County Public Library in Fort Lauderdale. There students from South Florida could earn a fully-accredited library degree while taking classes close to home.

The program had been established because of a critical shortage of librarians in Broward County—both in public libraries and in school library media centers. It was in this program that my classmates and I had to reckon with the likes of the Bad Brad.

In the back of my mind, there had been a nagging call to become a librarian. The fact that my mother had been a librarian for many years influenced me more than I had realized.

When I was an elementary school student, I converted many of my books to **library** books. I made pockets for the back of each book to hold my home-made *date-due* cards. I played **library** with a friend or alone with imaginary friends for hours upon end. [Aside: Libraries that I patronize print receipts for checked-out books indicating when they should be returned. I have nostalgia for the old *date-due* cards.]

As a child, it was more about the entertaining diversion of stamping and checking out books. Later I thought it would be fascinating to become a reference librarian where I could assist other people with research and learn simultaneously for my own enrichment.

Eventually, I envisioned transitioning from language arts teacher to school library media specialist, which is what I did in reality after earning my degree.

I spent eleven years in that position in one Palm Beach County middle school before my retirement. In that capacity, in addition to managing the library media center, I taught critical thinking and video production.

My talented students put on a daily telecast for the school and made videos for FAME, Florida Association for Media in Education, where they took frequent honors at local, regional, and state competitions.

My dependable assistant deserves much credit for supporting me in multitudinous ways for the duration of that time.

From 1995-1997, a language arts colleague and I met after school on Mondays and Wednesdays and again on Saturdays to drive to Broward county for our library classes. Florida State University has long held a high national ranking in the field of library science.

For our special arrangement, Ph.D. professors from Tallahassee flew to Fort Lauderdale each week to deliver their instruction to us. Together we formed a cluster of fifteen students, most of whom were teachers.

We took three classes per term and, as a rule, we had three different professors from the main campus. For the first year, we enjoyed and respected our instructors without experiencing problems. In the last term of our program, however, we became disenchanted with one class.

The professor, originally scheduled to teach us, cancelled because of illness in the family and, as a result, we were assigned a substitute instructor. He had earned an advanced library degree from Florida State University, but he was not affiliated with the university.

As an administrator in the Broward County library system, he was well respected in that field. But he was not a professor, and he had no teaching experience. My colleague dubbed him the Bad Brad for two reasons:

- **He had a bad system for grading the many projects required of us.**

- **There was a smart, friendly student in the class with the same name whom my classmate labeled the Good Brad.**

Unbeknown to the substitute, his nickname caught on with our classmates and stuck firmly to him as he continued following the error of his ways.

Brad's administrative skills did not transfer over to his teaching and grading practices. His assignments for us were library projects and accompanying presentations.

The Bad Brad lectured very little. He spent class time sitting and listening to our reports, placing the burden on us to teach the class.

The week after we delivered our presentations, the Bad Brad would give us our grades from the previous week. We worked hard on our projects, always trying to do our best to earn an A. We followed the general instructions he had outlined.

My partner and I received a B plus on our first project. Teachers like to earn A's, and we were no exception. My friend and I spoke to Brad about our grade after class. He held up the one A project completed by a classmate and told us decisively, *"This project deserves an A."*

He advised us that it was *"**better than the others**,"* but he gave us no concrete justification for labeling it an A project. We saw no more merit in that project than in ours.

For our second project, the same scenario occurred. Only one person earned an A, and the rest of us earned B's. The Bad Brad gave no rationale as to why.

When Brad learned that we were disappointed to earn a B on our projects, he went on to assure us that, *"**B is a good grade**."*

Still we were not happy to settle for a B after the work we had put into it. Incidentally, Brad's comment to us was *identical* to those offered to two of my grandchildren by their teachers.

Instead of helping their students determine why they did not earn an A, those teachers dismissively told them and their parents, *"**Don't worry about it. B is a good grade**."* Those teachers did not want to be bothered to find the root of the problem so that the children could earn the top grade.

No matter whether this attitude is found in grade school or at the university level, it is a patent example of inertia and dereliction of duty. If a child is receiving a B grade when an A indicates a perfect score, that child has a performance gap that must be addressed.

One elementary school teacher, referenced in the scenario above, kept dodging a parent conference because she did not wish to exert the effort to help the child raise her grade.

That teacher even convinced the child to tell her mother that she did not need a conference—thereby putting the child in the middle of an adult matter.

Unfortunately, these unprofessional intimidation tactics occur all too often. Parents must be aware of them and push through those bouts of resistance with continued attempts to reach a solution.

With regard to the Bad Brad's grading system, my classmates and I met one Saturday during our long lunch break and discussed how to address its randomness.

We came up with a list of grading criteria that the teacher could use for each project, and we presented it to him later that day in a straightforward but diplomatic manner.

The Bad Brad had no idea
what he had been doing wrong.

He was, however, receptive to our suggestions, and he accepted the rubric to use in grading all projects from then on. If students followed the criteria faithfully, they would earn an A.

We also suggested that if he felt that some students went above and beyond the criteria, he could feel free to give them an A+ as long as he did not penalize other students who had fully complied with his objective requirements.

Our collaborative brainstorming had produced an objective tool for him to use, and Brad was sincerely grateful to us.

We had actually made Brad's job easier. He was even willing to regrade our earlier projects using his new tool. We were all satisfied: teacher and students alike.

Advisory: Teachers with bad grading practices
can be found at all levels of instruction from
grade school on up to the university level.

Chapter 10
Dishonorable Honor Society Advisor #1:
Do-Little-or-Nothing Debbie

**"I'm sorry; I cannot do anything about it now.
It's too late."**

Family member: Nick

When Nick was about to complete eighth grade after continuing to be an outstanding student throughout elementary and middle school, I was surprised to receive a letter from the middle school inviting his brother Tony, a sixth grader at the same school, to become a member of the National Junior Honor Society (NJHS).

In ten days, the school would host an evening candlelight installation for all new members and their families. All of the previously inducted members would be recognized once again on stage and serve as sponsors to the new inductees.

Although I was thrilled to receive the news about this honor for Tony, I was taken aback that Nick had not received a similar invitation at the end of his sixth grade year. I reacted with an emotionally charged question, ***"Why had my son Nick been overlooked for this honor? "***

I had to admit, though, that I had not previously heard of the existence of this award at the middle-school level. Joy was a member of the National Honor Society (NHS) at the high school in that same time period, but I knew nothing about a junior branch of that organization. Perhaps, I thought, this ceremony might be ushering in its debut at the middle school.

When I began to investigate the matter, I learned that the society had been in place throughout Nick's tenure at the school, and that its history dated as far back as 1929.

Obviously, he had met the grading criteria because of his excellent academic record, but I began to wonder if there were some other reason why Nick had not been included in the selection process.

That very same year when I was teaching in a private high school, Daniel, one of my top students, was not invited to join the National Honor Society. From a gregarious, outgoing family, he was himself more introspective. A dedicated student, he consistently earned high grades. When I inquired of the school's honor society sponsor as to why he had been excluded from selection, she replied that the consensus of his teachers declared that Dan was not a leader. They believed that he was decidedly too quiet.

I felt that it was unfair to deny him admission based on a *superficial* definition of leadership, but I was new to the school and powerless to intervene.

In spite of Daniel's reserve, I could see that his classmates respected his intelligence, maturity, and good judgment. That young man later became a doctor and has continued to be a solid leader in the community for more than twenty years.

Since Nick and Tony were equally recognizable by their teachers, coaches, and classmates as all-round leaders in the traditional sense, I continued to be puzzled and racked my brain for answers, *"Why had NJHS excluded Nick from membership?"*

Before I approached the honor society's sponsor, I was able to conduct an undercover investigation through a friend who taught at the school.

He reported back to me that the main criteria for acceptance were grades, and specifically that of earning no grade lower than a B. My friend searched grade reports and learned that Nick was one of the highest ranked students in his class. He had habitually earned A's and had no grade lower than a B.

I spoke via phone to the National Junior Honor Society sponsor, Do-Little-or-Nothing Debbie, and asked why Nick had not received an invitation to join the society at the end of his sixth-grade year.

She responded that she would look into the matter and get back to me. It was customary for teachers to take turns as sponsors of the honor society, but I learned that Debbie had been in that role for the previous two years.

When she called the next day, Debbie confirmed that Nick was one of the top students. His omission from the honors roster had been none other than a *careless error.* Indeed, Nick should have been initiated into the society at the end of his sixth-grade year.

Compounding the matter, the sponsor had missed another opportunity to induct Nick after his seventh-grade year. In other words, his exclusion from the honor society had gone unnoticed for two years.

Furthermore, Do-Little-or-Nothing Debbie, chose to do nothing to rectify the mistake, *"I'm sorry; I cannot do anything about it now. It's too late."*

It was easier to disregard the injustice rather than come up with a way to make amends. No action could fully make up for the oversight, but some type of delayed recognition might express some good will toward the student. I scheduled an appointment with the school's principal to discuss the problem.

After many years of fighting for my children, I toughened up when talking to school personnel in authority positions. But in that era, I was inexperienced and emotional when I spoke with the principal about my son Nick, the model student, who had been given a raw deal under that administrator's watch.

My voice was shaking, and I was on the verge of tears. I asked that the school own up to its culpability in the matter and that Nick be recognized in front of his peers at the installation of the new NJHS inductees.

To me it was the only course of action to take. As was her custom, the principal was pleasant and polite to me. She expressed sincere regret at the error but calmly told me that there was nothing she could do to right the wrong.

On the way home, I was both dejected and angry. I went to the library and looked up the National Honor Society headquarters in Washington, D. C. I learned that the Executive Director was Owen B. Kiernan. Dr. Kiernan had been the Superintendent of Schools in Milton, Massachusetts, when

I was in high school. My classmates and I had been thrilled to speak to him personally when he came to visit our class.

From that position, he moved up to become the Commissioner of Education for the Commonwealth of Massachusetts. Subsequently, he went to work in the District of Columbia with the National Honor Society for many years. Within that same time frame, he also served as an education advisor to seven U. S. presidents.

In my still outraged state of mind, I was seriously considering calling Dr. Kiernan's office to enlist his help in setting things straight for one Nick Ryan, a former student in the Milton Public Schools. A kind and humble man, he cared about families and fairness.

Above all, he had a soft spot for the Town of Milton and for students who had, at one time in their lives, attended Milton schools. As it turned out, it wasn't necessary to make the appeal to this top educator.

Early the next morning, I received an unexpected call from the middle school principal to advise me that she had arranged a small celebration to redress the NJHS oversight. It would be held two days later after school.

As it happened, after she had met with me, the matter began heating up behind the scenes. My incognito, teacher informant, turned amateur sleuth, had mentioned the incident to a friend whose daughter was in Nick's class.

Coincidentally, that young lady, another highly-ranked student, had also been overlooked for both the sixth-grade and seventh-grade honor society installations. After the girl's mother notified the principal of their family's consternation, the principal suddenly realized that there was a firestorm brewing.

When mothers start talking to one another and comparing notes, word travels dangerously fast. The principal rightly cracked down on Do-Little-or-Nothing Debbie and urged her to scrutinize student grade reports with utmost precision.

In delving deeper into the matter, Debbie and the principal unearthed the names of five other students, **seven in all,** who had been similarly wronged. Like Nick, they had not received the honor they deserved. They and their families had been completely unaware of this inexcusable slight to their children.

In order to arrange a form of compensation for the students and to pacify unhappy parents before the big reveal got out of control, the principal held a private ceremony for the previously unrecognized honorees and their families.

First, the school's principal graciously and warmly congratulated the students for their outstanding scholarship and sincerely apologized to them for the school's error.

Next, students received official certificates of membership in the NJHS, and they enjoyed a special cake that the principal had generously ordered in their honor.

I would have preferred that the students receive their overdue recognition at the evening ceremony in front of all their peers, but I knew that was not going to happen. Clearly, the administration did not wish to call attention to this flub. We had to accept a compromise, and I was most appreciative of the principal's effort to make things right.

A few hours later, at the official evening ceremony and formal induction of new members, Nick and the other newly ordained members sat up on the stage with their eighth-grade classmates who had been admitted to the NJHS in a previous year. They were all part of the impressive candlelight ceremony in the dimly lit auditorium.

Each new member held a lighted candle while taking the oath of the NJHS. Nick was proud to be present in the background when his younger brother Tony recited the honor society pledge.

I was surprised to be the only mother present who had two honorees on stage. If it had not been for Tony's invitation to join the honor society, the entire matter would never have been brought to light.

In hindsight, I can see how this error might easily have been prevented. Debbie could have distributed the names of the designated honorees to all teachers. She could have instructed teachers to review the list for mistakes and to **add** or **delete** names as necessary. Teachers know those of their students who deserve honors, and they enjoy seeing them rewarded for their hard work.

Do-Little-or-Nothing Debbie earned a decent stipend for her sponsorship. Her significant error in this identification process calls into question the accuracy of her work and that of other sponsors in years past. How many other honor students had been so carelessly overlooked?

Ironically, Debbie discharged her honor society duties *without a semblance of honor.* When she had a chance to rectify her error, her immediate response was to slough it off and look the other way.

Without question, if it had not been for my inquiry, *seven* students would have left eighth grade without ever knowing they had earned membership privilege in the National Junior Honor Society. They and their proud parents would have been left permanently in the dark about this accomplishment.

**Advisory: National Honor Society
advisors are not always honorable.**

Chapter 11
Secret Slacker Sam & Others

It became apparent that Sam was looking for the easy slide with no confrontations. His game was up. He knew when to fold.

Family member: Fay

Once Fay had skipped over first grade, she did well in elementary school having participated in a gifted program part time. A full-time gifted program was available only to students living on Track C under a system known as CONCEPT 6, described at length in Chapter 13.

Her teacher for the gifted segment was *Meticulous Millie,* a consummately dedicated teacher, who emphasized a combination of mastering concrete, basic skills, while stressing the importance of completing assignments on time. Along with this approach, she encouraged creative projects that nurtured abstract thought.

It has been my experience that gifted students often prefer to avoid learning the basics on their way to engaging in more unconventional endeavors. Coincident to those behaviors, they may be weak in fundamentals, become distracted from tasks at hand, and have trouble meeting deadlines.

The latter is a habit which in educational jargon is known as the ***ability to delay closure.*** Unfortunately, many gifted students excel in this area of nonperformance, and that characteristic may carry over with them to their adult workplace. I was, therefore, most appreciative of *Meticulous Millie's* attention to details along those lines.

In middle school, as her two older brothers had done, Fay qualified for admission to the National Junior Honor Society after her sixth-grade year.

Her classes went well with the exception of one incident with Secret Slacker Sam when she received an 80%, or a letter grade of C on one of his tests. Sam taught *Academic Subject X.*

Slacker Sam had taught at the school for a number of years and was highly respected by his colleagues. It was unusual for Fay to earn a grade that low, and she did not understand how it happened. As was my custom, I wanted to analyze the test to learn where she had made errors and why.

Going over the test with me, Fay was surprised at her mistakes because the teacher had given similar material for practice, and she was certain that she had understood the work.

Fay had done a combination of classwork and homework for five days as instructed, kept her work in a file folder, and then submitted that folder to the teacher for his review and correction if necessary.

The day before the test, Secret Slacker Sam returned Fay's folder with his signature stamp of approval on the front. There were no mistakes noted in any of the work therein.

Believing, therefore, that she had mastered the new concepts of the lesson, Fay had taken the test with confidence in her comprehension of the material.

For our analysis of the test results, we compared the work in Fay's folder to the test questions. We noticed that all of the practice questions in the homework folder were duplicates to all of the questions on the test.

It seemed that her teacher did not test students on any material that he had not covered—*so far, so good.* Then we looked specifically at the four questions marked wrong on the test and compared them to Fay's work in the folder.

Her test answers reflected her answers to the questions in the folder. They were identical. We then determined that Fay had made *four mistakes* in the homework that Secret Slacker Sam had *not corrected*, and therefore, she made the *same four mistakes* on the test.

It became all too clear that Secret Slacker Sam had not actually read the answers to the questions inside Fay's folder. He had simply checked off the work as *completed* in his grade book and returned the folder to her with the mistakes still solidly in place.

Enlightened by that information, I wrote a letter to Slacker Sam outlining what had occurred and requested that a grade of A be given to Fay's test. Secret Slacker Sam quickly obliged.

It became apparent that Sam was looking for the easy slide with no confrontations. His game was up. He knew when to fold.

One of the most important aspects of a teacher's job is to give feedback to student responses. If this does not happen, students will not know where they made mistakes. They will not learn from them. Furthermore, students, too, may start slacking off.

When a teacher requires students to submit work, the teacher does not necessarily need to assign a formal grade to it, but the teacher must check the work for errors and return the work to the students to make any necessary corrections. Otherwise, there is **no point** to that exercise.

Studying this predicament from a teacher's point of view, I understand how difficult it is to keep up with the enormous amount of material to be graded each week.

Therefore, it is critical for teachers to develop a system that will prevent them from being inundated in paperwork while, at the same time, showing students their errors and how to rectify them.

Language arts teachers, who concentrate on essay writing, bear an enormous burden when it comes to correcting students' work. Many of them use a rubric along with a type of special shorthand to indicate errors. Those teachers deserve everlasting praise.

Other teachers use an overhead projector and a large screen every day accordingly:

- **to teach the lesson**

- **to enable students to correct their own work**

This technology is basic. Some schools may have advanced versions of this technology with students using laptops. Teachers project the classwork or homework problems onto the screen and demonstrate how to arrive at the answers as students take notes and make adjustments if needed.

While students are reviewing or correcting their work, teachers can walk around the room observing who is on task—and *who is not.* They can zero in on student slackers who may not have done the work at all or focus on those students who may seem lost and need assistance.

If a majority of students are experiencing difficulty, teachers will *reteach* the concept. They can work with deficient students individually or recommend that they obtain extra assistance before or after school.

Teachers may prefer that students keep their annotated work with them in their folders to use as study guides for upcoming examinations.

It is critical that students learn how to take accurate notes, meaningful to them. They need to develop their own *personal* test-taking strategies that will help them remember the material covered.

It is also their responsibility to *ask questions* if they don't understand. Often reluctant to do so, many students set themselves up for failure.

But, ultimately, it is the job of teachers to realize how well students are grasping the material. They must reach out to low-performing students in a variety of ways such as facilitating parental involvement, enlisting peer tutors, and notifying guidance counselors—all of this to identify and eliminate the comprehension gap.

In Secret Slacker Sam's case, he could have used the *Stand & Deliver* model described above to accomplish the objectives of the lesson. Using that method requires a considerable amount of physical stamina on the part of a teacher who teaches six classes or more each day.

Almost all teachers have had days when they need to take a break and remain at their desk for a significant period of time, but those days should be at a minimum.

In fairness to Slacker Sam, Fay did not have problems with his grading system previously. This lapse may have been an isolated incident. It was near the close of the school year. Perhaps Sam was getting tired. Nevertheless, this scenario with the Slacker had penalized a student for a teacher's mistake.

Most likely, other students scored poorly on this test for the same reason. As in other cases similar to this, I could not be a crusader for all students. Parents and guardians bear the responsibility for monitoring the work of children in their care.

It really bothered me that a teacher who presented a façade of organization and fairness could use such sloppy, careless tactics with students' assignments. Even if such a gaffe occurs only **once**, it is still an egregious error, and it points out how **vigilant** students and parents must be when students receive a low grade on a test.

This example further demonstrates that the practices of teachers held in high esteem may be circumspect in certain instances. Obviously, **no teacher is infallible.** Parents need to realize this, act accordingly when necessary, and work things out amicably for the benefit of their child.

If a student does not perform well on a test, it is **critical** for parents and students to obtain a copy of that test and determine if the cause was one of the following:

- **student deficiency**

- **teacher error**

- **teacher carelessness, indifference, or burnout**

Clearly, Slacker Sam's botched instruction method was due to one of the latter causes. Parents and students must discuss unsatisfactory test results with the teacher if they hope for maximum comprehension and improved grades.

Above all, tests should be **tools** for learning. It is important to know what happens to tests **after** they have been graded. Test scenarios **vary** as outlined:

- **Some teachers offer no access to graded tests. Students cannot learn from those tests.**

- **Some teachers return tests to students, not caring what their students do with them.**

- **Some students indifferently throw their tests into the trash. They learn nothing from them.**

- **Some students keep their tests to use as study guides. They can learn from these tests.**

- **Online tests should be made available to students after the fact for a review of the material.**

When I returned tests, I called each student up to my desk to see their results **in private** while the other students worked on an important written assignment due at the end of class.

This method eliminated students' prying eyes and comparing grades with one another on the spot. It further prevented students from bragging about high grades and from feeling embarrassed about low grades.

Also of prime importance, this system fostered peace and quiet in the classroom and enabled students to keep focused on the task assigned. I could walk around the room as needed to make certain that students were completing the work in accordance with instructions.

After students were apprised of their test grades, I stored their tests in my file cabinet until the end of the year in the event of a parent conference. If teachers use this system, tests should not get lost.

Moreover, students and parents can obtain copies of tests upon request. Equally important, if teachers are blameless, and students have made their own *legitimate* errors, parents can learn what their children are doing wrong and determine how to get them the help they need.

Slacker Sam's careless method reminds me of a *similar pattern* I witnessed when I was teaching in a school where a large percentage of students came from dysfunctional families living in extreme poverty.

The parents or guardians of many of these children seldom had any contact with the school beyond registering them at the beginning of the year. Some teachers took advantage of the fact that there were no parents to challenge their teaching methods.

On certain occasions, I visited classrooms of two teachers in that school where the teachers gave preliminary instructions to students at the beginning of class and then assigned remedial seatwork for the rest of the period.

Partners in a pilot program, they had the same management style. They were known for being excellent disciplinarians with a rigid system in place.

They instructed students to work alone *quietly* at their own pace and submit all work in a folder at the end of class. Their students did as instructed.

These non-teachers circled the room once *midway* through the class. For the remainder of the time, they sat at their desks, often attending to personal business like balancing their checkbooks.

Student folders appeared well organized, displaying each student's name on the file tab. A goodly amount of work was enclosed and plainly labeled as to each day of the week. Teachers made certain that the students would not finish all of the work in any given day.

At the end of the week, those teachers would *clandestinely* and *callously,* dump all of their students' work directly from the folders into a huge trash bin without reviewing it and without giving an ounce of feedback.

Demonstrating a complete disregard for their obedient students' wellbeing, they returned the folders to them, along with a new batch of busy work on the first day of the following week. Their students continued in compliance, and the cycle of illiteracy droned on.

With a lax principal at the helm, such practices would go on undetected. I worked at that school under three principals with distinctly different management styles.

The first was a strong principal who supervised teachers closely, visiting classrooms *randomly* and *frequently,* immediately putting a stop to unacceptable practices observed. Subsequent administrators at the school, however, were not as attuned to the habits of their teachers, and they created a climate of *careless indifference.*

There is yet another lesson to be learned from Secret Slacker Sam and these *same* teachers. All three of these teachers had the reputation of being impeccable dressers. Their wardrobe choices were beyond reproach. Without a doubt, they created the impression of the quintessential professional.

By no means, do I intend to indict all well-dressed teachers for incompetent teaching methods. But I have known several other teachers who hid their teaching defects and sly grading techniques behind a façade of good grooming and organization.

Each day, they staged a *masquerade* as they stood at attention outside their classroom doors waiting for their students to arrive. They were usually clever enough to deceive their inadequate supervisors.

Advisory: Guard against all Secret Slackers and their cunning contempt for best teaching practices.

Chapter 12
Broken-Promise Buddy

**Students' hopes and dreams,
their trials and their triumphs,
will heartlessly be forsaken by this charlatan.**

Family member: Nick

After Nick left middle school and went on to high school, he experienced four more successful years. Looking forward to being in New England once again, he applied to Boston College and to Bowdoin College in Maine. Both colleges accepted him. He chose the former and was pleased that he did.

His time at Boston College coincided with the thrilling performances of football phenomenon and Heisman trophy winner Doug Flutie, who was a member of the same graduating class. Nick's excellent record in high school, along with a solid SAT score had gained him admission to these outstanding schools.

Always enjoying the challenges presented, Nick devoted much time to sports. He was an excellent swimmer and an accomplished diver in elementary and middle school. He was a swimmer and a runner in high school. When he was sixteen, he ran the Orange Bowl Marathon in Miami.

It was a thrill for the family to see him cross the finish line in good shape and happy to have stayed the course. Nick hoped to complete the race in less than four hours, and he achieved his goal with seven minutes to spare.

Later, at Boston College, he was a member of the track and cross country teams. While in Boston, he ran the Boston Marathon twice—once with his brother Tony.

His high school offered a dynamic athletic program led by many dedicated coaches. The school had its share of super stars and state champs, but the majority of athletes, like Nick, enjoyed performing their personal best in sports they dearly loved.

Soon after Nick entered high school, Coach Buddy called a *special meeting* for all first-year athletes. New to the school, Buddy was trying to make a name for himself as Mr. Popularity. He sang the praises of participating in sports and offered an attractive reward to those who became involved in multiple sports during the four-year period. Buddy energetically explained that any athlete who earned a letter for three years in three, different, varsity sports, would be awarded an athletic jacket in the spring of twelfth grade.

Decades later, I still vividly remember when an animated, fourteen-year old Nick shared with me the enticing words of Coach Buddy,

"This jacket, bearing our school colors, will be

'no ordinary jacket'

but an expensive, classic, varsity jacket,
custom made of high quality fabric in bright
emerald green, with gold leather sleeves."

Although a mature, responsible student, Nick was still infused with the innocence and idealism of youth. Enthusiastically, he complied with the coach's challenge.

He *swam* for the school for three years, and he earned medals in *track* for three years. His strong participation with the *cross country* team qualified him for statewide competition in his last two years of that sport.

Even though all of the Ryans were involved in high school athletics, no other family member fulfilled the exacting, *three-sport, jacket-earning criteria.*

Joy and Fay excelled in swimming for four years. Tony was an outstanding swimmer for four years and ran cross country for two years. Thad was an excellent swimmer for four years in addition to keeping up a rigorous debate team schedule.

Knowing that Nick would remain steadfast in his quest, I made up my own private game in honor of Nick's winning the coveted prize. No one knew that I silently ticked off each sport and each year on the *countdown* to victory, reminiscent of,

"You can do it, kid—only two years more!"

"Attaboy, Nick; you've got this one. It's in the bag!"

"Nick, Ole Man, can't wait to see you sporting the

Green and Gold."

In early spring of senior year, modestly yet proudly, Nick stopped at Coach Buddy's office to notify him that he had in all respects met his rousing, *three-sport challenge.* Sadly, Broken-Promise Buddy remained true to his inglorious epithet. It was disheartening to realize that the coach was suffering from an acute case of amnesia.

Incredulously, Broken Promise Buddy professed to have no recollection of the event and of the words he had chosen to motivate the school's young athletes three and one half years earlier.

Realistically, that may have been true. Buddy had been known for his cavalier attitude. As recklessly as he had uttered the challenge, in all likelihood, he dismissed it from memory. I admire a teacher or coach who puts his mind, heart, and soul into his work, but Broken-Promise-Buddy was *not* that guy.

His coaching style seemed to be one of doing and saying whatever worked at the time in order to gain attention, and then moving on, completely disregarding his wake.

I cannot say for certain whether any other student fulfilled the *three-sport requirement* for the jacket as Nick did, but we know of no one else who came forth to claim it.

Generally speaking, many of the top athletes lettered in two sports, football and baseball, or they were standouts in just one sport like swimming or tennis.

Buddy could be charismatic and charming. He laughed things off as if his explicit challenge had never occurred, and he convinced the trusting school principal of same. But Buddy's lingering message was clear,

The words of a scholar/athlete have no credence with me. Students' hopes and dreams, their trials and their triumphs, will heartlessly be forsaken by this charlatan.

Broken-Promise Buddy went on with business as usual.

I have no doubt that Nick would have participated in three individual sports for three years even if Buddy had not dangled his transitory incentive.

Nick relished his involvement in each of those activities. Nevertheless, a promise is a promise, and Buddy had ***done him wrong.***

Although this segment of the book does not involve an academic travesty, the insensitive betrayal of a young teen's aspirations and achievements took place in a school setting where teachers and coaches are expected to serve as role models for their students.

Broken-Promise Buddy did himself a great disservice. My children and others learning about this incident no longer had an ounce of respect for him.

Parents cannot solve all of their children's problems or right every wrong that touches their lives. But in this case, I rejoiced in performing the simple and speedy remedy.

Bright and early one Saturday morning, shortly after the rejection encounter, Nick and I headed out for a hearty breakfast and then went on to a sporting goods store about fifteen miles away.

There we selected for him in colors of vivid ***green and gold***, the finest athletic jacket in the store that matched ever so closely the original specifications outlined to the last detail by Broken-Promise-Buddy.

Once the jacket was home, I asked Nick to bring out his collection of medals along with the varsity letters he had earned in recent years. For the jacket, Nick selected the award letter he had received from the *National Honor Society* which displayed the *Lamp of Learning.*

It was otherwise identical in appearance and size to the regular, eight-inch athletic letters. Accordingly, Nick attached to the letter all of the gleaming, gold-filled pins emblematic of his impressive athletic achievements. Next, with needle and thread, I securely affixed the stately, gold-colored letter to the left side of the new jacket.

As Nick calmly strolled the campus that following Monday with his long, confident strides, athletes and non-athletes alike stopped to admire him and the jacket. He was *King of the Halls* that day and for many more whenever the jacket was on parade.

Nick brought that jacket with him to Boston College where he continued to wear it for the next several years as weather permitted. Indeed, my purchase had been a priceless investment.

More than thirty years and countless challenges later, the GREEN AND GOLD jacket is but a compelling memory. Yet tucked away in Nick's closet among his most valued souvenirs is the chenille and felt AWARD letter, resplendent with its NINE GOLDEN WARRIORS, symbol of his commitment and success as a determined young athlete who made himself, his high school, and his parents proud.

Advisory: Be on the lookout for campus con artists who pose as teachers or coaches.

Chapter 13
Year-Round School: CONCEPT 6
&
Randall the Retaliator

It was then I realized that Randall the Retaliator was exacting a double revenge in one fell swoop.

Entire Ryan Family affected by CONCEPT 6

Tony affected by Randall the Retaliator

Part I. CONCEPT 6 - BACKGROUND INFORMATION

As I mentioned in an earlier chapter, the schools in Florida are run by counties, with each county being made up of several towns. In August of 1975, with an effort toward eliminating overcrowding, ending double sessions, and avoiding the cost of building new schools, the School District of Palm Beach County, decided to implement a system of year-round schooling known as CONCEPT 6.

In so doing, the school district chose *one town only* out of the entire district to be its sacrificial lamb in this experiment. That town was Jupiter, and each one of its schools was targeted in the process. All other towns in the county remained unscathed.

The school district borrowed the idea of CONCEPT 6 from Colorado Springs, Colorado. District officials sent representatives of the school board and members of the Jupiter Parent Advisory Committee to observe how the system functioned in Colorado. When all was said and done, it was a small group of proponents who set CONCEPT 6 in motion.

Jupiter's school children waded through that quagmire for seven problem-riddled years. In August of 1982, CONCEPT 6 met its welcomed demise.

At long last, Jupiter students began their school year on *a traditional learning calendar,* no longer out of synch with all of the other schools in Palm Beach County.

Under the experiment, the town was divided into three tracks, A, B, and C. Two tracks attended school, while one track was on vacation. More specifically, students in each track alternately attended school for four months at a time and then went on vacation for the next two months.

In sum, there were eight months of schooling and four months of vacation for each track. There was a loss of seventeen school days per year for each track, more than three weeks of school lost for all students. Each grading period, called a *mester*, lasted two months.

The following is a timetable of each CONCEPT 6 track depicting months *in* and *out* of attendance. The vacations are shown on the top line. An asterisk * placed *before* a month indicates the *start* of the new academic year.

Jupiter Schools Timetable
Track A
Vacations......... January-February; July-August
In School: March-April; May-June
                  *September-October; November-December

Track B
Vacations.......... March-April; September-October
In School: November-December; January-February
                  May-June; *July-August

Track C
Vacations........... May-June; November-December
In School: January-February; March-April
                  *July-August; September-October

Originally, county administrators told Jupiter parents that if CONCEPT 6 were shown to be successful, they would phase it in gradually throughout Palm Beach County. That did not happen.

It didn't take long for shrewd Jupiter parents to realize that they had been hoodwinked and that their town had been selected to implement this tentative pilot program because Jupiter was essentially *out of sight, out of mind.*

Jupiter is located in the northernmost end of the county, contiguous to Martin County, an appreciable distance from school district headquarters in West Palm Beach.

In 1975, Jupiter was considered to be a bit out in the boondocks, and it was less densely populated than many towns in the district. For these reasons, architects of the system agreed that Jupiter schools—*all on their own*—were uniquely suited to pilot the disruptive year-round plan. At the end of the day, it was **easier** for them that way.

They created a policy of containment and converted isolated Jupiter into a giant testing laboratory. Many of us—both parents and teachers—knew from the outset that CONCEPT 6 was a mistake.

We would have preferred that our children continue on double sessions. We felt helpless. Yet, we had no choice but to muddle through the morass and hope for the best.

Evidently, CONCEPT 6 landed in Los Angeles about the same time that it fizzled out of Jupiter. Hector Villagra wrote the following in his blog on August 29, 2012, for the Huffington Post:

"A new school year just began in Los Angeles Unified School District with all the typical fresh hopes and dreams, but this one will be different. For the first time since the 1980's when the district first implemented it, no LAUSD student will be attending a school on the calendar known as Concept 6. This is something for all Angelenos to celebrate.

Concept 6 was never more than an elaborate shell game . . .

Through this sleight of hand, Concept 6 expanded the capacity of a school by 50 %." [13]

Nationally renowned education experts have criticized the system harshly, citing direct links with CONCEPT 6 and low student performance—as well as imposing its own version of segregation.[14]

Many Jupiter teachers, putting their personal interests above all else, favored the system because they enjoyed the extended vacation time. There were, however, outstanding, dedicated teachers, who could barely tolerate it.

Those teachers could see how the long breaks in instruction were affecting the way they taught their subject matter and how students were being short changed.

Although many Jupiter teachers and some administrators opposed CONCEPT 6 privately, they felt obligated to support it publicly.

They could not speak out against the iron-clad policies of their employer. Still, not long after the program was launched, a covert network of teachers, adversaries of CONCEPT 6, stealthily passed on information to a group of parents who hoped to abolish the program by gathering evidence of its mounting inadequacies.

In sharp contrast to the shroud of secrecy and silence that most Jupiter teachers and administrators upheld for seven years, was the bold and candid comment made by Merle Price in 2002. Price, the Los Angeles Unified School District's Deputy Superintendent of Instructional Services, stated,

"Nobody is happy with the Concept 6 calendar, from the superintendent to the board, and every effort is being made to replace it." [15]

In terms of years endured, the impact of CONCEPT 6 on my children was as follows:

Joy-three years, Nick-six years, Tony-seven years, Fay-seven years, Thad-six years.

This system was far more than we had bargained for in our move south. My intense focus on education gave our family an advantage over those who found themselves without direction in the confusion that this ill-advised alternative had spawned.

When Tony was in high school, I was part of a highly *vocal* and *visible* group who frequently attended meetings with teachers, county administrators, and occasionally the Superintendent of Schools, in an effort to end this program. Several of my children's teachers were public spokespersons on behalf of CONCEPT 6.

They were well aware of my dislike for the plan. Among the supporters was Randall the Retaliator who eventually found a way to strike out at both Tony and me because of our combined opposition to this academic disruption.

My close friend, then and now, a former math teacher and mother of four children in the system, had the courage to run for school board in 1980, with the clever campaign slogan,

"Kids Do Better With TLC: Traditional Learning Calendar."

She was her own efficient and effective campaign manager. I accompanied her to several meetings to lend a degree of moral support and help distribute her informative pamphlets.

Because she was a newcomer to the area, having moved to Jupiter from Connecticut just three years earlier, she had limited name recognition in comparison to the other candidates. All of her opponents had been longtime area residents, much more well known to voters.

Although her election bid was unsuccessful, my friend made a strong showing in the race, and she, of all the candidates, brought greater awareness to the CONCEPT 6 debacle.

With her mathematics background, it took her little time to figure out that the cost of operating schools year round was far more than the county had foreseen and, in short, the experiment was not at all cost effective. She emphasized that fact in her campaign. Two years later, district administrators came to the same conclusion and dismantled the program.

It is important to understand the layout of Jupiter and how the tracks were physically assigned. Intertwined in the configuration were the demographics of the town in that era and its socioeconomic composition.

1. Track A - Description.

a. **Track A** was varied. One section of **Track A** was comprised of families who lived **"out west"** of the turnpike in a more rural section of town. Some families owned large parcels of property and stabled horses there. Some families lived in large, impressive homes like that of Hollywood actor Burt Reynolds. His adjacent property, managed by his father, was eponymously named the *Burt Reynolds Ranch*. Some families lived in comfortable, middle-class homes. Some families lived in very small homes. Some families lived in trailers temporarily while they were building houses on their property. Some families lived in trailers permanently.

b. In another section of **Track A,** was a small number of students, most of whom lived in moderately-priced homes within a few miles of the schools, slightly west of town.

c. In another section of **Track A**, was a larger group of students, most of whom lived in moderately-priced homes several miles south of town, off Route Alternate A1A.

d. In another section of **Track A,** was a small number of students living in upscale residences near the ocean.

2. Track B - Description.

a. A small group of students from **Track B** lived in high-end properties near the Loxahatchee River, a considerable distance from schools.

b. Another small group of students from **Track B** lived in moderately to highly-priced homes near the Loxahatchee River, closer to the schools.

c. Another small group of students from **Track B** lived in moderately-priced homes near the high school.

d. The most densely populated section of **Track B** was comprised of low-income property near the elementary school, home to students in the lowest socioeconomic strata.

e. On average, **Track B** parents were the least vocal of all parents.

f. A qualitative analysis of this track's collateral damage reveals that students in this track had the most disruptive schedule and lacked opportunity for full participation in advanced classes. They had, in fact, been thrust into the least conducive environment for student learning.

g. **Track B** students were the only students who began a *new school year* on the *very next day* after ending the previous school year. They missed the traditional break in transitioning from one grade to another along with a period of relaxing down time.

3. Track C - Description.

a. For the most part, **Track C** had the largest number of expensive properties because of its proximity to the ocean, to the Tequesta Country Club, and to the Loxahatchee River, its *southern boundary.*

b. **Track C** included all Palm Beach County public school students living in the *southern* part of Tequesta and its adjacent unincorporated areas. Also included were tiny pockets of Jupiter by the river and the Jupiter Inlet Colony by the ocean. **Reminder:** There are not now, nor ever have been, public schools in Tequesta. Students living in the southern part of Tequesta attend Jupiter schools if they want a public education.

4. Track Inequities.

a. **Socioeconomic segregation.** A profound overall defect of the tracking system was its socioeconomic segregation, plainly visible in the demographics as described above. CONCEPT 6 was reminiscent of a caste system aggravated by tracking labels.

Some students from affluent families on other tracks referred degradingly to Jupiter's poorer students as *"Track B types."* Thirty-five years after its demise, students from that era may inadvertently conjure up the same labeling terminology.

Admittedly, the town of Jupiter was itself divided along socioeconomic lines. But before CONCEPT 6 arrived with its inherent divisiveness, all students attended school at the same time, and students enjoyed the chance to meet and mingle more freely with the entire student body.

b. Course offerings. A major academic shortcoming was the striking inequality among tracks with regard to course offerings. It would seem that **Track C** students were given preferential treatment in deference to the disproportionate number of influential families on that track.

One overt example was the *Latin deficit.* With the advent of CONCEPT 6, the only certified Latin teacher taught on a different track from that of my children. I had wanted them to take three years of Latin, but only **Track C** students had that privilege. My children were limited to two years.

Another inequity was the administration of the gifted program in elementary school. **Track C** students had the advantage of attending gifted classes fulltime, but gifted students living on **Track A** or **Track B** were offered merely partial access to the program.

In the 2002 Los Angeles Times CONCEPT 6 news article previously mentioned, there is an unfortunate but recognizable criticism outlining problems of **Track B** students which relate to course offerings.

> *". . . Some complain there is even a stigma associated with being a B-track student. They say B-track is the dumb track . . . We're not those special magnet kids. So the most apathetic students are on B-track."* [16]

5. Vacation Problems.

a. Lack of supervision for vacationing students whose parents were in the work force. Our family was able to resolve this problem because my parents drove south from Massachusetts each year and rented a condo nearby for January, February, and March.

With great pleasure, my mother and father came over to the house every day for my children's two vacationing months. Had it not been for the loving care of their grandparents, Philip and Elinore Fay, the five Ryans would have remained home alone all day unchaperoned—no doubt getting on each other's nerves, or worse.

Other families were not as fortunate. Most parents could manage a traditional summer vacation, even if both parents worked, because ample recreation programs for school children were in place at that time.

Winter, spring, and fall vacations, however, presented problems. Some parents were forced to place children in daycare, hire sitters, or leave children home alone.

b. Lack of bus transportation for students who had switched tracks. This scenario would apply to all families who had a need to change their assigned track. The Ryan family was in this category. While Jupiter students were living in the shadow of CONCEPT 6, I had been teaching in both private and public schools taking the traditional summer vacation—the same vacation offered to all other school children in Palm Beach County.

In order that my children and I could share the summer vacation, I needed to petition the school district to transfer them out of **Track C,** our assigned track of *privilege,* and move them over to **Track A** which offered the summer vacation.

In so doing, I created an enormous transportation problem for my family in that there was no school bus service to any vacationing track.

In other words, since my children were **Track A** students living on **Track C,** there was no bus transportation for them in the months of November and December when **Track C** was on vacation.

During those months, it was a daily challenge arranging rides for five children in three different schools: elementary, middle, and high school. Not until Joy was a senior, was she old enough to drive herself to school.

For much of CONCEPT 6, Captain Joe was home only on weekends. On the occasions when he was in residence and forced into the driving/juggling act twice daily, he would say, *"This is madness! Change all of the children back to Track C where they belong!"*

Although I could certainly sympathize with his frustration, I was resolute in my decision that our family spend the summer vacation together. No changes were made.

On the bright side, Captain Joe enjoyed being our capable chauffeur in the summer when we drove to New England to be with our families and childhood friends. This luxury would not have been possible had I followed his sensible advice.

c. Lack of formal recreation for vacationing students who had switched tracks. There were no extracurricular activities in town for my children while they were on their January and February vacation.

Their only formal recreation occurred in the early evening when I drove them to their respective swim team practices at North Palm Beach Country Club's Olympic pool.

[Aside: One of the reasons we moved to Jupiter in 1974, was the Olympic pool *"soon"* to be built in the area. It would have been ideal for our children's swim program. For two years before the move, Captain Joe's friend Franklyn (Chapter 5) had sent us articles on the topic from *The Jupiter Courier.* Town fathers were considering placing the pool by Carlin Park and the beach. As it turned out, those discussions dragged out for *twenty* years. Eventually the pool was built near the high school in 1993, several years after our children had moved on. All was not lost, however, as Captain Joe enjoyed the public pool every day after his second retirement.]

d. Lack of transportation for vacationing students wanting to participate in school sports. While school sports programs continued, students on vacation could not take advantage of them unless they provided their own rides. For many, this was not possible.

e. Lack of continuity and cohesiveness. On a larger scale, CONCEPT 6 vacationing students were out of synch with countywide sports contests, music competitions, drama festivals, and more. Families would need to make special arrangements to offset this inconvenience. One track was always out of school for important events.

f. Lackluster student morale. With respect to the social dynamic, there were morale problems with regard to severed friendships. When students returned to school from a two-month vacation, several of their friends on another track went out on vacation for the next two months.

They would not see each other at school for *four months*. Best friends could work things out on weekends, but the easy-going spontaneity of seeing casual friends in class or at lunch was completely gone.

Part II. RANDALL THE RETALIATOR VS TONY

Another disadvantage of the system—that interfered with school friendships—was the distribution of high school yearbooks. Before CONCEPT 6 began, students received their yearbooks by the middle of May and attended a much-anticipated party where they signed each other's yearbooks.

Underclassmen bid farewell to graduating seniors. A festive, emotional event with laughter, tears, and youthful conviviality, it was a traditional rite of passage.

Soon after CONCEPT 6 took hold, the distribution of yearbooks dramatically changed. The yearbook sponsor and a few colleagues convinced the administration that yearbooks should be delivered in August from then on. Their justification was based on scheduling changes imposed by CONCEPT 6.

They decided to hold the yearbook signing party more than *three long months* after high school seniors had graduated and flown the coop. Organizers attempted to make the August event sound exciting, but the truth was that it never gathered momentum, student enthusiasm had waned, and the party was a down and out *flop.*

This practice went on for several years until Tony decided to tackle yearbook distribution reform when running for junior class president in April of his sophomore year.

I supported him in this effort because it was an important issue to students that other candidates had been reluctant to address—either through fear of **reprisals** from teachers, or because they simply didn't know how to approach the problem.

Tony was well liked, but the added incentive of receiving their yearbooks before graduation, prompted his classmates to give him an overwhelming victory. In effect, he had hit a home run with his campaign pledge.

But, **Whoa!** Hold the phone! There was a hitch. The election had taken place in April when **Track A** and **Track C** students were in attendance, and of necessity, a second election had to be scheduled for May when **Track B** students were back in school.

The result was the same, but, curiously, it was late September or early October before Tony was allowed to assume office.

Students had begun to complain and question as to what was causing the delay.

We learned later from inside sources that Randall the Retaliator and a few other teachers who favored an August delivery of yearbooks were instrumental in postponing the installation of class officers.

Deviously, they wanted to stall and thwart Tony's efforts to change the yearbook distribution date. Randall was a retired teacher from up North who had been acting regularly as a substitute teacher before he accepted a permanent position on **Track A.**

Randall had become very attached to the **Track A** vacations, enjoying January and February in sunny Florida, and visiting family and friends back home during the month of July. Involved in assisting several sponsors with extracurricular activities, he had ingratiated himself with certain teachers.

Randall was not one of Tony's teachers, so Tony knew him only in passing. None of my other children had a class with him. But oddly enough, as we learned later, he had developed an irrational grudge against Tony for his campaign pledge.

Once he had been officially pronounced class president, Tony began looking into the yearbook predicament with the assistance of *Teacher Y* who favored his plan. He soon found out that the publisher was most willing to move the delivery date back to April, before graduation, contrary to what students had been told.

Upon further investigation, it seemed that those in charge of yearbook distribution had made the change to August for their *own convenience* and not for that of the students. That was a revelation to Tony. When he took on that project, he did not realize that he would be clashing with teachers' ulterior motives.

Fortunately, Tony was able to effect the change by setting up a conference with the school principal and a few of his advisors.

At the meeting were the other class officers and some students from each of the tracks who wanted this adjustment.

After hearing the students' side, faculty members in attendance were receptive to the modification, and Tony was able to set the gears in motion with the yearbook publisher for the desired April delivery date.

The administration worked out **shared responsibility** for the yearbook with the original sponsor and *Teacher Y* who had been helping Tony look into the matter. That teacher was on a different track from the sponsor and on the **same** track as Tony.

The new arrangement made things convenient for Tony, and he welcomed the assistance that *Teacher Y* provided. With little thought, this same system could have been put in place at the onset of CONCEPT 6.

Students were absolutely thrilled to return to a normal **yearbook signing** event with its typical excitement and hoopla. As one would expect, Tony was exceptionally pleased that he had been able to make that happen, although it appeared that Randall the Retaliator and a few other teachers continued to be disgruntled about the unanticipated turn of events.

After the yearbooks had been issued, several students asked Tony if he intended to run for senior class president. They thought it was *"really cool"* that he had kept his campaign pledge.

Tony had decided against running. As a senior, he would participate in the **Executive Intern Program** (Chapter 17), and he would be off campus most of first semester. He would be working in the Engineering Department of Riviera Beach, a small city fifteen miles to the south of Tequesta. Tony was enthusiastic about that assignment.

For sports, he participated in cross country in the fall, and he was senior co-captain of the high school swim team. Outside of school, he swam year round for the **Amateur Athletic Union (AAU)**.

At graduation he was ranked #7 in his class. Life was busy, but he managed his time fairly well.

Not long after the yearbooks were issued, Tony was startled to receive a disturbing phone call from Randall the Retaliator at just about 8:30 in the evening on a week night. In the twenty-three year time span that my children attended school, not one of their teachers had ever called the house for them or me—although I wish that The Bugman (Chapter 8) had called.

Randall got right to it and lashed out at Tony in a rage. He told him that he had been the worst class president he had ever known, and he was really glad that Tony was not running for that office again. He then brutally chastised him for his involvement with the yearbook and advised him that he should have left things *"well enough alone."* He did not use profanity, but he hurled one insult after another.

And that wasn't all. Randall went on to reprimand Tony for not attending the junior prom about ten days earlier. It seems that Randall had been at the prom and noticed Tony's absence.

When I walked into the house shortly before 9:00 P.M, after returning from the supermarket, I saw Tony standing *stunned* and *speechless* in the living room.

He was silently listening to this teacher's deafening tirade and holding the phone out from his ear. Appalled, as I walked toward Tony, I could hear Randall's harsh monologue from twelve feet away.

I took the phone and introduced myself while Randall continued his harangue. He assured me that it wasn't a student's place to get involved in administrative decisions like yearbook distribution—that Tony had been *"wrong"* to do so.

Sarcastically, he added that were Tony to run for class president again, Randall could imagine Tony *"hatching plans for more unneeded reforms."* In his eyes, Tony was an irresponsible rabble rouser who had delved into matters that were none of his business.

Inasmuch as Tony had not responded about the prom, nor to any other remark, Randall the Retaliator brought up that topic again with me, saying, in essence, that Tony had abdicated his presidential duties by not attending. In those days, students did not go to the prom without a date. That's the way it was.

Tony was not dating anyone at the time, so he did not attend. On the day of the prom, however, he worked the entire day in a number of capacities to make the prom atmosphere as inviting as possible—from seemingly endless removal and stacking of chairs to placement of potted palms, to whatever else class sponsors asked him to do.

Good teachers can be excellent role models and mentors to their students. Mentoring allows for a **give** and **take** where teachers and students can learn from one another. Rather than choose that path, Randall took a different route and injected his own personal values into the equation.

Lastly, Randall scolded me sharply for voicing my opposition to CONCEPT 6. He told me that I too had been *"wrong"* to challenge the system.

> *It was then I realized that Randall the Retaliator was exacting a double revenge in one fell swoop:*

- **one against Tony for his yearbook reform**

- **one against me as an adversary of** CONCEPT 6

Not wanting to respond in kind, I quickly terminated the phone call. The disillusionment of it all was this teacher's **destructive desire** to shame an unassuming, young leader who had improved the morale of the entire student body.

I listened intently to **Randall's Rant**. Although I had never met him, I had heard him talk at meetings several times. It was his custom to speak distinctly in a perceptibly loud voice. That night he was speaking in his usual manner—but with even more intensity—when he unleashed a premeditated, *character assassination* against a blameless honor student, who had presented not one discipline problem since he began school.

Thankfully, Randall the Retaliator was not one of Tony's teachers, and they had no further dealings with one another from that moment on. Tony continued to enjoy his school activities, his friends, and his overall way of life.

I did not report the incident to the principal. Randall held prestigious membership in the inner circle. It would have been futile, and I did not want to prolong the verbal assault by recanting it.

After the fact, I learned from a teacher who had worked closely with Randall, that Tony's case was not unique. He knew Randall the Retaliator to be spiteful in dealings with colleagues and students if things did not proceed according to his wishes. Before this unpleasant experience occurred, I would not have believed such behavior of a teacher.

Fortunately, Tony got over this ugly scene in short order, but it left an indelible imprint on my memory. I have no idea how prevalent or isolated an incident such as this may be today. I report it here simply as a caution.

Advisory: At times, teachers do indeed retaliate against students—ever so ruthlessly.

Chapter 14
Paula the Perfect Pro

Her expertise guided them as they struggled out of the abyss.

Family member: Thad

Where was Piaget when I needed him? I began my doctorate with the study of Piaget in 1987. I could have used his help in 1982 when Thaddeus entered sixth grade.

Joy, Nick, Tony, and Fay had whizzed through Grade 6 without incident, but Thaddeus at the outset began to have difficulty with pre-algebra and earned a D on a test. I was **baffled.**

I scheduled a conference with his teacher, Paula the Perfect Pro, and we had a productive discussion. She was gracious and spent as much time with me as I needed.

She showed me the type of problems that were giving Thaddeus trouble and advised me that some students were not mature enough to understand how to solve them. They could not grasp the concepts quickly, but with remediation and extended time, they could work through them.

She eagerly offered her services after school, two days per week to help Thaddeus. He wasn't thrilled with that arrangement, but he went along with the program as outlined for him.

Gradually, he began to explain to his teacher exactly what he was **not** comprehending. She could then zero in on his specific weaknesses and on his thinking processes in general. As the weeks went on, Thaddeus started to grasp what the problems were all about, and he was learning how to solve them.

By the end of the first term, he was able to earn a low B for his final grade. During the second term, he needed assistance only one day per week. Paula the Pro was extremely pleased with his progress, and I was most appreciative of her dedication to helping my son.

Thad earned a high B for the second term. Understandably, Paula and I were happy about this improvement.

During the third term, *ambiguity gave way to enlightenment.* Thad no longer needed extra assistance, and he began to enjoy the challenges of problem solving. He earned A's for the third and fourth terms, and from then on, he was not stymied by the study of mathematics.

Five years later, when I was studying his four stages of cognitive development, Piaget made it all clear to me.

**"For *Piaget, intelligence* meant
exploring the environment."** [17]

The following is a *brief synopsis*[18] of Piaget's stages of cognitive development:

1. **Sensorimotor stage. Ages: Birth - 2 Years. Children learn through their instincts, sights, sounds, sucking, and grabbing.**

2. **Preoperational stage. Ages: 2 - 7 Years. Children cannot understand why events occur, so they make up their own rationale. (As an example, readers may remember the old explanation for thunder that God was bowling in heaven).**

3. **Concrete operational stage. Ages: 7 - 11 Years. Children begin to use inductive reasoning. They can remember where they left a toy instead of searching for it, but they still have trouble with abstract thinking.**

4. **Formal operational stage. Ages: 11 - Adult. Adolescents begin to think abstractly and logically about hypothetical problems; they begin to use deductive reasoning. They come to understand scientific concepts.**

To sum up, each person's brain develops and matures at a different pace within an overall framework of recognizable growth patterns.

When Thaddeus began the study of pre-algebra, he was still eleven years old, and his brain could not fully process the information or perform the required tasks needed to solve the problems. Once his maturation process had progressed farther on the continuum, he reached a higher level of comprehension.

As he neared his twelfth birthday in April, Thad's cognitive development coincided with Piaget's calculations. He was approaching the formal operational stage.

Apparently his siblings had progressed toward that stage of cognition ahead of schedule, but Thaddeus, according to Piaget, was on target.

I don't know if Paula the Pro was aware of Piaget's theory. She never mentioned it to me as a way of analyzing the gaps in Thad's comprehension, but she knew that it was common for students of that age to experience the same difficulty. *Her expertise guided them as they struggled out of the abyss.*

Although I believe that Piaget's studies are highly credible, I also give full credit to Paula the Pro for bringing Thaddeus out of the darkness into the light.

Without her guidance, he might have been grappling endlessly with the concepts of higher order thinking, not having any idea on how to proceed.

Paula taught him strategies and techniques that helped him find his comfort level with a variety of math-related assignments.

Moreover, she gave him confidence to tackle advanced math in each succeeding year. Unlike Zack's teacher **(Tip #16),** she did not label him as a student of limited ability. She facilitated his understanding of concepts he considered difficult.

Some teachers do not see why their students are having problems absorbing the material. And even though those teachers themselves fully understand the concepts of the lesson, they *cannot explain* them well.

Furthermore, they are ***incapable*** of showing their students alternative routes to problem solving. Many would agree that such teachers are better suited to a different profession.

Undeniably, Paula the Perfect Pro is an example of all excellent teachers who reach out to help their students and stay with them until they master the subject.

She represents the best of the best, and from reports of my friends, whose children she taught several years later, she was consistent in her student outreach throughout her teaching career.

***Advisory: Keep in mind that
some knowledgeable teachers cannot explain
difficult concepts to struggling students.***

Chapter 15
Manual-Bound Manny

Manual-Bound Manny had substituted a strict adherence to the teacher manual for lack of competency and common sense.

Family member: Thad

At the opposite end of the spectrum from Paula the Perfect Pro in terms of wisdom, attitude, and proper protocol was Thad's sixth grade literature/reading teacher, Manual-Bound Manny. I heard Manny address parents at the middle school's Open House at the beginning of the academic year.

Although he appeared to be well into middle age, he told his audience that he was new to the field of education. It seems that he had run his own business for many years and decided it was time for a change.

He assured all of us that he was looking forward to working with our children. As a late entry into the teaching profession myself, I was rooting for him.

Literature/reading had been Thad's strong suit ever since he began elementary school. Each year he and a classmate named Callie outshone their peers on national reading assessments.

In third and fourth grade, their teachers sent them up to read with students at the next grade level. During fifth grade, they were placed in a group of their own and maintained an accelerated pace all year.

In middle school, problems arose with Manual-Bound Manny in March of Thad's sixth-grade year. Thaddeus showed me three literature assignments bearing the grade of B with a few mistakes noted on each assignment.

He did not see any errors in his work. I studied the material carefully to determine where he had gone astray. Instead, I noted that Thad had answered each question thoughtfully and on point. I confirmed that his work was error free.

Reacting to those low grades, I wrote a note to Manny advising him that Thaddeus and I were wondering why so many of his answers had been marked wrong. Manual-Bound Manny, in accordance with his epithet, replied that Thad's answers did not correspond to answers in the teacher manual, and therefore he could not allow any credit for them.

I left a phone message for Manny requesting that he provide me with a copy of the manual. He told Thaddeus that he was unable to comply with my request because the teacher manual remained in the privileged domain of teachers at the school.

Not willing to concede that point, I contacted Thad's guidance counselor and asked if she could locate a manual for me. She arranged for me to borrow one, and I took it home for a few days to pore over it deliberately.

As I had suspected, some of Thad's test responses were at odds with answers in the teacher manual because the corresponding answers in the manual were incorrect.

What surprised me, however, was learning that above and beyond the errors involving Thad's tests, there were other errors in the manual. Inaccuracies were apparent in each chapter.

In my assessment of the teacher manual, I found two categories of faulty answers:

- **Some answers were incomplete or misleading.**

- **Some answers were just plain wrong.**

Whoever had written the questions and answers for the teacher manual had done a shoddy job of it. Very likely, it had been the work of several persons with little collaboration with one another. Throughout my career, I was never impressed with a teacher manual, but I realize that many teachers rely on them.

During one of my early years of teaching, my principal inquired at a faculty meeting,

"What makes a good teacher?"

I didn't answer aloud, but I was thinking, *intelligence, wisdom, knowledge of subject matter, planning, organization, patience, establishing a rapport with students,* and more.

One language arts teacher, however, replied without a moment's hesitation, ***"Having a good manual for the teacher to follow."*** The principal nodded forcefully in agreement.

I had not anticipated the teacher's answer or the principal's reaction to it. I always believed that teachers with a strong background in their field of expertise took precedence over a teacher manual any day.

Still, I would not rule out a carefully-crafted teacher manual that might offer an experienced teacher some additional ideas for presenting a lesson. Then too, it is quite plausible that Paula the Perfect Pro may have used a teacher manual providing answers to the textbook's math problems.

But Paula, without a doubt, had the expertise to recognize a mistake in the manual, and she knew how to evaluate, teach, and work through each formula to the last detail.

There are times when teachers are compelled to rely on a teacher manual if they are assigned to teach a subject that is *out-of-field*, one that they are not certified to teach.

Occasionally, in response to requests by parents, administrators create an academic course for which they have no officially accredited teacher on their faculty, and they randomly place any available teacher in that slot.

This is far from ideal, but it does happen. Teachers have no choice in the matter but to obey their principal and use the manual to teach the class as best they can. In that situation, a conscientious teacher can do the job under proper conditions:

- **The teacher must be highly competent.**

- **The teacher manual must be accurate.**

After reviewing the teacher manual for Thad's class, I verified my supposition that

Manual-Bound Manny had substituted a strict adherence to the teacher manual for lack of competency and common sense.

Whenever he administered a quiz or exam, he accepted only those student responses that corresponded **_word-for-word_** with answers in the manual.

One morning, I decided to call from work and talk to Manny during his planning period which coincidentally occurred at the same time as mine. Speaking to him as one professional to another, I told him that I had received a copy of the manual, and after comparing Thad's answers to those in the manual, it was evident that Thaddeus had responded appropriately.

As a result of finding errors in the manual, I asked if we could set up a date and time to conduct a thorough review of the material in order to revise Thad's grade. I had not foreseen Manny's immediate reaction.

Manual-Bound Manny abruptly hung up the phone. I could see that he was inexperienced and had a lot to learn. If he continued to teach, he would come up against parents with far more aggressive attitudes than mine, making much harsher demands than any I had made.

A reasonable person would have met with me to see what I had found in the manual. Furthermore, he could have discreetly benefited from the exchange.

Instead, by his own doing, Manual-Bound Manny besmirched his reputation with his superiors once they learned about the error-ridden manual and his refusal to acknowledge it.

Nevertheless, I did not convert his bad manners toward me into a personal vendetta. Even if he had denied my request with extreme civility, I would have pursued the matter further.

He should have sensed that I was focused on getting to the root of the problem no matter how much effort it would take.

After advising the guidance counselor of Manual-Bound Manny's response to my phone call, I left her a packet of information containing copies of Thad's tests along with several pages from the manual where I had located errors. I asked her to decide how I should proceed from there.

I then became a victim of the **Big Stall** and the **Big Run Around.** My report circulated among two assistant principals, the language arts department chairperson, and the principal with whom I had a brief conference explaining my concerns.

After telling me that he would get back to me on the matter, he did nothing. He was biding his time. It was the same old story.

He ignored me intentionally in hopes that he could wear me down, and that I would in the long run give up the ghost. I called him once again.

After yet another delay, I received a letter from the principal with the following message supporting the teacher in his system of grading:

- *"Manual-Bound Manny has treated your son fairly."*

- *"The grading of written work is certainly a subjective matter and could not necessarily be questioned."*

The second sentence made no sense whatsoever. It was obvious that no one in authority had read, addressed, understood, or even cared about the specific complaint regarding errors in the teacher manual that I had submitted for review.

In all likelihood, my letter passed from desk to desk with barely a glance. It would seem that the principal relied on his subordinates for their input, and he took no initiative on his own to intervene directly in the matter. After allowing considerable time to respond, he had given my communiqué little thought.

Having exhausted my remedies at the middle school, it was time to move up to a higher level of appeal. With my next step, I achieved the results that I had been pursuing for more than **three months.**

This time around, I submitted the same packet of material to the area administrator known for her intelligence, her efficiency, and her fairness.

After reviewing all of the paperwork, she acted swiftly. She saw an immediate need to rectify the wrongdoing stacked up against a student under her jurisdiction.

In her phone call to me, the administrator told me that she had met with the principal and Manual-Bound Manny and given them copies of the errors in the manual. She personally arranged for Thad's grades to reflect the A's he had earned via his **accurate** responses.

Who knew how many more students had been adversely affected by Manual-Bound-Manny's inexperience and inadequacy—coupled with systemic flaws in the teacher manual?

As a follow up to this time-consuming exercise in persistence, I learned from a friend who taught at the same school as Manual-Bound Manny, that the administrator addressed the topic of inaccurate teacher manuals at one of the monthly faculty meetings.

Speaking authoritatively and specifically, she advised sixth-grade language arts teachers that a parent had found many errors in the literature/reading manual.

In general terms, she cautioned the entire faculty to be on guard against mistakes in all teacher manuals in the future. Department chairpersons would need to set up a system for locating and weeding errors.

At long last, by sounding the gong, I hoped that I had made a difference—not just for my child—but for all students going forward whose teachers would be using the same, defective manual. Alert parents must always be part of the equation.

Although my message had fallen on deaf ears in the case of the principal and his assistants, I was fortunate to have been able to appeal to someone who was not threatened by, nor indifferent to, my request.

The area administrator was an experienced, competent professional who could clearly see all of the weak links in the chain of command that led to her door.

It is alarming to know that imprecise teacher manuals are not relics of the distant past. In recent years, working with my grandchildren or with school-age children of friends, I have been able to document mistakes in student worksheets that accompany teacher manuals.

Unaware of the errors, many teachers routinely use these inexact, prepackaged materials as a way to assign daily grades to their students. Teachers who fail to monitor and recognize such errors are not only causing their students to earn poor grades; even worse, they are compromising the integrity of the lesson.

These examples serve as added exhortations for **parental vigilance** which must play a critical role in seeing that children's schoolwork is subject to at least **weekly** if not **daily** scrutiny.

A few months ago, one of my friends told me about a problem with a mathematics textbook that her granddaughter was using as a first-year student in a public high school in Florida.

An all-A student since kindergarten, she asked her math teacher to go over Problem X one more time. She could not understand why the answer she had worked out methodically on her own did not agree with the textbook answer key.

Her teacher, a larger-than-life, 2016 version of Manual-Bound Manny, had no patience with her request. He refused to *"waste his time"* reviewing the problem.

Acerbically, he told the young lady to go home and prepare a PowerPoint presentation for the class, showing in detail why she thought that the textbook's answer key was invalid. From his myopic stance, he thought that his negative retort would be the end of the matter.

Intrepidly taking up the gauntlet, the conscientious student went home and fastidiously solved the problem showing her work every step of the way—via the suggested PowerPoint slide show. When she returned to school, she asked the teacher's permission to present her findings to the class.

Although noticeably unprepared for her resourceful rejoinder to his challenge, the teacher allowed her to proceed. In so doing, she demonstrated that her answer had been the correct one all along, and that the book's answer key for that problem was invalid. *What's wrong with this picture?*

Parents are smart enough to know that we live in an imperfect world where mistakes may be found from time to time in a cookbook, a technology manual, or even in a textbook. To counteract textbook errors, parents rely on teachers to set the record straight for their children.

Teachers hold their positions because they are alleged to be the experts in their academic disciplines. It is the duty of knowledgeable teachers to alert students to such errors. Instead, many teachers mindlessly and negligently conform to a flawed system without giving it a second thought.

The math teacher's behavior in the example above is an abomination. Quick-thinking students, forced to second guess their teachers, are dismayed and disillusioned by the lack of professionalism in teachers of this caliber.

Of even greater concern, students who are *slower* to *comprehend* can become seriously flummoxed by a teacher displaying this ineptness.

Just when those students believe that they are grasping a difficult concept, they may be thrown altogether off balance with a *wrong answer* provided by their own teacher. For all types of students, a Manual-Bound Manny is flat out demoralizing.

Advisory: Your children are counting on you to rout out and eliminate errors in their classrooms, whatever the source may be.

Chapter 16
Reign of Terror Tess

It appears that some teachers like Tess, in taking themselves and their subject matter seriously, lose sight of the student as a person.

Family member: Tony
Two Other Students

Soon after our family arrived in the Jupiter/Tequesta area, I began tutoring a few students who lived in the Tequesta Country Club community of homes. The majority of parents from that neighborhood set high educational goals for their children.

Many of them were engineers who had been transferred from Connecticut after 1958, when Pratt Whitney Aircraft Corporation opened a testing facility west of Jupiter in a rural area of West Palm Beach.

One afternoon in May of 1975, I received a frantic telephone call from a high school student named Katy, who was a friend of one of my pupils from the country club.

Her final exam was scheduled for the next day, and she needed help preparing for it. Katy was a senior looking forward to graduation in four days.

Just that very day, her teacher, Reign of Terror Tess, had advised her that she would not graduate if she failed the exam. As a result, she was exceptionally nervous.

In going over her test review study sheet, I could see that Katy was ill prepared. I helped her as best I could in three hours and wished her luck.

Two days later, Katy called to report that she had failed the exam. She would not graduate with her class, as her teacher, Reign of Terror Tess, had forewarned.

First she would be required to attend summer school. Then, she would need to pass a similar but different exam in order to earn a high school diploma *without ceremony* at a later date, sometime in August.

Although Katy was devastated about missing the pomp and circumstance of her graduation ceremonies, she was not upset with me but rather with her teacher. Katy told me that she had just talked with a friend who had the *same* experience with the **same** teacher the previous year. There were rumors of other victims over the years whose graduation ceremonies Reign of Terror Tess had powerfully and proudly blocked.

Still new to the area, I did not know many of the teachers at that high school. I was sorry that I could not have offered more help to Katy.

But I sensed that something was terribly amiss with a graduation bombshell that took this student so completely by surprise. With time, I came to learn of the reputation of Reign of Terror Tess who had failed my pupil on the eve of her graduation. Tess taught *Academic Subject X*.

Seven years later as a junior in high school, Tony was a student in the class of Reign of Terror Tess. Through that class, I learned firsthand about this teacher, her unorthodox tactics and her powerful status at the school.

Having been there at the same school for a number of years, she enjoyed her seniority among the faculty as a whole and at times when she acted as department chairperson.

In most disciplines, the department chair position seemed to rotate regularly among the teachers. There was no doubt that students feared Tess's stern grading policies.

At the beginning of the academic year, Reign of Terror Tess issued an austere proclamation with regard to deadlines for special projects:

> *"My project deadlines are firm and inflexible. Illness will not be an excuse. If you are sick when the project is due, send it to school with a family member. I will not accept a late project."*

I remember vividly the three-dimensional project assigned by Tess near the end of the first term. Tony and his friend Ben, another A student, even more conscientious than he, had teamed up to do that assignment together.

135

Because they were heavily involved in sports, had recently participated in a number of band concerts, and had been deluged with exams in other classes, they had neglected the project until the final moments. With a few small tools, rigid foam, and glue, they were piecing the project together on the tile floor of our living room.

At midnight on a Sunday, with the project due the next day, the model was far from complete. Ben appeared worried about the prospect of earning a bad grade, but both boys were exhausted and had not an ounce of strength left to finish their potential masterpiece. I sent Ben home and Tony to bed, and I assured them that I would complete the remaining work.

Ben was skeptical, but Tony had no doubt that his mother would come through for them on this important assignment. Even though I needed to be at work the next day, I stayed up to fine tune the project. Shortly after 4 A.M., I finished spray painting its intricate details,

Reign of Terror Tess was so impressed with the project that she gave it an A+ grade, and it was the only project she sent to the Library Media Center to be placed on display.

We were all relieved that Tess's deadline had been met in a timely manner. Both Ben and Tony earned A's for that term in Terror's class, and they vowed to themselves and to me that they would do better at organizing their time in the future.

There are some parents who believe in making their children assume full responsibility for their school projects without giving them any assistance. In a case like this, they would have let their children suffer the consequences of poor planning.

I look at it in a different light. There were many times when I had to lend a hand to save the day. Working together on school projects can be a valuable experience for parent and child where each can learn much from the other.

Of course, there should be a limit, to parental involvement. Some parents take over the entire project from start to finish, and students learn nothing.

In the case of **science fair** projects, I have seen parents go completely overboard with their own ideas and squelch most of the input their children might have. Intensely competitive parents turn such assignments into their own personal crusade for a blue ribbon. Many other parents and I came to dread and detest those science projects.

Yet there was one notable exception for me. It was Fay's middle school science project where I took photos of Fay **talking** to tiny trees in Gallery Square, Tequesta. After several sessions of stimulating conversation, photos indicated **significant** growth of foliage in three saplings. Fay and I had some fun with it.

As a bonus, her teacher was amused and rewarded her with a grade of A minus, imposing only a slight penalty for lack of strict, scientific muster.

I'd prefer that students be given a problem in some realm of science to solve at school by themselves with a modicum of guidance from their teachers.

- Students would be responsible for **their own work** with no one else leeching off them for help, as is often the case with group projects. Individual, random topics of equal difficulty would be assigned in the first class of the day.

- Students would remain in one classroom all day, and the project would be completed in all disciplines throughout the school—with one entire day being **dedicated to science.** Science teachers could visit each class to offer advice.

For several years, many science departments abandoned the routine, stylized projects. But, as with other lapsed initiatives, they have once again been reborn.

In recent years, my grandchildren have entered the science project arena, along with a little help from their parents, assorted relatives, or family friends. It can take a village to get the job done.

In sharp contrast to hovering helicopter moms and dads are those parents, previously mentioned, who do not become involved to the least extent with school assignments.

Their children, as a result, often earn bad grades on their projects—either for not doing the work at all, or for submitting a poorly done project for lack of parental guidance.

Parents who offer no help whatsoever run the risk of having their children ashamed of their projects in front of their classmates. As a teacher, I have often witnessed students humiliated for this very reason.

Even if other students did not ridicule those projects openly—as they might have done—the dejected students themselves knew all too well that their work was of inferior quality.

Unfortunately, there had been no one at home to get them started. Some students tried to laugh it off and look cool for not doing their work, but it was easy to see through their façade. They really did care about their image in front of peers.

Many students simply don't know how or where to begin a project. With a little support, parents can help their children tap into their creativity while following the specific directions set forth.

After a while, students will get the hang of things, go it alone, and take pride in their finished product. Beyond any doubt, I admire and applaud students who can create an excellent project entirely on their own.

Those students live up to the *ideal* of the responsible, resourceful student and, in so doing, they free up their parents from yet another time-consuming task.

Tony's next major assignment in Reign of Terror Tess's class was one that he worked on without anyone's help. He was on track to meet his deadline when he became ill with a fever and other flu-like symptoms. Our family's pediatrician called in a prescription and prescribed bed rest. Tony slept the better part of two days.

On the third day, Tony was still weak, and he tired easily. But he felt well enough to put the finishing touches on his project. Arriving back at school the next day with an excused absence, he submitted his project to the teacher, **one day late.**

At the end of class, Reign of Terror Tess returned the project to Tony attached to a clean sheet of white paper on which she had imprinted her formal decree along with a large, bold, black **F** for an impressive visual effect:

> *"Excellent project, submitted late. This project would have earned an A had student met teacher's assigned deadline. No credit. Grade: 0 = F (Failing)."*

Naively, I had underestimated the arrogance of Reign of Terror Tess. In spite of the harsh rule she had imposed, I had doubted that she would follow through with her warning exactly as stated.

Instead, she remained hard-nosed and inflexible as to her stance. It was obvious that she relished her reputation as a no-nonsense authority figure and did all that she could to preserve that image.

In those **pre-email** days, I sent my protest letter to Tess, via Tony, the next day. I did most of my communicating with teachers through brief notes or letters.

It was difficult to get a teacher on the phone, and since I was working, I did not want to spend time away from my students in parent-teacher conferences. Surprisingly, two days later, Tess sent a verbal communication with Tony indicating that she would be willing to give Tony a B on the project.

Her supposedly magnanimous concession was, nonetheless, unacceptable to me. At that point, I did not want Tony to continue in the awkward role of a go-between, so I left a note for Tess with the head secretary at the school, and I watched her put it in Tess's mailbox.

Just to double check that she received my correspondence, I left Tess a telephone message advising her of same. In the letter, I argued sensibly that Tony should not be penalized one point for his illness and that if I did not hear back from her within two days, I would take the matter to the school principal.

I always attempted to work things out with the individual teacher before speaking to a higher authority. In like manner, I hoped that my students' parents would extend me the same courtesy if there was a problem, real or perceived. Since Reign of Terror Tess served as the department chairperson at that time, the principal was next in the chain of command.

Not hearing from Tess after establishing *my* firm deadline, I made an appointment with the principal and advised him that Tess's rule was invalid. My rationale was simple: ***teachers' deadlines must allow for illness.***

After I left, the principal called Tess into his office for a chat. That same day, Tess begrudgingly changed Tony's project grade to an A. She did not like her word being challenged, but she had been forced to make things right. This confrontation need not have happened.

Reign of Terror Tess had been determined to keep her ***phony rule*** intact. In so doing, I could not understand why she would put herself in an unfavorable position with her students, their parents, and with her boss. Perhaps no one had challenged her on it before this incident.

For the remainder of the year, Tony felt as if he were walking on eggshells in Tess's class, and he took extra precautions with his assignments to keep them error free. He could not help but fear some form of retribution from Tess. Fortunately, he ended up with an A average in Tess's class each term, and he was not one of those who needed to be concerned about his graduation status.

Two years after Tony had graduated from high school, I received a phone call from my friend Maura indicating that Reign of Terror Tess **had struck again.** Maura, however, had known nothing about my past dealings with Tess. We were friends because her younger son and Thaddeus had been great pals since kindergarten.

Maura was distraught upon learning that her older son Matt, four days away from graduation, had failed the final exam in the class of Terror Tess. As a result, he would neither graduate later in the week, nor be permitted at the very least to walk in the graduation ceremony alongside his classmates.

Before she called me, Matt's mother had spoken with the high school principal. As a consolation, he told her that Matt could receive his diploma in August after he attended summer school and passed a different test in the same field. Since Maura felt that the principal was automatically backing up the teacher without an investigation into the matter, she scheduled a conference with him for the next day.

In a disturbing flashback, I was reminded instantly of my tutoring pupil, Katy, who had faced the same consequences with Reign of Terror Tess—ten years earlier, almost to the day. This time, I was able to make an impact and help Matt graduate with his class.

That evening, over the phone, I worked with Maura composing a letter to the principal, advising him that Matt had been a solid B student in all of his other academic classes for four years. Additionally, Matt had been an outstanding band member throughout high school, successfully representing the school in a variety of demanding competitions.

On his way toward becoming an Eagle Scout, he had also been involved in a number of community service projects. He had never been a discipline problem in any teacher's class. In short, he was an all-round good kid, well-liked by his teachers and his peers.

His parents and I believed that prohibiting Matt to graduate with his classmates would not only have been an insensitive act on the part of the school, but also a ***cruel and unjust punishment*** for him.

Before delivering the letter to the principal, Maura planned to read it aloud at the conference so that all those in attendance could hear her speak in defense of her son.

From our phone conversation, I learned from Maura that because Matt had been sick midway during the first term, he stayed home from school for eight days.

In that time period, he had missed some critical class presentations that had put him at a disadvantage when he returned to school. Matt didn't feel that Tess had brought him up to speed, but he put forth his best effort.

As a consequence of those absences, he earned an F in that course for the first term of his senior year. In the second and third grading periods, he had made a significant improvement, earning C's in Tess's class.

For the final term, he had been maintaining a C grade, and therefore believed that he was proceeding on course toward graduation. Then during the last week of school, out of the blue, Tess hurled her thunderbolt. Matt had failed her final exam.

The extra weight of the final lowered his average to a failing grade for the last term and resulted in a failure for the entire year, making him ineligible to graduate with his class.

There was, however, one all-important proviso of that process designed to prevent failures. If a teacher believed that a pupil was in danger of failing a term, that teacher was obligated to notify the parent/guardian as follows:

Warning: Notice of Possible Failure

District policy mandated that the notice be sent home along with the mid-term progress report, four and one-half weeks into a term.

The purpose of the warning was to allow students on the receiving end to take advantage of remediation. One step might be to set up a no-cost tutoring program at school, before or after classes, or private lessons elsewhere arranged by the family.

A parent needed to sign and return the warning notice to the teacher who would file it in the student's folder. If a student did not bring back the notice from home, the teacher was required to make a personal contact with the parent.

In more recent years, teachers have been required to submit further documentation to the administration at this juncture, but in the day of Reign of Terror Tess, the warning notice described above was sufficient.

At times there were **suspected forgeries** of parental signatures that the teacher needed to investigate. If a forgery passed the teacher's inspection, and the student forger subsequently failed the class to the confusion and dismay of his parents, in all likelihood, that forged notice would be enough to prove that a proper warning had been sent home.

The teacher's outreach would be confirmed, and the failing grade would remain. I imagine, however, that there might be exceptions depending on the circumstances, and if a parent persisted in challenging the decision.

Maura told me that she had **not** received a failure warning during Matt's first term in Reign of Terror Tess's class, and neither had she received one at the midpoint of the final term. She would have remembered receiving a notice of this magnitude. In general, she was unaware of the existence of these notices because in all other classes throughout his years of schooling, Matt had maintained good grades.

Moreover, Maura was confident that Matt would not forge her signature in an effort to cover up a bad grade. She had excellent rapport with her son and believed that he would have been honest with her from the outset if that scenario had occurred.

Maura asked if I would accompany her to the conference, and I agreed to do so, advising her to make the following inquiry the first order of business: *"On what date was the midterm warning notice sent home?"*

On the morning of the meeting, I sat with Matt and his parents outside the conference room waiting to be called inside. Already in attendance were the principal and the guidance counselor who had briefly acknowledged us earlier. Reign of Terror Tess glanced over at us as she walked past on her way to the conference room.

Although, I had never met Tess face to face, we knew each other by sight. I had seen her at school meetings where she had heard me speak in opposition to CONCEPT 6, of which she had been a staunch supporter. She also remembered my meeting with the principal which led to his reversal of Tony's project grade from zero to A.

Arriving at the conference room, I was the last person to enter after Matt and his parents. Quickly and quietly, the principal approached and asked me to *remain outside.*

He looked apologetic, but nevertheless he acceded to Tess's demands, and I promptly obliged. Reign of Terror Tess had requested that I not be present.

Matt's parents wanted me there as an *advocate* for their son, and I should have been allowed to participate. But the principal preferred to placate Tess. *Her power prevailed.*

Still I recognized the significance of keeping everything on an even keel. Matt's scholastic standing was that which mattered most. In today's world, advocates for students can be necessary and commonplace at school conferences. Thankfully, a teacher like Tess **cannot prohibit** their attendance.

On a positive note, Matt's conference lasted less than fifteen minutes. Matt and his family emerged calmly triumphant, graciously suppressing the urge to break out in a victory dance. After the extensive preparation for the conference, it all came down to one simple fact. Reign of Terror Tess had neglected to issue a failure warning to Matt at the midterm.

Two days later, after a little tutoring by Mom and a makeup exam administered by Tess's assistant, Matt took his **rightful place** at graduation with his classmates.

I was markedly surprised that Tess had forgotten to send a failure warning because she had seemed to be such a stickler for rules. Taking a different view, some of my colleagues believed that Tess deliberately avoided sending home a warning to failing pupils because she did not want those students to have time for remediation.

She was intent on targeting them for failure in accordance with her **predetermined quota.** If she could get away without sending the warning, she chose that route. For more than a decade, she had transmitted a loud and clear signal to the entire school, **"Don't mess with Tess!"**

Reign of Terror Tess had demonstrated no concern for Matt or Katy in helping them to ward off failure. On the contrary, it seemed as if she were playing a game of **Gotcha.**

There was a serious flaw in the system if teachers like Reign of Terror Tess could create such a devastating impact on students so close to graduation. How many graduation ceremonies had Reign of Terror Tess improperly but successfully prevented on the eve of their occurrence?

It appears that some teachers like Tess, in taking themselves and their subject matter seriously, lose sight of the student as a person.

Good teachers, in contrast, **agonize** over the plight of a failing student. Good teachers know how to prevent a graduation crisis. Good teachers know that summer school followed by a make-up exam is nothing more than a **sham** at that late date in the academic year.

Good teachers realize, from a purely human perspective, how important the high school graduation ceremony is to a teenager. Categorically, hands down, it is a supreme **rite of passage.**

Oddly enough, there seemed to be a **culture of acceptance** at the school where administrators and guidance counselors alike succumbed to Tess's all too frequent malpractice scheme. They allowed her to hold the reins. Today's counselors would be infinitely more **proactive** and **protective** of students who might suffer a similar fate.

Tess was considered to be an expert in her field, and it seems that a string of principals deferred to her with regard to much of her biased decision making. Tess **reveled** in her power. She was confident and well aware of her position of prominence, and it made her **Reign of Terror** a very long one. Her safe environment shielded her, cultivated her, and allowed her to flourish.

In a similar manner, other teachers strive to become empowered. Some volunteer for thankless tasks around the school in order to ingratiate themselves with the principal.

As a rule, these **self-serving sycophants** have their own agenda to pursue, and they hope for **favoritism** from the principal at an opportune time. Experienced principals understand exactly how these games are played. Depending on their leadership, they will ignore them, join them, or crush them.

Three of the eleven public school principals for whom I worked, operated with a **blatant crony system** in full force. It is readily apparent to all who work at a school when such relationships are permitted and even encouraged. Cynicism will prevail among those teachers who value fairness. Enthusiasm for their profession may be diminished.

In the name of sound educational practices, school principals are expected to conduct themselves above the fray in accordance with the following behaviors:

- Principals must symbolize integrity.

- Principals must evaluate all teachers impartially.

- Principals must promote strong morale among faculty and students.

- Principals must guarantee that all of their teachers treat students fairly.

Assuredly, more parents should have questioned the tyranny of Reign of Terror Tess. After the graduation incident with Matt, I hoped that the principal took it upon himself to neutralize her power and to keep other teachers like her in check.

Advisory: Parents, look for power plays by tyrannical teachers and resolve to stifle their influence over school principals before they affect your child.

Chapter 17
Dishonorable Honor Society Advisor #2:
Malicious, Malevolent Max

**His spiteful, aggressive actions had already
alerted me to his militant agenda.**

Family Member: Fay

Joy and Nick had been inducted into National Honor Society (NHS) in the spring of tenth grade, as was the tradition of the times, but after a policy change, Tony, Fay, Thaddeus, and other eligible members were inducted in the spring of ninth grade.

Fay's admission was based on her high academic grade point average which she maintained throughout the four-year period. During her sophomore and junior years, Fay attended honor society meetings regularly and participated in what few events or fundraisers the sponsors had scheduled.

Fay continued to be active in other extracurricular activities. At the end of her junior year, she was honored by **American Legion Post 271** in Tequesta, to represent both the local post and her high school at **Girls State** in Tallahassee, Florida's capital. While attending the week-long program, she was elected to the position of Comptroller.

Fay was an excellent swimmer on her school's seasonal swim team, and she also competed twelve months in **Amateur Athletic Union (AAU)** swimming competitions. She played the flute for both her high school band and for the *Symphonic Band of the Palm Beaches*. Rounding out her activities, she took on a variety of roles in school drama club productions.

By the time Fay was a senior in high school, she and Thaddeus were the last of the Ryans at home. Joy had graduated two years earlier from Brown University in Providence, Rhode Island. Nick and Tony were attending Boston College in Chestnut Hill, Massachusetts, two years apart.

One Saturday morning in September of her senior year when Fay, Thaddeus, and I were having a leisurely breakfast, the postman rang the doorbell and delivered a certified letter from the high school to the **Parents of Fay Ryan.** Up until that point, no school had ever contacted us by mail in such dramatic fashion. By nature of his profession, Captain Joe was not home in times of family crises. He had returned to the high seas several years earlier to cover college expenses for the children. I signed for the letter and quickly opened it.

We were advised that Fay had been **expelled** from National Honor Society for failure to comply with NHS rules. The letter was signed by the honor society sponsor at the school, Malicious Malevolent Max, and his assistant. No other specific information was given. Fay knew of no rules that she had supposedly violated.

The following Monday, I spoke via phone to Malevolent Max. He told me that because Fay had missed two meetings, she was being taken off the roster of National Honor Society with all privileges permanently revoked. He and his assistant sponsor had just taken over the society on behalf of NHS members at Jupiter High School.

Their rationale was that they wanted to streamline and revitalize the organization and, in so doing, **"eliminate dead wood."** Together, they had *officially* decided to place Fay in the **dead wood** category. When I spoke to Fay later that evening, she told me that she was unaware of any missed meetings. Until then she had received no notices from either sponsor.

Next, I talked with front office personnel who were responsible for the announcements and learned that all announcements with regard to club meetings and other activities were delivered at the same time each day over the intercom just before seniors went to lunch or left school for the day. A small percentage of students had an abbreviated schedule for their senior year and took their leave at lunch time.

Fay was one of the few students at the high school participating in the districtwide **Executive Intern Program.**

She was **on the job** with that program five days per week for the first half of the academic year. For the duration of her internship, she was **not** on campus when announcements were made.

The **Executive Intern Program** was a career-exploratory program that made it possible for high school seniors to work in a field of interest at the executive level along with top administrators of the organization. Guidance counselors and program coordinators had a longstanding, official agreement that students would not be assigned clerical tasks, and this accord was strictly honored.

I considered this program to be the *crème de la crème* of the School District of Palm Beach County. By way of comparison, at the time, I saw no counterpart to it in any school, public or private, that my friends' children had been attending in other states.

Fay wanted to become an **Executive Intern** because her sister and her brothers had enjoyed their roles as interns. Additionally, college counselors had advised us that admissions officers looked favorably on this program. From another aspect, I was impressed with the professionalism of the program's director, who coincidentally was an alumna of Mount Holyoke College, my alma mater.

She continued to forge strong partnerships with business communities so that students could choose from a number of professions when making their selections. Only outstanding students recommended by their teachers were admitted. They were required to spend a minimum of four hours each weekday on the job.

Accordingly, during the first semester of senior year, my children took only one class at the high school—first thing in the morning—and spent the remainder of the day at their internships where they earned additional credit toward their Grade Point Average (GPA). During second semester, they took their final classes at the high school.

For their internships, Joy worked as a reporter for *The Palm Beach Post*, Nick worked in hospital administration at Jupiter Medical Center, and Tony worked in the Engineering Department of the City of Riviera Beach. Fay, like her sister, chose to write for the *The Palm Beach Post*. When Thaddeus' time came, he worked in broadcasting at a radio station in nearby Lake Worth. Arrangements for the internships had been set up before the end of junior year and approved by senior class academic advisors and guidance counselors.

When I learned why Fay had not heard the announcements advising students of National Honor Society meetings, I sent word to Malevolent Max as to the reason and assumed he would rescind her expulsion notice immediately without further ado. On the contrary, Malicious Malevolent Max decided that he was more justified than ever for giving Fay the boot.

If Fay could not attend meetings because of her internship away from the school, the advisor was convinced even further that Fay should no longer be a member of National Honor Society. From his perspective, attending meetings was of prime importance for NHS membership.

Malevolent Max would not reverse his decision. I could not believe that I was once again facing a challenge that involved one of my children being rejected for membership in National Honor Society.

In those years before the internet, I researched via public library and located the Constitution of National Honor Society. **Article X, Sections 1-5** follows, indicating procedures for discipline and dismissal which still exist today.[19]

Section 1. The Faculty Council, in compliance with the rules and regulations of the National Honor Society, shall determine the procedure for dismissal. A written description of the dismissal procedure shall be available to interested parties.

Section 2. Members who fall below the standards that were the basis for their selection shall be promptly warned in writing by the chapter advisor and given a reasonable amount of time to correct the deficiency, except that in the case of flagrant violation of school rules or the law, a member does not have to be warned.

Section 3. The Faculty Council shall determine when an individual has exceeded a reasonable number of warnings.

Section 4. In all cases of pending dismissal, a member shall have a right to a hearing before the Faculty Council. (Note: This hearing is required and is considered "due process" for all members – Ed.)

Section 5. For purposes of dismissal, a majority vote of the Faculty Council is required.

My investigation revealed that honor society sponsors had acted in either bold defiance of or shameful ignorance of the NHS constitution. In all scenarios, Fay had ....

- Not fallen below the standards that were the basis for her selection.

- Not exhibited a flagrant violation of school rules.

- Not been issued a warning of her *alleged* wrong doing by the chapter advisor.

- Not been given a hearing before the Faculty Council; and that same council had

- Not been notified of the sponsors' unilateral action against Fay.

Once Malicious Malevolent Max had led the duplicitous campaign to oust Fay from the society, it was up to me, to launch my own counter offensive in order to demonstrate how this seemingly well-respected teacher had unjustly proceeded against a dependable, defenseless student.

I scheduled an appointment with the principal and the chapter advisor, Malevolent Max, who had sent word to me through the principal's secretary to have Fay attend the conference. I had no intention of bringing Fay along with me to the meeting because I knew instinctively that Malevolent Max would attempt to lash out or intimidate Fay in some manner.

That sounds like a harsh indictment of a teacher, but ***his spiteful, aggressive actions had already alerted me to his militant agenda.*** More important, there was no need for Fay to attend the conference. She was busy with her internship.

At the conference, representing the school were the principal, Malicious Malevolent Max, and the assistant sponsor of NHS. Max appeared confident that he was holding all the cards and that he would retain the upper hand.

As we were taking our seats, Malevolent Max looked all around the room dramatically in a much bewildered manner and then turned to ask me, **"Where is Fay? I requested that she be here today."**

I told him matter-of-factly that she had an important commitment each day with her internship. Malicious Max's expression indicated his displeasure that I had not yielded to his request.

Instead of Fay, I brought along my close friend who had run for school board on a platform of dismantling CONCEPT 6 (Chapter 13). I knew better than to attend the conference alone.

I wanted an outside witness. I am reminded of Strickland's comment in his book**, Bad Teachers,**

> *"And make no mistake about it: Confronting a teacher requires a great deal of backbone. Marching alone into battle against a teacher and his whole army of supporters is a terrifying prospect."* [20]

In a situation like this, I knew that I needed to educate the school principal:

- First, I presented an overview of what had occurred, and I gave everyone in attendance a copy of the **Discipline and Dismissal Policy** of the National Honor Society on which I had highlighted the key discussion areas.

- Secondly, with the principal's permission, I took the initiative of reading **aloud** from that section of the constitution, *slowly* and *distinctly,* emphasizing established procedures.

- Thirdly, I shared my disbelief and disappointment that an honor society advisor would be unfamiliar with the constitution, and I expressed my quiet outrage at how Fay had been treated.

- Lastly, I ended with the request that Fay be fully reinstated in National Honor Society, although technically by the rules, there had been no grounds for her dismissal in the first place.

After I finished talking, Max's assistant continued to remain silent. In contrast, Malevolent Max, still unremorseful, made an unsuccessful attempt to blame Fay for a communication problem between them.

- Then I reminded him that every year the guidance department sent a notice to all teachers listing the names of students who would be participating in the **Executive Intern Program.**

- Next, I handed him a copy of that list. It had been his responsibility to review it and make a note of any students who were also NHS members. Max had not done that. Insensitive to the needs of high school students in his care, he had been **preoccupied solely with their expulsion.**

By the end of the conference, Max had no recourse. The principal had said almost nothing, but he ordered the deflated, yet still Malevolent Max, to arrange for Fay's readmission into National Honor Society.

I suggested to the principal that if any other students had been similarly victimized, he needed to make it right for them; however, I had no power to follow through with that aspect of the case.

The student president of National Honor Society had told me in confidence that other students had received letters of dismissal for the same reason and in the same manner as Fay, but I could not involve him in the matter.

Not having names, I could not advise those students or their parents of Max's transgressions. I could only hope that the principal learned from Fay's unfortunate experience and made certain that all students were treated fairly. I thanked him for his time, and we said our "goodbyes."

What the principal should have done, after I left his office, was request from Malevolent Max a list of all students to whom he had sent honor society expulsion notices. The principal then would have needed to set the matter straight, ***once and for all.***

From my personal experiences in such matters, I find it disconcerting and, more to the point, ***unethical,*** that most of these incidents are handled individually on a ***hush-hush*** basis—only ***if*** and ***when*** a parent complains. [One exception to this, that I am aware of, was Nick's incident involving NJHS outlined in Chapter 10.]

In a majority of cases, you will not find the principal acting like a town crier spreading the news of misdeeds and urging victims to come forward for redress. Unlike in a class action lawsuit where all parties are notified of a possible wrong doing, victims of injustice at a school often remain ***unenlightened*** in order that errors made by teachers or administrators stay ***shrouded in secrecy.***

Two nights later, I received a phone call from an unrepentant, but subdued Max inviting Fay back into National Honor Society and letting me know about a special meeting of NHS the following week. I politely thanked him for the information and kept our exchange to a minimum. Max had been instructed by the principal to rectify the situation, and he had no choice but to make the call.

It is conjecture as to whether or not Malicious Malevolent Max knew that National Honor Society had a practical, working constitution. If he did know about it, then he had committed a flagrant violation of its guidelines in seeking Fay's expulsion.

If, on the other hand, Max had been unaware of the constitution's existence, he would have neglected his duties by not researching the history of the organization in order that he . . .

- **Learn of its bylaws**

- **Understand what values NHS upholds**

When I conducted my investigation, I learned that National Honor Society is extremely tolerant of students who do not follow the traditional path. As an example, I found a section of the constitution stating that even if some of its members are using drugs illegally, they need to be *counseled extensively* before advisors could consider taking any drastic action like expulsion. Following a model of integrity, National Honor Society advocates *due process.*

By virtue of its existence, National Honor Society is an honorable organization. Accordingly, all of its chapter advisors throughout the United States, in upholding the wellbeing of its members, are expected to conduct themselves in an *honorable* manner.

The attempted ouster of Fay and several of her classmates under the *guise of legitimacy*—via United States Postal Service certified mail—was a shifty, underhanded move that defied all sense of decency on the part of the school's National Honor Society sponsors.

Further, it was an assault on the dignity and ideals of some of the high school's most distinguished scholars who deserved praise and encouragement from the sponsors instead of *humiliation* and *exile.*

Author's commentary:
Shame on Malicious Malevolent Max!

Chapter 18
Illiterate Liza & the Literati

Unabashedly, the illiterate Lizas of the teaching profession conceal their ignorance with bravado.

Family member: Fay

Overcoming another obstacle, Fay became the *first* eleventh-grade student at Jupiter High School to enroll in the *Advanced Placement* (AP) literature class. Fay and I believed that waiting another year to take the class made no sense. In spite of a short-sighted protest from the AP teachers, the school principal granted Fay's petition for entry.

In existence for just a short time, the AP class had been reserved *solely for seniors.* Two years earlier, Tony was the first Ryan to take the class. Furthermore, it was the only AP class offered in the entire school—out of all the disciplines. In that era, the school's AP curriculum was vastly different from today's full menu of AP classes—with some APs now being offered in ninth grade.

Many seniors took the AP literature class with an eye toward supplanting a college literature class when that time came around. It was a way to save both time and money at the university level. Neither Fay nor I considered that option. Rather, we both agreed that the AP class would help Fay to become more informed and competitive in her SATs which she planned to take in September of her senior year.

The teachers of the AP class promoted the idea that it was reserved for a select group of twelfth graders. They denied Fay's attempt to register for the class at the end of sophomore year.

My letter to the principal, however, convinced him to override the teachers' opposition. Fay confidently held her own in the class. As she had hoped, the rigorous AP curriculum better prepared her for the SAT exam than any of the other language arts classes offered. We were appreciative of the principal's wise and practical decision.

In the fall of her senior year in high school, Fay applied for admission to Boston College via the Early Action process. She was accepted before Christmas, and she chose not to apply to any other schools. A *Florida Academic Scholar,* Fay was an honor student with solid SAT scores and a portfolio of extracurricular activities.

Circumstances dictated that after Fay had completed her **Executive Internship** at *The Palm Beach Post* for the first semester, she was assigned to *Academic Subject X* of Illiterate Liza for the second semester. She needed that class and one other to graduate. Having taken difficult classes in other disciplines, she had anticipated no problems. She had planned to earn an A in the class.

Illiterate Liza was a veteran teacher but new to the high school where she stayed only a few years. She was another teacher who made up her own rules and had the false confidence to use them even if they penalized students. Apparently, Illiterate Liza was able to badger students and deceive parents in this regard and would continue to do so until a parent complained.

Illiterate Liza and some of her colleagues throughout the school were fond of using the **Big Scare** tactic to influence class size. Over the years, I had witnessed its use by college professors and even among several of my fellow teachers in different schools where I had worked.

Every day, during the first week of school, certain teachers of **advanced classes**, would emphasize how difficult their classes were, how much extra homework there would be, how **extremely qualified** and demanding they were as teachers, and how only a very small percentage of their students would earn A's in those classes. Nowhere in their presentations was a pep talk encouraging students to step up to the academic challenge.

Inevitably, those teachers intimidated several capable students into dropping down to a lower-level class for fear of jeopardizing their GPA and class rank. Illiterate Liza and her counterparts had become accustomed to masterminding and executing a cunning process of **attrition** in order to obtain a small class, one of the most highly coveted rewards for public school teachers. With this strategic maneuver, they preserved their disingenuous image as a veritable corps of the teaching **elite.** And so it was that after Liza's **Big Scare,** her advanced class dwindled down to twelve students.

Before I enumerate Illiterate Liza's deficiencies as a teacher, I want to note that I do not equate the use of good grammar with wisdom or intelligence. Many wise, clever people use incorrect grammar.

Speaking grammatically correct has far more to do with proper training than it does with intelligence. Nevertheless, I expect teachers to use proper grammar and maintain appropriate word usage in the practice of their profession.

Illiterate Liza tarnished her credentials with me when I noticed a subject-verb agreement error in the syllabus which she had distributed to students and parents on the first day of school. In the same document, she made two mistakes in word usage when she confused the words *affect* and *effect* and *accept* for *except.*

These sets of words may frequently be used incorrectly by the general public, but I could not overlook those mistakes when they came from a teacher who bragged about her high level of expertise.

After reading the syllabus, I did not address those errors with Illiterate Liza, but I filed them away as a reminder of paradise lost—along with generations of teachers who brought impeccable credentials to their profession. I took her blatant blunders as a warning that there might be a problem with Illiterate Liza's teaching along the way.

Although her class was not a language arts class, Liza chose to incorporate vocabulary and writing into her curriculum. She referred to it as *Reading & Writing in the Content Area.* Liza informed students that English was her minor field of study in college. I was impressed. I thought things might be looking up.

As it turned out, Liza's deficiencies were manifested in several ways:

- **Giving inadequate and misleading directions on tests**

- **Refusing to correct her own errors that penalized students**

- Adhering to a faulty teacher manual

- Having an inferior knowledge of vocabulary

- Demonstrating weak writing skills

Fireworks erupted with the ***first*** test. Fay received her ***only failing grade*** in all her years of schooling because of Liza's poorly worded instructions. Illiterate Liza had designed a test comprised of four parts:

Parts 1 - 3   Directions: clear
                            Fay earned full credit - 60 points.

Part 4   Directions: unclear

Fay earned **0** points out of **40** for her answer to **Part 4.** What she thought was a precise response was unacceptable to Liza and, consequently, she earned the ***failing grade of* 60%** on the test overall.

Fay was not the only student in the class who had fared poorly. She and the others spoke to Liza wanting to know why they had lost so many points, but Illiterate Liza would offer no explanation, nor raise any grades. She told them that the test was self explanatory.

In stark contrast, was Liza's ***second*** test in which she had used the same formula as the previous test with one big exception:

Parts 1 - 3 were the same as the earlier test, but for this next exam, Illiterate Liza had constructed a major overhaul.

Part 4 contained a ***detailed revision*** of her directions, in essence, what she should have written for the first test.

This time, all students knew with certainty what Liza was looking for by way of a response. Fay earned **100%** on that test. Mentally, I applauded Illiterate Liza for amending the test directions.

But in the interest of fairness, it would also have been appropriate for Liza to adjust her students' grades on the first, defective test. She chose not to do so. Yet, I waited before contacting her. I wanted a more comprehensive picture of her teaching methods.

The **third** and **fourth** tests, involved defining and using selected vocabulary words correctly in sentences. The problem was that Liza accepted only **rote memorization** of answers that she had reproduced from her poorly-prepared teacher manual. All I could think of was, **"Here we go again!"** It was evident that Manual-Bound Manny had become reincarnated at the high school level.

For test three, the word **"sesquipedalian"** stands out in my mind. Fay gave an excellent definition of the word, but it did not match the definition in the manual. Liza gave her no credit for it.

In test four, the problem word became **"literati."** Illiterate Liza issued the definition as **"the educated classes."** Fay gave a more encompassing definition: **"a learned or scholarly group of people, the intellectual elite."** She wrote the following sentence to indicate that she understood the meaning of the word, **"Some believe that the literati of Harvard University feel superior to others."**

In keeping with her adherence to definitions supplied by the teacher manual only, Illiterate Liza allowed no credit for either the definition or for the explanatory sentence. It was clear that Liza did not understand the word or its historical context.

Like Joy, Fay had been an avid reader since she was very young. She had acquired and maintained an extensive and advanced vocabulary for her grade level. Some of Liza's definitions were moderately accurate, but they were nonetheless **wooden** and **stilted.**

Fay's definitions demonstrated that she knew the meanings of the words, not only from the assigned textbook readings, but also in a larger context from a wider range of literature.

In vain, Fay spoke to Illiterate Liza about her tests. Liza would not budge an inch. For the moment, I was leery of speaking to the department chairperson. I knew that along with another teacher, Liza and he carpooled each day and ate lunch together. I was worried about cronyism.

Next came problems with Fay's essays. Liza told students that she would grade their writing assignments as if she were an English teacher because it was important to express themselves well in writing, no matter what the subject. I agreed with her professed philosophy, but Fay told me that Liza's alleged corrections were grammatically incorrect. At that point, I sent a note asking for copies of the essays which Liza kept at school in her files.

To my surprise, Liza initiated a request for a conference with me. By that time, I welcomed the opportunity to address all of my concerns, but I was still doubtful about obtaining the results I wanted. Again, I brought along a **third-party** silent observer to take note. Regrettably, this time, I had no honor society constitution to hold up as my ultimate defense.

As I had predicted, my misgivings about the tests were rejected and invalidated immediately by the department chairperson. Another ardent devotee of the teacher manual, he supported the teacher's position.

When I read over the essays in the principal's office, I agreed with Fay's conclusion about Liza's erroneous corrections. But the department chair stood solidly behind Liza and succinctly dismissed my concerns.

I knew that the school principal would not get involved in the substantive issues in question. Instead, the principal conferred **resident expert** status on the department chairperson and willingly abided by his decision on all of the disputes. I understood his position.

His teachers liked to work for him because he backed them up in confrontations with parents. This can be a good thing, but if the department chair is in cahoots with the teacher and incompetent, the student suffers as a result. Fay's case had been abruptly **shut down on all counts.**

The above incident is another conspicuous example of how an inferior teacher can be supported over an outstanding student who had the knowledge and the courage to challenge that teacher's credibility.

I was left with **no** alternative but to contact the area administrator from the school district who, two years earlier, had resolved all of the problems created by Manual-Bound Manny. Once again, she came to the rescue. I sent a packet of material to her with evidence of the many poor teaching techniques that I had compiled:

1. Illiterate Liza's syllabus with usage and grammatical errors

2. Illiterate Liza's grading system at times at odds with district policy

3. Three tests graded improperly by Liza

4. Two essays displaying Liza's inaccurate grammatical corrections

About a week later, the area administrator visited the school to meet personally with Fay. She apologized for Fay's unfortunate experience with her teacher. She remarked that there had been problems with teachers interpreting items too literally from teacher manuals, and that more training was needed. As we had expected, the administrator told Fay that her grades would be recalibrated to an A.

She further advised Fay that she had spoken in person with Illiterate Liza and requested that the teacher herself notify me of the grade changes. Liza did this by leaving me a telephone message while I was working. That was sufficient for me. There was no need to talk with her again.

The administrator told Fay to thank me for recognizing things in the system that needed to be revamped. She, like me, believed that parents should be **more vigilant** in supervising their children's assignments.

She had done the same with her own children. I was fortunate to have benefited twice from her keen insight, her command of the English language, and her manner of working authoritatively on behalf of students whose neighborhood school had, to a certain degree, let them down.

Reflection: Although I was satisfied that the area administrator took the proper course of action on behalf of Thad at the middle school and Fay at the high school, it is troubling to reflect upon the reasons why I was forced to seek her assistance. In the predicaments stirred up by Manual Bound Manny and Illiterate Liza, there were the following common elements:

- An inferior teacher who relied on a faulty manual for answers

- An incompetent department chairperson who covered up for the problematic teacher

- A principal who deferred to the department chairperson

- A student who had been treated unfairly

- A parent whose plea for help was ignored

- A higher level administrator who stepped in to solve the problems

This was and is an intolerable situation wherever and whenever it might occur. In an ideal world, parents should be able to send their children to school without worrying about teachers' mistakes. In instances, too numerous to mention, that is not how it works. Both the administrator and I also knew that in the case of many teachers, old habits and attitudes die hard.

Parents need to know, however, that they have the power to **stop** bad practices in the classroom. They must put continual pressure on principals or on higher level administrators when any of these educators are **deficient, defensive, defiant,** and plainly **deceitful.**

Ironically, Fay began first grade with *Sesame Street* Sadie and finished up twelfth grade with Illiterate Liza. She weathered an incredibly bad **beginning** and **ending** to her public education in Palm Beach County.

Fortunately, she encountered many dedicated teachers and enjoyed any number of worthwhile experiences along the way so that she did not become embittered about school.

I thought it was bizarre that both Malevolent Max and Illiterate Liza did not take time to know Fay, either as a student or as a person. Her accomplishments and quiet, mature demeanor attested to her integrity:

- **Fay was a hardworking, soft-spoken, respectful student.**

- **Fay was well liked by all of her other teachers.**

- **Fay had an outstanding academic record.**

- **Fay had a strong sense of right and wrong.**

- **Fay had the courage to stand up to unfair treatment.**

- **Fay had the resiliency to stay the course when advocating her position.**

Teachers of this type upset me more than they bothered Fay. ***Unabashedly, the Illiterate Lizas of the teaching profession conceal their ignorance with bravado.*** They establish inflexible, inconsequential rules that act as their first line of defense for keeping anyone who questions them at bay. Sadly, this course of action serves its purpose more often than not.

Advisory: Savvy students will expose a teacher's flimsy façade and help bring about needed curriculum revisions.

Chapter 19
Wretched Retread Reeba

I was about to encounter and expose one of the strangest examples ever of teacher incompetency.

Family member: Thad

For the academic year 1985 – 1986, I took a leave of absence without pay from my Palm Beach County middle-school teaching job. I wanted a break after eleven years of full-time teaching and preparing my four older children for college. This hiatus coincided with Thad's first year of high school.

Needing a source of income, I worked in the evening as an adult education teacher of migrant workers in nearby Martin County just north of Tequesta, a twenty five-minute drive from my home. Captain Joe had returned to the big ships several years earlier and was again away most of the time earning money for all of the college expenses we had incurred (Chapter 22).

After my father died, my mother moved from Milton, Massachusetts, to live nearby. We were lucky to have her with us in excellent form and spirit into her nineties. She was very close to my children and almost always worried as to whether or not they were getting enough to eat. Fortunately, they were healthy and physically fit.

When I took the night job, I arranged for her to arrive at our house by four o'clock on weekday afternoons, Monday through Thursday. She made certain that Thaddeus ate a good dinner, and she loosely supervised his homework.

As a rule, when I arrived home at nine thirty, my mother told me that Thad had finished his studying and was already asleep. Although I was somewhat skeptical that he had completed all of his homework, I went along with his schedule.

Nevertheless, Thad earned excellent grades until the last term when he brought home his midterm progress report with the alarming news that he had a D average in Academic Subject X with only four weeks remaining in the academic year.

Accompanying the grade report was the dreaded advisory that Reign of Terror Tess (Chapter 16) had neglected to issue to Matt,

Warning: Notice of Possible Failure

Up until that point, Thaddeus had earned an A in this subject for each preceding term. I was puzzled to learn that his grade had taken such a dramatic dive.

Naturally, I was not pleased that Thad had hidden some low grades from me before receiving the failure notice. Upon questioning, he admitted their existence saying that he had been hoping to pull them up before I found out about them.

He insisted that he fully understood the subject matter, but the **tests** presented problems for him. As I set out to salvage Thaddeus' grade and prevent a failure for the term, I did not realize that *I was about to encounter and expose one of the strangest examples ever of teacher incompetency*, in the person of Wretched Retread Reeba.

During the fourth quarter of ninth grade, Thaddeus' class in this discipline had a change of teachers. The **new** teacher, Wretched Retread Reeba, was actually the **same** teacher who had taught the class for ten years or more.

She had just returned to work after an extended medical leave. I thought that perhaps Thaddeus had problems adjusting to her teaching style. In any event, no matter what it took, I needed to determine why his grade had deteriorated so drastically. Wanting to assess his knowledge of the material, I decided to study with him each night.

The next evening, I initiated a **crackdown policy** which would remain in place until the end of the school year. Thad was at liberty to go to bed while I was working, but I advised him that I would wake him up as soon as I arrived home, and I would review the lesson with him.

Each night, Thad and I went over the material for about sixty minutes depending upon the lesson's degree of difficulty. I was happy to note that Thad thoroughly enjoyed our work sessions which incorporated lively discussions on the issues at hand. Having joined the debate team at the beginning of ninth grade, he was often at the ready for a provocative argument.

171

Before the next test, two weeks later, I was confident that we both knew the material inside and out. Thaddeus would surely earn an A, if not a perfect score. To the contrary, after the test was graded, Thad learned that he had received a C on the test.

Startled by this mediocre grade, I tried to obtain the test from the teacher in order to scrutinize it, but she would not release it. She sent home a message, **"Study harder."**

Toward that same end, I wrote a note to Thad's guidance counselor. She, too, gave me the cold shoulder, stating that the school must preserve the *integrity* of the test for the benefit of all students.

Lastly, I contacted the school's principal requesting that Thad receive a copy of the test and the answer key for both of us to review. By then, he knew me well because Thaddeus was the fifth Ryan to attend the school.

Moreover, he had been a guidance counselor at the high school for several years, and in that role, he was a strong *advocate* for Joy when she applied to Brown University.

Up to date on the status of many former graduates, he was aware that Joy had finished college and was doing well in the workforce. Obligingly, a few days before the final exam, the principal arranged for me to receive a copy of the most recent test along with its answer key. I inspected both with a fine-tooth comb.

The result of my analysis was hard to believe. By being very familiar with the content of the test, I was able to discern that many of the questions contained factual errors or were worded in *illogical doublespeak*, or both. Disgracefully, there was no *integrity* of the test to protect.

Suddenly, my memory flashed back to a comment Tony had made about this same teacher's tests six years earlier, **"My teacher makes up weird test questions, but I figured out how to answer them."**

To check up on this, I called Tony at college in Boston and read him parts of the test. It all came back to him. He remembered that Retread Reeba had given faulty quizzes and exams, expecting one answer to some of her questions but literally asking for a different answer through her flawed wording.

Almost ingeniously, Tony had figured out the answers that Wretched Retread Reeba expected. Deliberately then, he put *wrong* answers on his exam papers and did well in each of them.

Accordingly, *ignorance was bliss* for me in that time period. I knew nothing about problems with those tests, and I never had to request an appointment with Reeba about Tony's grade.

After talking with Tony, I was convinced that these were the same *retreads* she had used when Tony was in her class, albeit with considerably more wear and tear.

My advice to Thad was to continue answering in his own way for the final exam, *"Let the chips fall where they may."* I pledged to pursue the matter in depth after school closed for the summer.

Thaddeus received a C on the final exam and a C for the term. It was time to regroup. I scheduled a conference with the principal, outlined my suspicions, and requested copies of all tests that Wretched Reeba had given during the term— complete with their answer keys.

My extended study of the tests revealed that Retread Reeba had invalidated every one of her tests by several peculiar *cut and paste* transpositions.

To begin with, all of Reeba's tests required answers of *true* or *false*. It didn't take much inventiveness, to crack her code. Dates on the tests helped me to determine earlier versions from later ones. I found two original tests along with their distorted versions.

When I placed these tests side by side, I noticed her method. First, Reeba had moved entire questions by placing the first question of each test last, and the last question of each test first. Carelessly, she did not update her answer keys to align with the alterations.

Secondly, she **tampered** with the wording of two questions in the middle of each test to make them look different from the original questions. Her changes, however, negated the validity of the answers.

For example, where the original question required a response of *false*, Reeba's rewording logically demanded a response of *true.*

She was oblivious to all of it, and again her answer keys did not reflect her modifications. This sounds **convoluted** and **crazy,** and indeed it was all of that. The following is my theory as to how this test snafu evolved.

Going back in time, some of Reeba's students caught on to the fact that she used the same faded, worn-out tests year in and year out. In one way or another, her tests had been compromised.

Perhaps student assistants had seized an opportune moment, copied them, and shared or sold them to their buddies. Upon discovering the nature of the beast, Retread Reeba, may have guarded her tests more closely from then on.

But, in the meantime, Wretched Retread Reeba needed to revise them. Her original tests likely came prepackaged along with the textbook.

Making up new tests on a typewriter in those days before the computer would have been far too time consuming for *lazy*, sidestepping Reeba. Therefore, to confuse would-be cheaters, she resorted to a poorly executed **cut** and **paste** fabrication.

I myself had learned the **cut** and **paste** trick from a colleague in my third year of teaching, and we both used it occasionally on **true** or **false** or **multiple choice** tests.

We resorted to this strategy to prevent information sharing among students sitting in crowded classrooms. In that private school, cheating ran so rampant that I was forced to give alternate tests to students sitting behind one another and to students sitting beside one another.

When they glanced at each other's tests from either direction, the tests appeared to be different. One of my students even had the audacity to yell out, **"Hey this is not fair! He has a different test!"**

In truth, they were identical tests labeled Test A and Test B, but the top half of one test had become the bottom half of the other test and vice versa.

The important thing to remember when making the switch was to adjust the answer keys to correspond with the change. In my case, I needed to prepare two separate answer keys, A and B. Unthinkingly, Retread Reeba had not taken that extra step.

Usually, Reeba's tests contained twenty-five questions worth four points each. If a student made mistakes on four questions that had been realigned, then the highest grade a student could earn was an 84%, or a C, according to the school district's grading scale at the time. This was exactly what had occurred with Thaddeus on the last test of the term and on the final exam.

After completing my examination of the tests, I took several pages of findings to the principal along with copies for the department chairperson who was not present at the meeting. I gave the principal an **item-by-item analysis** of each test, indicating which questions were written incorrectly.

For each bad question, I found the intended answer in the textbook and provided verification as to the page number. I did not have originals for all of the tests, but it was evident that the **pattern of distortion** in all of the adaptations was the same. The principal told me that he would give the material to the department head and call me within two days.

It didn't take either one of them long to rule in Thad's favor. The principal notified me later in the day that he had arranged for **all** of Thaddeus' test grades, his final exam grade, and his overall average for the term to be changed to an A. **Mission accomplished.** I thanked him, and there was no further discussion. I had achieved my immediate goal on behalf of my son.

Even though I was infuriated at the teacher's lack of concern for her students, I had no power to reach out and act on behalf of every student. It seemed irrefutable that the administration had both a responsibility and a **moral obligation** to rectify the damage done to all other students in Wretched Reeba's classes.

I could only hope that school administrators did not fall back on several age-old adages as binding administrative practices:

- **Don't rock the boat.**

- **Don't upset the apple cart.**

- **Bury your head in the sand.**

- **Grease only the squeaky wheel.**

Or, in somewhat more formal terms, it is common practice for school administrators to follow strict, self-preservation procedures and a philosophy of **laissez-faire** while enshrouding and perpetuating unrighted wrongs.

About three weeks later, Thaddeus spent the day at the house of a friend who had been in the same class. During lunch, his friend's mother told Thaddeus that she was unhappy that her son Andrew had received a D in Retread Reeba's class.

She was curious as to Thad's grade. He explained to her about the bogus tests, and he added further that he had been wondering if the school had followed up with any other students to adjust their grades.

His mother promptly called me to verify the information. She had been duly concerned because up until that juncture, Andrew had been an Honor Roll student.

As to be expected, she knew nothing about the inaccuracy of the tests. After talking with me, she told me that she was anxious to have her son's grade changed, but she was worried about being labeled as a *troublemaker.*

I advised her that if she met with the principal and told him that she had spoken with me about the adulterated tests, I was confident that he would help her. She did so, and her son's grade was also changed to an A. I was glad that I had been able to pave the way.

I had no way of knowing if all of the other students in Wretched Retread Reeba's class and their parents remained uninformed, without a clue, as to Reeba's substandard, recycled tests.

Because Reeba had finally been caught in the act, I doubt that she used her *retreads* again. All I could do was hope that the administration and the department chairperson took precautions so that Wretched Reeba could no longer continue her punitive charade.

I suppose that there are other parents of like mind, not wanting to be labeled a *troublemaker* or a *whistleblower.* To my way of thinking, as long as I could demonstrate that the facts were on the side of my child, I did not hesitate to do the right thing by that child no matter how many feathers I might ruffle.

The incident with Wretched Retread Reeba brings up the topic of students' responsibility to follow through with any test on which they do not earn 100%. It is also the parents' obligation to review test results and determine why their children do not earn a perfect score.

- Did the student prepare adequately for the test?

- Did the student experience text anxiety?

- Did the teacher prepare students adequately for the test?

- Did the teacher give complete and exact directions for the test?

- Did the teacher design the test properly?

It is important that students learn how to evaluate tests and be test *critics.* If a teacher explained the material in expert fashion and administered a fair test, students should perform well on that test. In that case, the burden falls on the student.

Students must be absolutely **honest** with themselves as to whether or not a test is fair. A good test should cover the lessons taught but challenge students as well. Under no circumstances, should a student be blindsided by new material. [Diagnostic tests are exceptions.]

Although, in some instances, a super simple test might be good for student morale, teachers should not make a practice of giving easy tests just to please students or parents. At the end of the **retread** incident, I was perplexed and left with lingering questions:

- Why had it taken over six years to uncover Wretched Retread Reeba's bad tests?

- Where was the oversight of department chairpersons?

- Why had Wretched Reeba's students not questioned their low grades?

- Why had parents placed unwavering faith in this wretched teacher?

On the one hand, I am adamant that school administrators be more attuned to cracks in the system on their own home front. Curiously, Wretched Reeba's *retreads* had an unusually long shelf life.

On the other hand, I urge parents to be *relentless* in probing for underlying causes of their children's unsatisfactory performances. [And, yes, I understand that families generally trust the school to do right by their children.]

Taking a positive outlook, competent administrators do respond to parent pleas. Admittedly, some attempted reforms like CONCEPT 6 die an excruciatingly slow death, but in other circumstances, improvements can be made in a relatively short period of time. Parents and caregivers have a duty to bring about much-needed changes at their children's school.

Advisory: Pay close attention to and probe into the validity of teachers' testing instruments.

Chapter 20
Working the System:
Reaching for the Stars

**It didn't take him long to develop a
silver-tongued, oratorical voice.**

Song: *Reach for the Stars*
Singer, Songwriter:
Will.i.am (William Adams)

Family member: Thad

For me, it is fascinating to ponder the reality that in spite of his later arrival to the abstract domain back in sixth grade, (Chapter 14), Thaddeus, of all my children, was the only one who went on to engage in high-level logic and abstract thought as a champion debater in high school and at the university level.

A precursor to Thad's debate years was his participation on a popular talk radio program in the summer after eighth grade. During the school year, I had chaperoned a few of my junior high gifted students at a nearby radio station each Friday at the end of the day.

I was inspired to set up this arrangement by a group of high school students who joined the radio program one day a week. Highly-skilled debaters at their school, they were known as the *"A-Team"* on the show. They discussed current events at a sophisticated level of understanding.

The dynamic host, a prominent, Emmy award-winning television personality in Boston, had recently relocated to West Palm Beach. I often listened to his program when I was driving home from work.

Initially dubious about my proposal, the program director, nevertheless, agreed to allow my students to take part in the program on a trial basis in the *same time slot,* but on a different day, from that of the older students.

The host of the show was so impressed with these young students' speaking ability and their high level of vocabulary that the *trial* was but a fleeting one. He praised them live, on air, and welcomed them to the very first junior *"A-Team"* only minutes after appearing on their first show.

Two of my students wanted to continue visiting the station during the summer, and radio personnel were delighted to have them. I brought Thaddeus and his super smart friend along to see if they would enjoy the challenge. They fit right in and could not get enough of it.

In that era, Iran Contra dominated the news. The young enthusiasts read up on the scandal on their own time and prepared to discuss it intelligently on the show. Along with other hot topics, there was plenty of material to research and plenty to say.

My mother was happy to join us. During the program, we waited outside the studio in the lounge area where we could hear the young students demonstrating their quick wit and critical thinking abilities. That's how it all began.

After the summer, when Thad entered ninth grade, I suggested that he sign up for debate. That elective class was a relatively new addition to the school's curriculum. The coach was marshalling his forces from scratch, and although I respected his superior intellectual prowess, there was no depth to his team.

I coached Thad myself at first, but I knew nothing about the art of debate except to advise Thaddeus to stand up straight and speak distinctly which he already did.

It didn't take him long to develop
a silver-tongued, oratorical voice.

Thaddeus specialized in **Lincoln Douglas Debate.** The following is an example of a resolution which calls for extensive research on the part of debaters:

**Resolved: The People's right to know outweighs
the government's need for confidentiality.**

In this category of debate, it is incumbent upon debaters to be prepared to argue forcefully, convincingly, and winningly both the *affirmative* and *negative* position of each resolution. Debaters are officially notified as to which side they will *fight to defend* or *fight to defeat* only moments before the debate round begins.

Debaters will often be required to argue a positon that is directly opposed to their personal beliefs. If they want to win the debate, they must effectively conceal their bias. ***Winning*** is the name of the game.

This exercise is a complex and intriguing intellectual challenge that brings about great rhetorical poise in the most talented and sophisticated of debaters.

In the days prior to internet, debaters spent uninterrupted hours in the library and debate room conducting research. Poring over a myriad of reference materials, they compiled countless details of major and minor importance.

They ***cut cards*** on current topics to include and organize in their imposing, leather file boxes which they authoritatively lugged into each formal debate.

Thaddeus took to this intellectual exercise with ease and began winning many debate rounds along with shiny silver pins that symbolized each achievement.

As he competed more extensively, he observed and interacted with top debaters in the area. It soon became obvious to him that a school in downtown West Palm Beach outperformed all other schools in terms of their accomplished debaters and their training.

Some of these students were original members of the talk radio show's ***"A-Team."*** Masterminding the strategies of the debaters was the coach recognized in high school debate circles across the country as the ***Grande Dame of Debate.***

Taking it further, by talking to coaches, parents, and students at debate tournaments, I learned that a number of debaters customarily attended the National Debate Institute Summer Program at American University in Washington, D.C., then directed by the illustrious and flamboyant debate coach, Dr. James John Unger now deceased.

A graduate of Harvard Law School, he was a former national champion debater while at Boston College where he was class Valedictorian. He had successfully coached

Georgetown University's debate team to several winning seasons.[21]

I looked into the program and learned that there were some scholarships for students who could demonstrate financial need. For two consecutive years, Thaddeus received a small stipend which paid much of the air fare. He attended the two-week intensive course after his sophomore and junior years of high school. Those summer institutes helped elevate Thaddeus to a high level of debate.

Since Thad's high school, at that time, did not participate in all of the larger, more inclusive and challenging tournaments, I petitioned the School District of Palm Beach County to allow Thad to transfer to Twin Lakes High School, the inner-city school previously referenced.

To plead Thad's case, I was summoned to meet with the guidance director and other administrators at the district level who were involved with the transfer. At the meeting, I explained that Thaddeus had become proficient in the intellectual exercise of debate.

In order to maintain and fine tune those skills, he needed to attend a school where his talent could continue to develop. The panel granted my request without the slightest bit of discussion.

Thad then transferred to Twin Lakes High School after his sophomore year. Being in the city as opposed to a small town, the school projected a more cosmopolitan flair. Among a diverse group of classmates and debate partners, Thaddeus thrived in his new surroundings.

Unlike today where magnet schools flourish in the Palm Beach County school system, they did not exist when my children were in attendance. Back in 1987, by virtue of Thad's transfer, I had created his own personal debate magnet.

Transferring into Twin Lakes High School had not been a trend. I know of no other debater who lived outside of the

185

school's established boundaries. In general, families who lived in the suburbs wanted their children to attend schools close to home.

Twin Lakes High School began in 1908 as Palm Beach High School, the school on the hill. It underwent a number of name changes as integration and urban development became a reality. With a beautiful **Mediterranean Revival** style of architecture, it was the oldest high school in Palm Beach County.[22] Thad arrived there just in time—before the school experienced yet another transformation and name change.

Thaddeus loved that school. On the same campus, across from the high school, was the Gardenia Street debate room. Debaters had their own separate building where they met every day for class in addition to long hours after school.

Inside was a unique club of young intellectuals who spoke their own exclusive language as they made seemingly infinite investigation and inquiry into a world of ideas from the safety of a cocoon.

In January of 1989, Twin Lakes High School metamorphosed into Palm Beach Lakes Community High School. Students moved to a brand new building and a different location several miles away.

The latter's sterile modernity was no substitute for the original school's alluring antiquity. Later in 1997, the historic Palm Beach High School, remodeled and again renamed, became the now highly acclaimed Alexander W. Dreyfoos Jr. School of the Arts.

Thaddeus' greatest triumph and proudest moment in high school debate was achieving top honors at the **Bronx High School of Science** amidst some of the best debaters in the country.

Thad continued to debate successfully in college. He began on a small scholarship to Southern Illinois University whose debate team had been Number #1 in the country for five years just prior to Thad's arrival.

Later he accompanied his debate coach to the University of North Dakota where he remained until graduation. The team traveled repeatedly to tournaments at the University of Texas at Austin and the University of Kansas. Although the national championship eluded Thad and his teammates, they came strikingly close to capturing the crown on two occasions.

Unequivocally, I am convinced that the art of debate was by far the most important factor in shaping and advancing Thad's education once he became a young adult.

Prompting him to seek and understand all sides of an argument in every discipline, it laid a solid foundation for his pursuit of a master's degree in Latin American and Caribbean Studies at the University of South Florida.

I am an enormous proponent of debate for students who want to expand their intellectual curiosity, stretch their capacity for critical thinking, and enrich their comprehension far beyond that of the banal.

When I was finalizing the paperwork for Thad's transfer to Twin Lakes High School, one of his teachers, who had known three of my older children, coincidentally witnessed and overheard the transaction. Without hesitation, he approached me and remarked with a sardonic smirk, *"Ryans always do what they want."*

He spoke derisively yet enviously. I said nothing but was simultaneously annoyed and amused by his glib, thoughtless remark. That teacher was single without children. He failed to realize that Ryans made their choices out of necessity. Mindfully, Strickland appeals to us with a realistic and powerful exhortation,

"You are the only person in the world who really cares whether your child learns anything, so you must take responsibility for your child's education." [23]

187

In accordance with that line of thought, I could not allow incompetent, indifferent, or mean-spirited teachers impede my children's progress.

I hope that if teachers exhibiting that aloof, unconcerned disposition, **had become parents,** they would have pushed on tirelessly for their own children in an effort to support their continued growth, no matter what the circumstances.

And, whether they became parents or not, how much more responsive they could have been to work for all of their students in a caring manner.

Advisory: Draw upon your ingenuity to plan a challenging course of studies for your talented child.

Chapter 21
Identifying Gifted Students
Unintelligent Intelligence #2:
Rigid Robot Rob

Curiously enough, Rob was anointed with the title of ESE Coordinator, but he had no training in any of the exceptionalities he was assigned to represent.

Family member: Susan
Challenges to Gifted Criteria

In 1984, I earned the degree of Educational Specialist (Ed.S.) in Gifted Child Education from Nova Southeastern University in Fort Lauderdale, Florida. The program required thirty-six credit hours of coursework beyond a master's degree. My instructors prepared me well academically, and I was required to initiate a practical component working with students in the field.

After that, I taught language arts to gifted middle-school students for a number of years. I worked under the direction of and learned much from a brilliant and versatile woman who had earned a doctorate of education in Early and Middle Childhood.

She inspired me to do the same a few years later. In charge of the gifted program for The School District of Palm Beach County for many years, she was an outstanding leader and advocate for gifted children.

Invariably on the forefront of new trends, she broke down barriers of exclusion. After many years of service in the system, she retired and established her own successful learning center.

GIFTED ACHIEVERS ARE IDENTIFIED

My specialized education along with my years of experience in the classroom gave me added insight into recognizing **not-yet identified** gifted students in my regular or advanced classes.

The main indicators for me were the students' provocative questions in class, their ability to grasp concepts quickly, and their creative, extraordinary ways of thinking.

In one category of gifted students were pupils like Ida. They were conscientious and enthusiastic about their schoolwork. They followed traditional patterns of high achievers and possessed an inherent zest for learning that was remarkable. When engaged in silent reading, Ida, for example, would become immersed in the literature, smiling or scowling expressively in response to events as they unfolded. She took immense pride in her work.

As I worked with students of this type, I witnessed their **giftedness.** It was plain to see. They completed their assignments with care, and they would score high on all types of exams—from teacher-prepared tests to national assessments. Yet, for some peculiar reason, other teachers had failed to notice their exceptional abilities.

GIFTED UNDERACHIEVERS ARE IDENTIFIED

In another category of gifted students were those of the same intellectual caliber, who would **not** score well on teacher-prepared tests. Those students were underachievers who usually paid scant attention to their teachers' instruction.

They carelessly rushed through their work to read high school or college-level literature during class. Overall, their grade reports were average indicating a lack of interest and effort.

Unconventional critical thinkers, they were **not intimidated** by the rhetoric of administrators who tried to convey the importance of nationally-normed exams. Taking those tests was tedious and tiresome for them.

But because of their passion for reading, they scored well on all segments involving reading comprehension. Discussions on controversial topics sparked their interest, and they demonstrated an ability to put forth uncommon but logical arguments to win impromptu class debates.

None of those students in either category came from homes indicating financial hardship, but a few families were troubled by problems that made life difficult to some extent for the children.

In general, their parents were unschooled in matters concerning education and were not even remotely aware of classes for gifted students. Their interests lay in other directions. As long as their children kept out of trouble and brought home a respectable C average, they were content.

Customarily, I would submit those students' names to the school's guidance counselor at a brief conference where I also provided, in writing, detailed anecdotal data to support my referrals for gifted placement. She, in turn, believing that my reasons were valid, forwarded my requests to the district level for review.

After conducting an intellectual assessment of those students described in both of the above categories, the school psychologist determined that their Intelligence Quotients (IQs) qualified them for admission to the gifted program.

All of my referrals came to fruition without complications. It simplified matters that these students did not have special needs which some gifted students may have. Subsequently, the students entered my gifted class with a smooth transition and remained there until they moved up to high school.

NEWLY IDENTIFIED GIFTED STUDENTS THRIVE

A new development for them was attending classes with other exceptionally intelligent students. Those who had been shirkers began to participate enthusiastically in verbal and written assignments. Their school work took on added meaning, and they enjoyed socializing with their new-found classmates both *in* and *out* of the classroom.

They all had an offbeat, sophisticated sense of humor which they brought to our discussions in the study of literature. This engaging group of students learned a lot and laughed a lot. Above all, I was pleased that I was able to help them get the attention they needed.

Through other colleagues, I was able to keep track of those students for several years after they left my class. I determined that the majority of them went on to excel in high school, college, and graduate school. Ida earned a Ph.D. in psychology and did post-graduate work at Yale and Harvard.

Twenty-five years after being my student, Ida wrote me a thoughtful and analytical letter of appreciation. She believes with all certainty that I initiated one of the most dramatic changes in her life by arranging her placement in the gifted program when she was in seventh grade.

Neither she nor her parents had any idea that she was a gifted child. From then on, she had the confidence and the will to excel in any endeavor she attempted.

THREE MORE STUDENTS DISTINGUISH THEMSELVES

Several years later, while working at another school in Palm Beach County, I had a disheartening experience when I recommended three of my sixth-grade students for the gifted program after observing them for three grading periods in my *advanced* language arts class.

Those students, referred to here as **J, K,** and **L,** were exhibiting almost identical behaviors to those of my students previously mentioned. In truth, each of them outshone all of my other, one hundred twenty-five students in ways that made them uniquely gifted. My impassioned hope was that all three of those students would be admitted to the program.

Student **J** was productive like Ida—although amusingly and annoyingly absent minded. He did his homework faithfully in almost illegible handwriting but could seldom locate it in his burgeoning backpack.

It would eventually be found among a heap of papers (several loose class assignments from all disciplines) mingled in with short stories of his own creation and an epic poem that he worked on at home every evening.

In his spare time, he read a full-length version of Moby Dick and drew detailed pictures of whales. A music lover, he played saxophone in the school band. He scored well on all tests and found humor in most situations.

Students **K** and **L** were friends. Several teachers considered them to be nothing more than *goof-offs.* If I did not separate them, they would be huddled together working on their independent mini-newspaper for the duration of class.

They were both writers and cartoonists. Completely absorbed in their own world, they would laugh hysterically when they thought of a new idea. Some of their teachers had confiscated their work.

For all of my classes, I set up the majority of lessons to integrate literature, vocabulary, and grammar. Students **K** and **L** were not interested in the grammar, but they were especially intrigued by the units I had developed with themes of nonviolence.

They picked up new vocabulary with ease. As one example, they were fascinated by an assigned story about Mahatma Gandhi. Wanting to know more about him, they went to the library media center and checked out Gandhi biographies.

From there, Students **K** and **L** began another newspaper. They wrote editorials and comic strips contrasting school bullying with the concept of nonviolence, illustrating them with Manga-style artwork. At home, they ignored much of their homework in all classes while they made **I-movies** on the same topic.

Focused on their craft, they experimented with artful changes to their voices for the video characters they portrayed. Also band members, they would sometimes play their instruments as background music to their movies. When we studied Martin Luther King, Jr., they launched a similar project.

In a gifted setting, extended activities of this type could have been incorporated into course objectives along with an interdisciplinary approach that would have allowed more flexibility of time. There was no doubt in my mind that all three of these students needed a *special program* as opposed to the regular classroom.

Protocol, this time around, required me to submit my students' names to Rigid Robot Rob, the Exceptional Student Education (ESE) coordinator. He would conduct a preliminary screening of these students.

Unlike the system with my previous referrals, the school's guidance counselor was *not* part of the identification process. Rob's job title gave him the authority to play the ever-powerful trump card. If he put the kybosh on my referrals, the matter would go no further.

RIGID ROBOT ROB BREAKS OUT STANDARD CHECKLISTS

Through these new referrals, I was made aware of gifted student identification criteria as outlined on the website of The School District of Palm Beach County.

These guidelines found at the end of this book (*Citations & Reference Notes*) are largely the same in 2017, as they were when I worked with Students **J**, **K**, and **L**. After I referred my students to Rigid Robot Rob, he looked at their grades and their results on standardized tests.

Student **J** with his outstanding grades represented all that was right and good, but when Rob looked at the report cards of Student **K** and Student **L**, he frowned.

When I explained my reasons for the gifted referral, Robot Rob was not impressed. Nonetheless, he advised me that he would distribute a copy of the *Gifted Characteristics Checklist* [24] to all of their teachers.

STUDENT J REACHES A HIGHER PLANE

Because Student **J** had excellent scores on standardized tests and superior grades on his report cards, his teachers gave him favorable rankings on the *Gifted Characteristics Checklist.* Robot Rob immediately agreed to have that high-performing student evaluated by a school psychologist at the district level.

That was easy—exactly the way Rob liked it. When all steps had been completed, Student **J** entered the gifted program in the following academic year, although undoubtedly his ability and talents should have been recognized several years earlier.

STUDENT K AND STUDENT L REACH A DEAD END

Students **K** and **L** had performed well on their FCAT reading tests because they spent a great deal of time reading independently at a high level. In spite of this, however, those students fell victim to the *domino effect* with regard to gifted placement.

It was most apparent that if students showed little interest in a teacher's class and earned low to average grades in that class, the teacher would automatically give them insufficient ratings on the *Gifted Characteristics Checklist.* That's exactly what occurred. Students **K** and **L,** with all of their innate intelligence, had reached a dead end.

THE CHECKLIST PREDOMINATES IN SPITE OF FLAWS

Rigid Robot Rob dutifully reviewed the *teachers' responses* on the checklists and promptly denied Students **K** and **L** the opportunity for further evaluation. No sooner had the process begun, when it was terminated. Rob chose to disregard my detailed anecdotal data describing the students' giftedness.

Like Superficial Screener Sal (Chapter 7), Rob had become an *intractable roadblock,* disallowing my students' access to the district psychologist—the one professional in the school system who was officially licensed to provide a thorough and discriminating measurement of their intelligence. Rigid Robot Rob's rationale was as follows:

- **The students held C averages on a majority of their grade reports.**

- **The students did not score high enough on the Gifted Characteristics checklists.**

Up until that time, I had admired the work ethic of this man. On the surface, he appeared to conduct his duties efficiently. Our school had a large ESE population, which included a wide range of students from trainable mentally handicapped (TMH) students to gifted students.

At parent conferences, Robot Rob was organized, professional, and attentive to details in reviewing checklists related to students' Education Plans (EPs). Before this incident, I had worked with him on matters of *form* only and not those of **substance.**

An analysis of the **Gifted Characteristics Checklist** indicates that it is **ineffective** when it comes to identifying gifted underachievers. For starters, at least eight of the questions on the checklist address high performance, and many of them concentrate on motivation.

Understandably, gifted underachievers do not score well in either of those areas if they lack interest in the subject matter. Moreover, if an underachieving gifted student is shy or introverted, checklist questions related to verbal interaction cannot be measured with any legitimate rationale.

TEACHERS IGNORE GIFTEDNESS

It is also a fact that the majority of teachers are **not** trained to recognize gifted students, and that their focus is a narrow one. The case of Student **J** bears witness to this statement.

If Student **J** was so obviously gifted in all of the required categories, why had none of his other teachers recommended him for the gifted program in elementary school or after the completion of three academic terms in middle school?

Most likely, those teachers were preoccupied with their own agenda and did not have gifted education on their minds. Amidst this *myopic classroom culture*, it is understandable how gifted underachievers would remain far below their teachers' radar.

Students **K** and **L** were highly capable students who had deserved *early years identification* and certainly more than a cursory checklist appraisal in middle school.

I was upset that Rob had robotically followed district guidelines without questioning their validity. In so doing, he was denying children their right to participate in a program that had been primarily established with their needs in mind.

Although he appeared highly competent to other faculty members, Robot Rob was oblivious to the needs of low-performing gifted students whose *parents did not know enough* to petition on their own children's behalf.

Outspoken parents will resoundingly make their voices heard, but these students needed a strong advocate, and there was *none.* School districts typically find checklists convenient when employing *shallow* methods of assessing intelligence. As a result, students suffer an ongoing educational disadvantage.

ESE COORDINATOR LACKS CREDENTIALS

To be fair to Rigid Robot Rob, he followed his superior's orders as directed. Soon I came to realize that Rob the Robot had not studied beyond a bachelor's degree in general education. He had *not,* at the very least, earned a certificate in Gifted Child Education.

He had no intention of challenging the system. On the contrary, he **embodied the system!** Haplessly, he lacked expertise regarding entrance criteria that really mattered, and he was not concerned about furthering his knowledge in the field. He had become enmeshed in a bureaucracy of implementation that had gone awry.

Rob the Robot began his career as a classroom teacher. He, like many other teachers and administrators in the system, become facilitators of programs that they are **not** qualified to facilitate. It is unfathomable how they are given exalted powers with no substantial preparation for the position.

Curiously enough, Rob was anointed with the title of
Exceptional Student Education Coordinator,
but he had no training in any of the exceptionalities
he was assigned to represent.

Instead he was without vision, a perfunctory **gatekeeper,** whose focus did not extend beyond the checklists he was assigned to review.

ELIGIBILITY CRITERIA NEEDS A FACELIFT

Undeniably, the School District of Palm Beach County is more advanced than many school districts across the country as relates to its gifted programing. But its method of identifying gifted underachievers—as prescribed by the Florida Department of Education—will continue to leave a blemish on the system until the following reforms are put in place:

- **The school district must expand its guidelines for identifying underachieving gifted students.**

- **The Gifted Characteristics Checklist must be stripped of its power to block underachieving gifted students from an official psychological evaluation.**

Students **K** and **L**, rejected by an untrained program coordinator and untrained teachers, were ***deprived*** of an energizing opportunity to revitalize their education. Countless others will experience the same loss as long as this condition prevails.

OTHER STATES OFFER MODELS
OF ELIGIBILITY CRITERIA

- In a refreshing comparison, the state of Connecticut demonstrates a more inclusive and more reasonable approach to identifying gifted students:

  "The identification process should be based on the use of multiple criteria including, but not limited to teacher recommendations, student work samples, a portfolio review, checklists, a parent nomination, peer or self nomination, and/or standardized assessment scores." [25]

- In a similar vein, the state of Washington presents expanded guidelines for identification of their gifted students whom they refer to as ***highly capable*** students:

  "Districts shall use multiple objective criteria for identifying students who are among the most highly capable. There is no single prescribed method for identification..." [26]

PALM BEACH COUNTY IMPLEMENTS
COMPREHENSIVE PROGRAMMING

The School District of Palm Beach County offers one of the top gifted programs in Florida. Full-time gifted programs are available at elementary schools from kindergarten through fifth grade. Three of my grandchildren have benefitted from attending them for a number of years.

Middle schools in the county also offer strong programs for gifted students. Contrastingly, some counties deliver only a few hours of gifted enrichment per week at elementary and middle schools. In Palm Beach County high schools—and other high schools throughout the state—a variety of magnet programs offer sufficient challenges to gifted students.

LEADERS CAN MAKE POSITIVE CHANGE

It would be appropriate for Palm Beach County educators to lead the way in eliminating *exclusionary gifted child identification procedures.* Maintaining the status quo is ever so easy. It is also profoundly unacceptable.

Taking action may seem formidable, but it is not mission impossible. Bold, strong leaders supported by solid research and a genuine concern for students can effect this change for the identification of and edification of gifted underachievers in Palm Beach County.

Indeed, policy changes can be initiated at the local level. Not long after the *Florida Writes!* assessment was implemented in 1993, two of my language arts colleagues and I were perturbed that the Florida Department of Education did not return copies of student essays after they had been graded at the state level. We wanted our students to *receive feedback* and learn from the writing experience.

First, we contacted our supervisors at the district level requesting that they plead our case with the state official in charge of the program. When they were unwilling to do so, we collaborated on a letter and sent it to the program administrator in Tallahassee on our own—with a copy to our district supervisors and to our principal.

Those same supervisors were not pleased that we had taken this action and wrote us a letter to that effect. Our principal, however, commended us for our courage. Her letter, expressed in an upbeat tone, championed our cause. *In time, our voices were heard.*

As a result of our efforts, the official administrator of *Florida Writes!* responded favorably to our appeal in another personal letter. Unmistakably, he did not write to offer superficial patronage. He followed through with our request. Within a few years, every school in the state received a CD with copies of the students' personal essays for their review—along with a grading rubric for analysis and further refinement of the students' writing skills. ***Bravo for local leadership & initiative!***

TRAINING MUST BE MANDATED

With regard to the identification of underachieving gifted students, it is most important that all ESE coordinators and all classroom teachers be given training on how to recognize the *highly capable* characteristics of super-intelligent, *low-performing* students. They should welcome the opportunity to have these students evaluated rather than to misjudge them and set them adrift.

GIFTED UNDERACHIEVERS ARE VARIED

It is important to emphasize that there are degrees of underachieving gifted students. When students are identified as *gifted underachievers* in middle school, as my students were, there is no guarantee that they will become full-fledged A or B students from that point on. But it is the first step.

It was especially rewarding for me that my students responded positively to a change in their intellectual environment. Yet, it is troubling that some students will continue to remain low performers in spite of their apparent ability.

Regrettably, there are children identified as gifted students in elementary school whose performance rarely matches their intelligence. On separate occasions through the years, three of my students who had been in the gifted program since kindergarten, arrived in my middle-school class with reputations as hard-core underachievers.

With brilliant minds, they presented a continuing challenge to their parents and to their teachers (*Twenty-Two Timeless Tips*, APPENDIX A, **Advisory #8**). I did not keep in touch with them after they moved up to high school, but I have never forgotten them.

GURUS OF GIFTED EDUCATION
SHARE THEIR THOUGHTS

Two prominent educators in the field of gifted education for more than three decades are Joseph Renzulli, Ed.D. and Sally Reis, Ph.D., a husband and wife research team at the University of Connecticut. Among other topics, they write at length about students who think creatively and often have a passion to study one topic in depth.

Renzulli reflects upon the dilemma of educators preoccupied with underachievers who do not earn the high academic grades that one would expect them to earn.

"I view all of our work in this field as a war against the forces of mediocrity, conformity, and the societal institutions that knowingly or unknowingly contribute to the suppression of creativity, social justice, and the liberation of the human mind and spirit. I view myself as a soldier in this war, and there are still many battles to be fought before we achieve the equity that gifted youngsters need and deserve." [27]

Seeing the high intelligence of gifted underachievers fail to materialize to any degree of productivity can be dispiriting. Reis and McCoach write, *"**The underachievement of gifted students is a perplexing phenomenon.**"* [28] In some cases, this behavior may also incorporate the added dimension of special needs.

Of necessity, is the stipulation that these students be assessed by expertly trained evaluators who will put together a team of knowledgeable and caring educators to help them. All in all, maintaining *high hopes* for these students is essential.

203

Matching such students with the proper mentors can make all the difference in the world. Those students often bring with them bright new ideas for the rejuvenation of society and the ability to find pathways to an enlightened future that no one else could envision.

Advisory: Teachers and parents, trust your intellect and your instincts to bring forth the finest effort from all children in your care.

Chapter 22
Loans 'R Us

**We gradually took on the staggering
number of eleven loans to get our children
through their undergraduate years.**

Song: *Fools Rush In*
Songwriters: Johnny Mercer, Rube Bloom

Singer: Billy Ekstine

By way of review, this chapter offers a capsulized history of the Ryan family and explains how we fared overall after relocating to Florida. It is also important at this juncture to offer more insight into Captain Joe's profession and to see how his life's work impacted our finances when our children were accepted into college.

Young Joe Ryan grew up in Cambridge, Massachusetts. His parents sent him to a technical high school for which he was not suited. He had no affinity for the curriculum and was especially put off by activities offered at the *forge.*

To compensate for this aversion, he ducked out of school almost every afternoon and headed for the Widener Library at Harvard University where he passed the time reading history and literature.

Later, for love of the sea and for love of country, my future husband set sail as a runaway teenager during World War II. With a falsified birth certificate making him two years older, he enlisted in the U.S. Merchant Marine as a Messman on the *S.S. Acme.* Soon he became a Wiper and an Ordinary Seaman.

Within a short time, Able Bodied Seaman Joe found himself serving on one of several perilous convoys to *Murmansk.* Those legendary convoy ships sailed laboriously around occupied Norway in mine-filled waters to Soviet ports. [29]

They were on a mission to deliver vital supplies to the Soviet Union under the United States *Lend-Lease Act of 1941.*[30] Historical evidence indicates incontrovertibly that the convoys of the United States Merchant Marine and our Allies contributed greatly to the Allied victory.

Our government was *shamefully slow* to recognize the achievements of these valiant, American mariners. But at long last, in 1988, those unsung heroes were awarded official U. S. Veteran status.

Next, Joe enrolled in intensive training at the United States Maritime Service *Officers' Candidate School* at Fort Trumbull, Connecticut, where he became a U.S. Merchant Marine officer at the age of eighteen. A number of years later, he passed a series of rigid examinations lasting six days to earn his unlimited license for *Master of United States Steam or Motor Vessels of any Gross Tons upon Oceans*. In simpler terms, this license qualified him to command ships of any size that traveled on *any ocean* in the world.

He participated in countless hours of continuing education throughout his tenure, conducted seminars, read avidly from the diversified collections of ships' libraries while out at sea, and traveled the globe. [Wherever and whenever a ship docked in the United States, the public library was there to restock its shipboard shelves.]

During Joe's years of service, he was involved in several military operations from World War II to Vietnam, to activities in the Persian Gulf, and more.

Captain Joe and I were married in 1960. He was out at sea for the births of Joy in 1961 and Nick in 1962 but home for Tony's delivery in 1965. When Fay arrived in 1968, Joe was shipping out of Oakland, California as Master of the container ship *S.S. Gateway City*, delivering wartime replenishments to Vietnam.

In 1970, he decided to retire. Enough was enough. As referenced earlier, it was that decision that precipitated our move to Florida where Thaddeus was born in 1971.

Once we arrived in Tequesta in 1974, we decided to make it our permanent home. After spending our second year in a modest rental house, we located a much larger rental a few miles away in Waterway Village where we lived most comfortably for several years.

An unusual tri-level, four-bedroom home with a roof deck off Joy's second-floor bedroom, it had a dock and was on a salt water canal directly adjoining the intracoastal waterway running alongside Jupiter Island.

Fay was friendly with four sisters who lived next door and spent many happy times with them in their Zodiac inflatable boat. We especially liked the house and relished being on the water. We would have bought the house if it had been for sale and if we could have afforded it. Neither was the case. When the owners returned from Chatham, Massachusetts, we moved once again.

With two of us working, our income had improved since we left Cohasset, but, to be expected, we incurred many additional expenses as the children grew older.

When we first moved to the Jupiter/Tequesta area, Joe opened his own independent business called *The Captain's Chair* (Chapter 6). It was a noble effort. We all liked the title of the shop and the idea that the indefatigable mariner could break away from his demanding years of going to sea.

The economy, however, was equally as bad in Florida as it was in Massachusetts. The only way to earn a significant profit with that enterprise, would have been to purchase an entire railroad car of furniture from North Carolina and offer each piece at a sizeable markup. With our budget, buying a boxcar was out of the question.

The business lasted barely two years. The harsh reality was that going to sea was the only way that Captain Joe could make a decent living to support our large family. Ironically, he could never be free of his first love. Yet the fruits of his enduring labor nurtured his children in limitless ways.

In the summer of 1976, knowing that college expenses for Joy would be upcoming in two years, my husband returned to sea. He began working for *Atlantic Undersea Test and Evaluation Center,* maintained and operated by *Radio Corporation of America Service Company*, more commonly known *as* RCA-AUTEC. His *Top Secret* Security Clearance issued by the Department of Defense made him a valued employee.

Company headquarters was located in West Palm Beach, Florida, thirty minutes from our home in Tequesta. But the project's testing range was off Andros Island in the Bahamas. Of necessity then, Captain Joe lived on Andros. We visited him there, or he came home to be with us every two weeks.

His job involved taking a ship out from Andros to the *Tongue of the Ocean* (**TOTO**) where United States Navy specialists monitored the deep water tracking portion of the weapons range. These maneuvers were in connection with anti-submarine and undersea research & development programs in the same location.

In the spring of 1978, Joy's senior year in high school, two RCA officials on Andros Island invited Captain Joe to their office for a special announcement. They advised him that his daughter Joy was the recipient of a ten thousand dollar *National Merit Scholarship* sponsored by RCA. Funds from the award would be dispersed to her university in equal segments over four years.

Indisputably, Captain Joe was thrilled at this news bulletin. He was pleased that he had been a part of the process .... although, all the while .... unknowingly. He immediately telephoned us on the mainland to relay the message.

It was an impressive honor for Joy. To us, the money seemed *far* more than it actually was. On the following weekend, RCA arranged a special ceremony on the island for our family and a photo-op with Joy, her dad, and officials of the company. They then sent the pictures along with an announcement of the award to local newspapers and to Brown University.

In those days, our family was unaware of the mechanics of corporate scholarships. We knew only that Joy had been selected initially as a *National Merit Finalist* about two months earlier.

We learned later that many finalists do not become **National Merit Scholars** because there is no corporation to sponsor them. In Joy's case, she was fortunate that her father had been in the right place at the right time. This distinction gave us all a boost of energy and pride.

From 1980 – 1991, Joe rounded out his forty plus years at sea with *Military Sealift Command Atlantic* (MSCA) based in Bayonne, New Jersey. Because his work was restricted to Key West and Cape Canaveral, we were able to see him regularly.

His very last ship, the *USNS Redstone* was manned by the U.S. Navy, the U.S. Merchant Marine, and civilian research scientists. Among other responsibilities, that ship was assigned to **monitor missile launches** fifty miles northeast of the cape.

On one occasion in July of 1989, Captain Joe invited me to come along for a ride on the *Redstone* to witness drama on the high seas. Green Peace environmental and peace activists thwarted a **Trident 2** missile launch from the nuclear submarine *USS Tennessee*. It was the only time I was aboard one of his ships when it was in motion. That incident attracted attention **worldwide.**

Whether we rented or owned a home, Captain Joe and I had always been drawn to the unconventional near the water. Our first home was a tiny garage apartment on Rice Island, Cohasset. In 1980, when Joy was in her second year of college, we bought a charming, Spanish style home in Tequesta that was within our means and **very near**, but not on, the Loxahatchee River.

It featured a spacious living area with white-washed Mexican tile flooring, an attractive screened patio with a graceful fountain, an expansive yard with a garden of Florida wild flowers, and well-trimmed hedges that provided privacy.

Two small dogs were phased into our family after the larger breeds we brought with us from Massachusetts succumbed to old age. Not being boat owners, we did not take advantage of our convenient neighborhood dock, but its access added considerable value to our property when it went on the market twenty-four years later.

All of the children were well adjusted—busy with their studies, sports activities, and compatible friends. Their names and photos frequently appeared in brief news articles in *The Jupiter Courier* upon receiving an academic or athletic award.

Six years after they entered the Jupiter school system, the high school principal requested that a reporter writing for that same newspaper, put together a more inclusive, human interest story about the Ryan children which she thought would provide good publicity for the school.

The article, entitled **Ryans Building Jupiter Tradition,**[31] focused in detail on the academic and athletic accomplishments of the three older children and ended by mentioning the names of middle school student Fay and elementary school student Thad.

With time, each child in turn, moved on to college: Nick, Tony, and Fay to Boston College; Thaddeus to the University of North Dakota. Many families may be in disbelief upon learning that . . .

We gradually took on the staggering number of eleven loans to get our children through their undergraduate years.

Their loans supplemented their scholarships. Nick, Tony and Fay, like their sister Joy, also earned one-time scholarships for ten thousand dollars, all distributed in four equal segments for the four-year period. Their sponsor was Captain Joe's union, *Masters, Mates, & Pilots Association* (MM&P) whose members were ship masters, ship's officers, and harbor pilots.

By the time Thaddeus was ready for college, MM&P discontinued its college scholarship program. Joe and I thought to ourselves that because our children had been triple recipients of the award, our family may have prompted and accelerated the scholarship's demise. Fortunately for those who qualify, the program is up and running again, but the monetary distribution has been considerably diminished.

There is no doubt that the scholarships of our first four children would have carried them through Florida's state universities for their undergraduate years at a very low cost to us. Yet we **never** considered that option. At that stage of my life, I did not think favorably of junior colleges or state universities.

In truth, I was a college snob. My New England, private college bias had taken a powerful hold on me. With time, I changed my mind on that score after becoming more informed and open minded. Indeed my own family eventually benefitted from attending state schools:

- Fay earned her Juris Doctor degree at the University of Florida College of Law, renamed the Frederic G. Levin College of Law in 1999.

- Thaddeus earned his Bachelor of Arts degree at the University of North Dakota.

- Thaddeus earned a Master of Arts degree in Latin American & Caribbean Studies at the University of South Florida.

- I earned a Master's degree in Library and Information Studies at Florida State University.

- I took several Spanish classes at Palm Beach Community College, now Palm Beach State College.

- I took an advanced Spanish class at the Honors College of Florida Atlantic University.

When Joy began college, tuition at private universities lay in the range of ten to fifteen thousand dollars per year, significantly lower than today's exorbitant college costs, but still a great hurdle for us. With each year and each child, the tuition mounted. From our perspective, we had no alternative. Our children had worked hard to gain admission to the colleges of their choice, and we would gladly send them no matter what the sacrifice.

That had always been our position. We knew many families who earned far more money than we did, who would not take out college loans for their children. They insisted, **perhaps wisely**, that their children attend the local community college for two years and then transfer over to a state university for the remaining two years.

My children lived a no-frills lifestyle at college. There were no ski trips to Vermont or sojourns through Europe. They worked in their free time and during every summer vacation to pay all of their extra living expenses.

We struggled paying those undergraduate loans for years. When Nick, Tony, and Fay obtained their full-time jobs, immediately after graduate school, they willingly took over the remainder of that debt.

By that time, they had assumed sizeable graduate school loans as well. Nick and Tony entered law school not long after their undergraduate studies. Fay began law school three months after college graduation.

Joy was the exception. At the start of her junior year at Brown, she insisted upon taking over completely the loan installments we had been paying toward her tuition. She knew that her siblings were fast approaching college age.

Suave, super cool, Captain Joe, broke down in tears when I told him about Joy's resolve to do this. We had not expected this magnanimous gesture on her part, and we never would have asked her to take on such a burden. But Joy had calculated that it was feasible, and she set out with great determination to make it work.

Having given up varsity swimming after sophomore year, Joy instead worked part-time jobs at Brown in order to pay the student loan. After graduation, she went to Boston for her first full-time job and making those payments was less of a strain.

Before she began law school, she had paid off all of her undergraduate debt, only to take out a graduate loan in its place. In a relatively short time, the sale of a real estate investment allowed her to pay off that new loan as well.

All in all, it was a never-ending cycle of loans which placed a tremendous encumbrance on all those involved. Yet, student loans provided our children with the opportunity to attend excellent schools and pursue their careers with a solid resume behind them.

Even though my children had two educated parents working nonstop to provide for them, they did not enjoy the luxury of having parents who paid their tuition outright. Nor, could they borrow money from their parents.

On a different trajectory and not saddled with as much debt, Thaddeus had become the General Manager of a large Borders bookstore in Minneapolis after college. Later, he returned to Florida to begin a master's program at the University of South Florida, most of which he paid for as he went along, while holding down a job.

Seeing my children achieve their career goals has been a priceless gift to me—along with knowing that they have been responsible borrowers, meeting their loan obligations as promised. In essence, we took care of college expenses *after the fact.*

Having learned from *our* experience, my children started college funds for their own children as soon as they were born. Most important, with regard to their children's education, they have peace of mind.

Advisory #1: Ideally, you will be able to maintain a college fund for your children beginning with their infancy. But recent setbacks in the economy, make it difficult for many parents to save toward the cost of higher education. When your children reach their first year of high school, their guidance counselor may be able to assist with an overall plan for locating scholarships (see **Tip #22** for pros and cons of counselors).

Advisory #2: Schools like Brown University and Harvard University have large endowments which can be a source of significant financial assistance for students with a genuine financial need. Because students are accepted on their merit without regard to their family's financial status, the high cost of tuition should not intimidate low to moderate income students from applying.

Advisory #3: When those college years arrive, you and your children may be called upon to make great sacrifices. Together, you can decide upon the most prudent way to proceed, keeping in mind, that there is no time like the present.

Advisory #4: In general, if students postpone college, they take much longer than usual to complete their studies once they return to them—often taking only one class per semester for several years. As a result, their starting salaries will likely lag noticeably behind their university educated contemporaries who earned a *head start* in the job market many years earlier.

Chapter 23
¡Ay Caramba! #1:
Middle School and High School
Learners of Spanish

Their attractive, regional, Spanish dialects gave them an air of professionalism and credibility that disguised the fact that they were inadequate or lax teachers.

Canción: Disimula
Song: Conceal (cleverly)
Compositor/Composer: Rafael Pérez Botija

Intérprete/Singer: José José

From studying Spanish at intervals for more than a decade, my experience has been that teachers whose native language is Spanish are not necessarily better at teaching their language than are native speakers of English at teaching their own language.

This is likely how it is with all language teachers around the world. As with any area of study, quality in teaching depends on the education, ability, and dedication of the individual teacher.

I have studied Spanish with native Spanish speakers and with non-Hispanic, non-Latino, American teachers, some of whom began their study of Spanish in elementary school.

In my quest to learn the language, I have encountered among my teachers of Spanish a wide range of abilities from inferior to outstanding, no matter what their native tongue.

It is noteworthy to comment that I have observed a number of native speakers of the language, who were clever enough to **conceal their ineptitude** as instructors from students, parents, and administrators.

Their attractive, regional, Spanish dialects gave them an air of professionalism and credibility that disguised the fact that they were inadequate or lax teachers.

Students, parents, and administrators need to realize that this scenario could surely occur anywhere, any time when students study a foreign language. Teachers who are native speakers need to be held to the **same** high standards as all other teachers.

Parents and administrators should not allow themselves to be **intimidated** by the foreign accent. They need to look beyond the façade and observe teaching techniques and attitudes.

Over the past few years, I have had an opportunity to volunteer my services as a tutor via telephone with two of my friends' grandchildren who were studying Spanish. One of my pupils, Barbara, was a student at a *private* school in the Northeast. My other pupil, Paul, was a student in a *public* school in northern Florida.

Tutoring Barbara

Most recently, I worked with Barbara. By using her school password, I was able to access her **Spanish II** textbook online along with all of her assignments, and I established communication with her teacher via email.

The teacher graciously assisted me in identifying Barbara's weaknesses. A native Spanish speaker from Venezuela, she prepared and presented the lessons clearly in a logical sequence intended to facilitate student success.

But that teacher, nevertheless, failed to notice two egregious grammatical mistakes *written in Spanish* in a worksheet which accompanied the students' textbook.

With my relatively new skills in the language, I found them right away. The teacher confirmed the errors when I brought them to her attention.

Coincidentally, I learned that my identical twin granddaughters in a Florida public school were studying **Spanish II** at the same time as Barbara. They were, in fact, using the *same edition* of the textbook along with its corresponding worksheets.

I discussed the inaccurate worksheet with them. They had done the same exercises, but neither of them had noticed the errors. Nor had their teacher, a native Spanish speaker from Colombia, advised them of the mistakes.

Reminiscent of teacher workbook problems with Manual-Bound Manny (Chapter 15) and with Illiterate Liza (Chapter 18), this incident with Barbara has shown me that everything old is new again. I found history repeating itself with my current discoveries:

- **A flawed workbook, vintage 2016—this time in a foreign language edition**

- **More teachers asleep at the switch**

Despite the fact that the ¡ *Avancemos* ! textbook, published by Holt McDougal in 2013, was still being used in **public** and **private** high schools across the country in 2016, the editors overlooked mistakes in the textbook's companion worksheets.

And there was no addendum to amend those errors. More to the point, all teachers of Spanish should have recognized the inaccuracies and alerted students as to their existence.

These errors, not merely typo mistakes, are located in student instructions at the top of the page. The instructions demonstrate **incorrectly** how to use indirect object pronouns.

As a matter of course, many students experience difficulty with these pronouns. They do not need to become further confused by seeing incorrect grammatical constructions **posing** as model sentences.

This latest example is yet another case of **gaffes** in teacher manuals and their corresponding worksheets which directly affect student learning. It must be emphasized once again that these errors do not hark back to yesteryear. They exist in the **here** and **now**.

It bears repeating that knowledgeable department chairpersons and teachers have a duty to find the errors, point them out to other faculty members and students, and correct them. They should also notify the publisher and **demand revised worksheets**. Textbook publishing is big business. Accuracy must prevail.

Tutoring Paul

Three years ago, I worked with Paul. He was assigned a native speaker of Spanish to teach his **Spanish I** class in eighth grade. The teacher had recently moved to the United States from Madrid, Spain.

It seems that the school had hired him at the last minute and would not otherwise have been able to provide Spanish as a course offering if he had not been available.

At the ***Open House,*** in the beginning of the academic year, the school's principal had proudly introduced the new teacher. Parents felt fortunate that their children would have the benefit of a teacher, who, they thought, was a highly qualified Spanish linguist. [Since this person does not merit the designation of teacher, I will assign him the label of NT, No Teacher.]

Parents boasted about his credentials to their friends. NT made his class fun, and students enjoyed it. That was all well and good, and indeed, it would have been fine for a class of introductory Spanish enrichment.

Paul's class, however, was intended to be a fast-paced, ***intensive*** course granting high school credit to those eighth grade students. NT's job was to prepare his students for an end-of-the-year, districtwide exam that would enable them to proceed directly to **Spanish II** in ninth grade. If students did not pass that exam, they would need to repeat **Spanish I** in high school.

Even if NT had truly been a highly qualified Spanish linguist, he proved himself to be incompetent in this teaching position. His students found the final exam hopelessly difficult, and when the results were published, it seems that ***none*** of the students in Paul's class qualified for **Spanish II.** Some disconsolate students even thought that the low scores were their fault. They felt guilty for not doing better on the exam.

Since my own child was not in this class, it was not my battle to fight. But I imagine that parents would express their disappointment at the test results to the school's principal, who would already be comparing his school's scores on that test to those of other schools in the district.

To protect himself and to indicate that he had taught in accordance with proper guidelines, NT should have kept a portfolio of his major assignments and tests.

Once the principal accumulated all the data, he would decide whether or not to rehire that employee. Having taught only one year in the United States, NT would not have held a continuing contract.

Easily enough, I had predicted this somber outcome very early on from my own observations. Knowing that I had been studying Spanish for several years, my friend's daughter asked me to help Paul by phone and walk him through assignments. Paul had been an honor student throughout his schooling, but Spanish was not his strong suit.

To maintain his high grade-point average, his mother did not want to leave any stone unturned. I was able to purchase a copy of the same textbook so that we could literally be on the same page. How much time we talked each week depended on his need for assistance. The assignments were basic. There wasn't much to discuss.

From the outset, I was concerned that NT had **not** posted an online course syllabus—complete with course objectives, corresponding exercises, carefully-worded instructions, and a timeline for tests, projects, and exams.

Neither had he distributed printed guidelines for parents and students to follow. When I was on the job, my colleagues and I were required to send out all of the above in order to ensure maximum communication between school and home.

It was all *off-the-cuff* as to what NT and his students would do in Spanish class on any given day. I could not see any step-by-step progression of content matter. I couldn't help Paul much because there was little to do.

NT skipped around in the book. I assisted Paul with two small projects and quizzed him over the phone for some vocabulary words, but he never brought any verbs to my attention.

It goes without saying, that learning verbs and their tenses is a major part of studying Spanish. Even though I had warned them that NT was not adequately preparing his students, Paul and his mother were pleased that he was earning A's in the class. They did not seem worried about the doomed final assessment.

In sharp contrast to NT, are two of my former colleagues who taught the same *Spanish* **I** class each year. They worked energetically and intently for the entire academic year preparing eighth-grade students for the same placement exam.

One of the teachers is female and a native of Ecuador. The other is male and a native of the United States with no Hispanic/Latino ancestry. Working for the Peace Corps in Latin America had strengthened his proficiency in the language.

Both teachers took pride in their work and in their successes. Exam results indicated consistently that a majority of their students had scored well enough to begin the study of **Spanish II** in ninth grade.

My first reaction was that parents of students in Paul's Spanish class should have been following their children's progress more closely and held periodic conferences with NT.

With more reflection about NT's nonperformance, I realized that parents were *intimidated* by the fact that he was a native Spanish speaker with an impressive and distinctive dialect from his country of origin.

The way he spoke made him appear highly credible. They felt that he was the **expert,** and that they were not qualified to judge how much progress their children should have been making each term.

Parents without a Spanish language background may be somewhat awed by a teacher of Spanish—even if the teacher has **no** Spanish accent. But there seems to be even more uneasiness when the teacher is a native speaker with an accent. (Those parents would probably have the same reaction with teachers of any foreign language.)

In parents' eyes, the teacher is **all knowing** and **unapproachable.** Paul's mother confirmed that feeling of inadequacy in this situation. Neither she nor her husband had studied Spanish. They and other parents had indiscriminately **placed their trust** in NT. The administration, as well, may have been buffaloed by him.

Additionally, it became obvious to me that NT had kept students and parents happy through a process of **grade inflation** as evidenced on the students' report cards.

Routinely, NT meted out good to excellent grades. In turn, parents were given **false hope** as to their children's performance on the districtwide exam. As a consequence, they were rather stymied by the results.

Parents need to know that **grade inflation** is another gimmick that bad teachers sometimes use to keep students and their parents at a comfortable distance. Good grades should be earned fairly and squarely.

If teachers choose to award them gratuitously, there is **no** need for parent conferences, and there is **no** need to justify their teaching methods—whatever they may be. This device often gets teachers out of the hot seat. Teachers using such sly tactics are engaging in willful **neglect of duty.**

I have observed this practice among colleagues in several academic disciplines and also within classes that I myself have taken. For example, if a number of students are doing poorly, teachers may circumvent the problem by curving their grades rather than by patiently leading their students to full comprehension of the subject matter.

Grade inflation is a two-fold *strategy of avoidance:*

a. Teachers who curve grades for low-performing students *avoid* a barrage of complaints by students or parents.

b. Teachers who inflate grades *avoid* taking the time to teach low-performing students how and what they should be taught.

- Students in the short term will find themselves with undeservedly good grades, and parents may be appeased.

- Students in the long term will be *woefully* unprepared in comparison to their counterparts who were taught by capable, conscientious, caring professionals. NT had blindsided students, parents, and administrators by his accent and by his apathy.

In this situation, I place the blame squarely with NT's immediate supervisor. New to the school, NT should have been subjected to a *series of check points* along the way. There needed to be more classroom observations, a thorough appraisal of the teacher's methods and an analysis of students' progress as they headed toward the district exam. Even from my distant vantage point, I had noticed a number of well-defined warnings leading with precision accuracy to the final outcome.

Teachers like Paul's may or may not face a day of reckoning. And, if not held accountable, those indolent teachers will continue to shirk their moral obligation to do the job for which they were hired.

Advisory: Beware of grade inflation in all disciplines and all lapsed practices that adversely affect student performance.

Chapter 24
¡Ay Caramba! #2:
Older Adult Learners of Spanish & More

It is important to warn such students that bad teachers can be found at any level of instruction and in any field of study.

[Canción: *Perdido en la oscuridad*]
Song: *Lost in obscurity*
Compositor/Composer: Alejandro Jaén

Intérprete/Singer: José José

Many adults, after a long absence from school, are returning to college to finish a degree, or they are just beginning to take classes for the first time since high school.

I have met many such students in my Spanish classes at the local community college—now a four-year state college—who were about thirty-five to forty years old. In most instances, they were studying Spanish, not because they loved the language, but because it met the language requirement that would lead to their degree.

It is important to warn such students that bad teachers can be found at any level of instruction and in any field of study.

For starters, it would be beneficial for them to review the information offered in Chapter 9 regarding older adult learners and in Chapter 23 regarding teachers of Spanish. My observations and advice for them can apply not just to their Spanish classes, but to all of their other classes as well.

When I write about bad teachers, I am not referring to their personal teaching styles. Not all teachers are by nature dynamic. Many may be out-and-out boring. But, they may be notably competent in their field and care genuinely about their students.

Some excellent teachers may lack a charismatic mode of presentation. Clearly, one teacher's personality may appeal to some students and not to others. This interaction involves a personal judgment on the part of students. In a similar vein, academic disciplines like English grammar and statistics hold little interest for many students, while others may find them fascinating.

Yet sophisticated students realize that certain teachers and their classes must be tolerated in order to fulfill a course requirement. Understandably, students need to learn to **_adapt_** to different teaching shticks. It's all part of the game. Instead, my warning about inferior teachers involves more **_serious_** concerns as itemized below. Add to this list if you choose. Students, be on the lookout for the following:

- **Teachers with limited knowledge of their subject matter**

- **Teachers who do not explain each lesson clearly, no matter how many advanced degrees they hold**

- **Teachers who dislike taking questions from students**

- **Teachers who offer disorganized, poorly prepared lessons**

- **Teachers who test on material they have not taught**

- **Teachers who give improperly worded tests or confusing directions on tests**

- **Teachers who do not establish objective criteria for their grading systems**

- **Teachers who are unfair to students**

In one of my Spanish classes, my teacher was a native speaker from Ecuador who refused to take questions from students. He just wanted to barrel on with the lesson.

In another, I had an American born, non-Hispanic, non-Latino teacher who taught each lesson thoroughly, using a variety of methods to get his point across. He was a first-rate teacher, but his professionalism was marred by the low quality of his tests.

Like Retread Reeba, he used old, faded, recycled tests that were difficult to read. Even worse, there were mistakes on them that he did not bother to change for a number of years.

I was aware of the defects in his tests because I took his class several times—once for credit, and four more times without credit—when there was no other class available.

Repeating the class helped with my fluency, but the teacher's **flawed tests** caused trouble for his first-time students. When that teacher eventually modified his material, the tests were the same in form and substance, minus the errors. I do not object, however, to a recycled test if certain criteria are met:

- **The test, in its original design, was well planned.**

- **The test continues to be relevant throughout the years.**

- **The test contains no errors.**

- **The test is clearly legible.**

[On a side note, I am a fan of **Open Book Tests** for learning reinforcement.]

My strong background in the field of English gives me a distinct advantage for studying Spanish. There are a number of similarities in the grammatical structures of the two languages.

In my classes were many native speakers of English who were studying Spanish for the first time. After a long hiatus from school, their background in English grammar was shaky. Spanish grammar was understandably a far greater challenge for them.

Confounding the problem was a teacher who did not explain the lesson well. As a result, students became confused and dejected, not knowing why they were having comprehension problems. This is an all-too familiar occurrence.

In addition, many older students, not unlike students in elementary, middle, or high school, are often reluctant to ask questions of their teacher. They do not want to appear ignorant. Others simply want to get by unnoticed and maintain a low profile.

Good teachers develop special radar that enables them to hone in on such students and assist them. If a teacher fails to do this, adult students—***without parents to fight their battles***—must learn to fend for themselves.

If they feel uncomfortable addressing a problem in class, students should arrange to meet with their teachers individually or in small groups and work through their difficulties.

Good communication is essential to learning. Responsible, caring teachers know this and make it a priority in their class. I offer the following advice to **all** learners—with a special emphasis in this chapter for those returning to school after a long absence.

- **Remain confident in your ability to do well.**

- **Let your teachers know whenever and whatever you do not understand.**

- **Be watchful for bad teaching practices that could impede your success.**

- **Share your concerns with other students, remembering that there is safety in numbers.**

In my Spanish classes, I have met students born in the United States whose parents came from a Spanish-speaking country. From birth they learned to speak both Spanish and English, but because they were fluent in speaking Spanish, they did **not** study the subject formally in school.

Now, as adults, some cannot read Spanish well, and many cannot write Spanish correctly. They had difficulty learning the grammar in our classes. As I see it, their precious gift was **squandered**, which, if nurtured properly when they were young, would have bestowed upon them a high level of proficiency.

It is important for people of all nationalities, who brought their native language with them to this country, to cultivate that **gift** faithfully in their children.

Experts emphasize the need to focus on informal and formal training in **all modalities**—listening, speaking, reading, and writing—so that the next generation will experience full participation in the language of their parents.

In my quest to learn Spanish late in life, I am surprised that some of my acquaintances and colleagues cannot understand why I would be interested in learning this language or any other language for that matter. They are content to speak one language and leave it at that.

Believing that everyone should speak at least two languages, I work every day toward increasing my competency in Spanish. Of course, I realize that it is best to study and assimilate such disciplines in the bloom of youth, but I know firsthand that it is never too late to enjoy the **thrill** of learning a second language.

Advisory: Experience the exhilaration of studying, speaking, reading, and writing another language.

Conclusion

My role as a mother was simplified because my children enjoyed school. They eagerly took on challenges. With assurance, I attribute their rewarding academic experiences to the *Twenty-Two Timeless Tips* revealed here in the *flip* section, *Literacy & Love Go Hand in Hand.*

Contributing to their never-ending desire to do well, these motivational, yet practical, strategies—launched when my children were very young—and enacted throughout their public school years, were the keys to their academic success.

Those early *Tips* remain with them still as the basis of a smooth-running operating system. They carry that same strong work ethic with them today in their professions, and they pass it along in their daily living to my grandchildren.

Much like my own children, countless teachers in public schools maintain those same values. They strive each day to make the subject of their lessons clear and meaningful.

In so doing, they facilitate their students' ongoing progression to a higher level of understanding. Often they do this while protesting unjust practices in the school system that hinder or penalize their students.

Sadly, many teachers do not personify that integrity. They look for the easy way out whenever possible. Master teachers enjoy going to work each day because they love teaching. Other teachers show up at our nation's schools because they love long vacations.

If I had been a mother with unlimited financial resources at my disposal, I would not have gone to work outside of the home. I was happy there. My life would have been entirely different. Now I cannot imagine that other life.

During my career, I worked for eleven public school principals. One of them frequently delivered the following exhortation at faculty meetings,

"If you don't like teaching, don't teach. There is no place for you here. Find another line of work."

One afternoon, after hearing her articulate those sentiments yet again, it came to me plainly that my job had evolved into a profession. I recognized the varied and valuable contributions that I was able to make in students' lives, and I realized that my career had enriched me immeasurably.

Through the years, several of my younger female colleagues expressed to me their preference for remaining home indefinitely after the birth of their children. But money was tight for them as it was for me. They needed outside income to raise their families. Nevertheless, while they were on the job, they took great pride in their work, and they put their students' needs first.

Their work habits were **identical** to mine in that I always tried to teach my students to the best of my ability, in the same conscientious and professional manner that I would want my own children to be taught.

Quite obviously, being a parent is not a prerequisite for being an outstanding teacher. As referenced earlier (Chapters 3 & 6), the majority of my teachers were unmarried women with no children. They upheld the highest of standards.

Above all, the teaching profession is one of service. To reiterate, even the finest of teachers can make occasional errors. An alert parent or guardian will be able to address those mistakes diplomatically with the teacher and resolve them in short notice. Matters of this sort present no problem with an honest and attentive teacher who operates **fully above board** with nothing to hide.

As students mature, they will learn to become their own advocates. If they are working with a reasonable teacher, they will solve problems by themselves without help from a parent.

Acutely distressing is the fact that many teachers harbor a secret stash of dirty tricks, artful subterfuges, and devious short cuts which they wield for their own convenience.

On the defensive, they discourage open dialogue. At the same time, they remain *inept, inflexible, and insensitive,* without adapting their teaching styles to student needs.

Advisory: Parents and guardians, this is where you pick up the unrelenting torch for positive change.

A Real Life Story
Laced with
A Bit of Exaggeration

South of the Border
One Phase of the Journey
By
Thaddeus Broward Ryan

[Note: This story took place in the pre-seat belt era.]

I clung to the first rung of the ladder in the deep end of the hotel pool. I watched my two brothers who stood at the top of the metal slide leading down the fiberglass boulder into the water.

"It's Midnight at the Oasis!" My brother Tony shouted the words of Maria Maldaur's evocative, popular song as he hit the slope. He tucked into a cannonball when the slide dropped off and hit the water with a splash that gushed down on my head.

I took a deep breath and stepped off the ladder while not letting go of the rail. I dropped below the surface and opened my eyes. It wasn't midnight, but the sun had set before we had arrived at the **Days Inn: Oasis** outside of Savannah, Georgia. We were headed north on our summer vacation to visit our relatives in Massachusetts.

I saw Tony swimming at high speed under water like Aqua Man, and then he disappeared into the flickering shadows at the edge of the cone of light. I pulled myself back up the ladder and watched Nick descend the slide, head first, with his arms outstretched. He dropped from the slide and dived smoothly into the water.

"Come on, Thaddeus," my sister Joy gently coaxed,

"I'll take you up."

I climbed out of the pool and onto the deck. I took Joy's hand and let her lead me through the winding canyon up toward the top of the boulder. The path was poorly lit and slippery. Several older kids pushed past us on the way up. There was a breeze at the top and a slight chill in the air that reminded me I was no longer in Florida. Fay stood waiting for us.

"Scared, Thaddeus?" she asked.

I shook my head. I looked down toward the pool where Nick and Tony were treading water in the deep end, just to the side of the slide. They faced each other about ten feet apart, squirting water in arched streams from their clasped hands. When one succeeded at spraying the other in the eye, he was the champion of the moment.

The loser ducked under the water and resurfaced with a fresh spray for the next contest. They seemed much farther away than they had when I was still in the pool looking up at them on the slide.

"N-o-o-o," I replied, clattering my teeth unintentionally, "just cold."

"Last one down's a circus clown," Fay pronounced.

She sat down facing away from the pool and leaned backwards. She slid down head first on her back and dropped into the water with a backwards dive.

"I'll go down next," Joy said, "so I can help you to the wall."

"I can swim," I told her.

"Surf's up!" she yelled to Nick, Tony, and Fay watching below.

She stepped onto the slide in a slightly crouched position and rode down standing up. I sat down on the concrete deck and dangled my legs onto the slide. Three little spouts at the top of the slide sent jets of water down the metal. I thought about letting go and pushing off the concrete, but some older kids kept swimming right beneath where I planned to hit the water. I wasn't sure this was such a good idea after all. I was about to stand up and walk back down, to try again when the pool was less crowded, when I suddenly felt myself lunging forward.

I was airborne for a second and then I hit the slide. I slid down the rest of the way like the *Six Million Dollar Man*, seemingly in slow motion but actually really fast. I was sideways when I reached the drop off and nearly upside down when I hit the water. I turned a few underwater somersaults before righting myself, swimming to the surface, and gasping for breath. I looked up and saw my brothers Nick and Tony back at the top of the slide. Nick was doubling over with laughter. Tony was patting him on the back.

"The clown comes tumbling down," I heard my sister Fay blurt out. I put my face in the water and kicked to the wall.

"*Massachusetts, here I come*," Joy started singing in the station wagon the next day.

"*Right back where I started from*," Nick and Tony, seated on either side of her in the middle seat, joined in.

Fay and I rode in the back, in the seat that faced out the rear window. We couldn't sit upright because of the suitcases packed where our feet should have gone, so we sat sideways, our legs pointing in opposite directions with our backs up against the side of the car.

"*Massachusetts, here I come*," I sang, but the others fell silent.

"You can't sing that, Thaddeus," Fay scolded.

"It's not where you started from," Nick reminded me.

"You were born in Florida," Tony pitched in.

When they resumed singing, Fay joined them. I stared ahead and watched the telephone poles race past the side of the car. I was running along the wires down the slopes between each pole and then up again. I was a *Flying Wallenda*, an honorary member accepted into that great family because of my agility and daring. I gave up the high-flying trapeze-without-a-net act for the long-distance-speed tightrope where I discovered that speed eliminated the need for the long balancing pole.

The singing stopped abruptly, and I was no longer a *Flying Wallenda* but a *Grounded Ryan* in a station wagon headed right back to where I hadn't started from watching Nick, Tony, and Joy scrambling to the front of the car. Tony got through the opening between the driver and passenger seat first, crawled to the dashboard, and reached his arms out,

"First one in South Carolina!" he shouted.

He crawled back to the middle seat humming, *Stars and Stripes Forever* and doing his best to dance a victory dance within the confined space of the station wagon. Joy had been the first in Georgia the day before. I went back to running along the telephone wires for a while. I must have said something about being a *Flying Wallenda* out loud because Tony and Nick began a conversation on the subject.

"Did you hear about the Wallenda in Puerto Rico?"

"The one who tried to walk the tightrope between two buildings?" Nick responded.

"That's him," Tony nodded.

"That is **he**," my mother corrected Tony from the front passenger seat.

"Yeah;" Nick continued, "the wind blew him right off the wire."

"He didn't make it." Tony explained.

The conversation was interrupted when Nick shouted, "South of the Border!" and began humming a confident solo version of *We are the Champions* by Queen.

I stood up on the seat and looked out the front window of the car in the direction where all of my family members seemed to be looking. I saw a billboard come into view on the right hand side of the road that depicted a chubby man wearing a brightly colored poncho and a large straw hat. The words **South of the Border** were printed in black and orange letters.

Joy informed me that **South of the Border** was a roadside attraction located just south of the North Carolina border. The game was that to earn a point, when you saw one of the signs, you had to call, "South of the Border!" before any other family member called the sign. If you called, "South of the Border!" in error, you lost a point. When we arrived at **South of the Border,** there would be a tall water tower. When you saw the tower, if you were first to call, "Sombrero!," you would earn five points.

"What's a sombrero?" I wondered aloud.

"A large hat," Fay answered, "like the one on the billboard, worn by the big guy, **Pedro.**"

Nick added, "He's the mascot."

"Oh, um . . . what's a mascot?" I inquired.

"Someone who kind of stands for something, like *Tony the Tiger,*" Tony chuckled and nudged Nick on the arm.

I remained standing up to watch for more **South of the Border** notices. I had a good view from each side of the car, but it was difficult to see very far ahead down the road.

Persuasively the signs continued. Joy called one. **Pedro's** black and white striped sombrero, similar in this advertisement to a conductor's hat, was announcing a train ride for kids with an inviting, *"**All Aboard!** "* I looked forward to riding it.

Nick then called a sign. **Pedro** had too much tequila and the sign was printed upside down. Tony called another. **Pedro** was taking a siesta beneath a tree. The sign said something about "**Catching some Z's**" at the **South of the Border** motel. I thought it sounded like a great place to stay—maybe even better than the **Oasis.**

242

Not yet being able to call a sign, I knew I was at a disadvantage due to my place in the back of the station wagon. I tried to crawl into the next seat, but Nick blocked my path. When Fay managed to score a point, I believed that I too had a chance. I paid attention to each bend in the road and thought I found a pattern to the placement of the signs. When we approached a cluster of trees on the right hand side of the road, I could see a billboard behind the leaves but couldn't make out what was on it.

"Look, Gang," my father shouted from the driver's seat, "a paper mill!"

"Gross! Where is it?" Tony questioned him.

We started looking frantically around. We had passed a paper mill the day before in Georgia. The putrid smell had penetrated the car and lingered for hours. We could even taste it in our snacks. That day, though, I didn't smell anything.

"Down there," my father pointed to the left of the car as we crossed over an overpass. I looked out to the left but still didn't see or smell a thing.

"South of the Border!" my father called out.

I looked back to the right and saw **Pedro** announcing the *'World's best meenature golf'* from behind the cluster of trees I had seen a minute ago. We crossed another overpass, and I got a good view way out in front of the car. I saw an orange and black sign in the distance and what appeared to be **Pedro's** sombrero sticking up over the top of it.

"South of the Border!" I exclaimed.

I started humming *Stars and Stripes Forever* with a bit of *We are the Champions* thrown in. Before I could add some victory dance moves, though, I stopped to wonder why everyone was laughing.

"Minus one," Nick observed.

"He fell for it," Tony emphasized.

"The old **Thunderbird** decoy," my mother added, advising me that the other motel took it upon itself to attract visitors by using some of the same colors as its competitor.

As I watched the sign draw closer, **Pedro's** sombrero transformed itself into the head and wings of a bird. The color scheme was similar, but there was no **Pedro**—just the going rate for a night at the **Thunderbird Motel**. The game continued, and I got farther behind. After my father's sneaky tactic put him on the board, he called a series of signs that put him in good position to win the game. A long time passed without anyone calling a sign, and then suddenly everyone but me seemed to be shouting, "South of the Border!" at once. I couldn't tell who was calling what. I saw **South of the Border** signs on either side of the road.

"The grand finale," my mother declared.

I started shouting, "South of the Border!" myself a few times, but each time I did, someone said

"Already called it."

Then my father cried, "Sombrero!" and secured his victory. He didn't sing or dance but just kept driving. The water tower shaped like **Pedro's** sombrero grew larger as the station wagon drew nearer.

Any frustration I had about not being able to call signs eased as I took in the view from the overpass. I saw a giant statue of **Pedro**, his legs straddled like a single **Golden Arch** except that his baggy trousers appeared to be more of a beige color.

I saw a giant ape and lots of little buildings like those you see in Westerns. I saw the miniature golf course and the train that wound around it. And then I noticed the sombrero tower getting smaller.

"Wait! We're driving right by!" I alerted my parents in the front of the wagon.

"Oh, I am sorry, Thaddeus," my mother replied nonchalantly. "We don't stop there. Too expensive."

"Tourist trap," my father grumbled.

I turned around and sat back in my seat. I watched the sombrero until it disappeared from view beneath the overpass. I saw another cluster of **South of the Border** signs, the finale for travelers headed south.

"South of the Border!" I tried one more time.

"Doesn't count!" Nick retorted. "Wrong direction."

"Game's over," Tony decreed.

My father rolled down his window and stuck his hand outside of the car.

"First one in North Carolina!"

245

Ryan children cerca 1990. From Left to Right:
Tony, Fay, Thad, Joy, Nick

Citations & Reference Notes

Part I. Chapter introductions...A: Seventeen chapters are introduced with **caricatures** of teachers. Above each caricature is a brief commentary written by the author taken from the text of that chapter. All of the caricatures are abstractions and exaggerations created in the stylistic technique of the illustrator. They were not designed to reproduce actual physical features of any teacher.

Part II. Chapter introductions...B: Seven chapters are introduced with illustrations and song titles that correspond to the subject matter. For each song, I have given the name of the composer and the performer who sings the original version or the rendition I prefer.

Part III. Citations: direct quotations & reference notes.

Within the text, I use **end-of-citation superscripts** to alert readers to the complete citations listed here. In this *Citations & Reference Notes* section, I have numbered each quotation with an Arabic numeral in the beginning of the citation—along with its matching superscript number from the text—at the end of the citation.

Above the citations, I indicate their location within the text as to **preface or chapter**. Each quotation is displayed here in ***bold italics*** to distinguish it from other notations. The source of a quotation is indicated directly below it.

Citations 1, 2, 3. PREFACE

1. "*. . . only education is capable of saving our societies from possible collapse, whether violent, or gradual.*" [1]

The original pronouncement made in French dates back to 1934 in Piaget's Rapport *du Directeur: Cinquième Reunion du Conseil*. Genève: Bureau international d'éducation. (1934c, p. 31).

Alberto Munari referenced this remark in an article he wrote for the following journal: Prospects: *The quarterly review of comparative education.* (Paris, UNESCO: International Bureau of Education), Vol. XXIV, no. 1/2 1994, 311-327. UNESCO: International Bureau of Education, 2000.

2. ***"Most teachers are nurturing, self-sacrificing, and inspiring, but it would be naïve to pretend that they all are. Some are indifferent, some are incompetent, and a few are downright destructive."*** [2]

Strickland, G. (1998). *Bad teachers.* New York, NY: POCKET BOOKS, a division of Simon & Schuster Inc., p. 3.

3. **". . . (5) if your child ever disagrees with a teacher or coach, you must always take the side of the teacher or coach; "** . . . [3]

Chua, A. (2011). *Battle hymn of the tiger mother.* New York, NY: PENGUIN BOOKS, p. 5.

Citations 4, 5. CHAPTER 2

4. ***"Pedro's Weather Forecast: Chili today, hot tamale! "*** [4]

South of the Border website:
http://www.the southoftheborder.com/

5. Captain Joe became an avid fan of the activity and soon adopted Doc Counsilman's book, *The Science of Swimming* [5] as his bible.

Counsilman, J. E. (1968). *The science of swimming.* Englewood Cliffs, NJ: Prentice-Hall, Inc.

Citation 6. CHAPTER 4

6. Having been a political science major at Mount Holyoke, I was **gung ho** in 1960, to get involved with local politics. I followed the advice of my esteemed professor

Victoria Schuck, Ph.D. and staged a robust, one-person, grass roots campaign two months before my wedding. A nearby printing press made leaflets with my picture on them, and I went door-to-door distributing them in person while espousing my platform. Additionally, I took out a fairly large ad in the local newspaper, also with my picture, and I stood at the polls for the entire day of the election soliciting votes.

My victory garned a significant amount of attention. I had won a coveted position for a small town, and I received the highest number of votes for the **newcomers** that were elected to that precinct. I was told that several others had tried in vain for years to accomplish what I had done in one try. Captain Joe bragged about it to all of his friends, *"Sue got elected!"* After serving two three-year terms, my family and I took up permanent residence in Cohasset, and that was the end of my political career.

Citation 7, 8. CHAPTER 5

7. In this period of *"economic stagnation* " [7]
Wikipedia.

8. *"Take it easy on the road of life."* [8]
South of the Border website:
http://www.thesouthoftheborder.com/

Citation 9. CHAPTER 6

9. Radcliffe College . . . completely absorbed by Harvard University in 1999.[9] *Wikipedia.*

Citation 10, 11. CHAPTER 8

10. *"Scholarship winners represent fewer than 1% of the initial pool of student entrants . . ."* [10] *Wikipedia.*

11. "Lotus Eaters" [11]
Homer (Translated by Fitzgerald, R). 1992.
The Odyssey. New York, NY: Alfred A. Knopf, p. 147.

Citation 12. CHAPTER 9

12. *"Better that ten guilty persons escape than that one innocent suffer."* [12]
Sir William Blackstone, 1765. *Wikipedia.*

Citations 13, 14, 15, 16. CHAPTER 13

13. *"A new school year just began in Los Angeles Unified School District with all the typical fresh hopes and dreams, but this one will be different . . . "* [13]

Villagra, H. (August 29, 2012). "Ding, dong, Concept 6 is dead." THE BLOG. *The Huffington Post.*

14. Nationally renowned education experts have criticized the system harshly, citing direct links with CONCEPT 6 and low student performance as well as imposing its own version of segregation.[14]

Two experts Dr. Jeanne Oakes and Dr. Ross Mitchell are noted as follows:

a) The reference to Dr. Jeannie Oakes' comment—also noted below—is cited, **not** in the body of this book, but in an extended version of the same Villagra newspaper article above. Ibid.

> *"Dr. Jeannie Oakes concluded that students who attend schools on the Concept 6 'calendar' suffer several clear disadvantages as compared to students at schools on traditional calendars."*

Dr. Jeannie Oakes, among her other credentials, was a Presidential Professor in Educational Equity in the Graduate School of Education and Information Studies at UCLA. Much of her research centered on inequalities in school systems.

b) Dr. Ross Mitchell, an educational researcher at Gallaudet Research Institute in Washington, D.C. made a study of **CONCEPT 6** as noted in the following journal article which addresses the issue of segregation created by year-round schools.

Mitchell, R. E., & Mitchell, D. E. (2005). Student segregation and achievement tracking in year-round schools. *Teachers College Record*, 107(4), 529-562.

15. *"Nobody is happy with the Concept 6 calendar, from the superintendent to the board, and every effort is being made to replace it."* [15]

Pierson, D. (December 8, 2002). *"The bad side of 'B-tracks' criticized."* *The Los Angeles Times.*

16. *". . . Some complain there is even a stigma associated with being a B-track student. They say B-track is the dumb track . . . "* [16]

Pierson (2002). Ibid.

Citations 17, 18. CHAPTER 14

17. *"For Piaget, intelligence meant exploring the environment."* [17]

Singer, D. S. & Revenson, T.A. (1996). *A Piaget Primer: How a Child Thinks.* Revised edition. ©A PLUME BOOK. p. 27.

18. *Brief synopsis of Piaget's Stages of Cognitive Development.* [18] Ibid. pp. 12-26.

Citations 19, 20. CHAPTER 17

19. . . . **Article X, Sections 1-5** follows, indicating procedures for discipline and dismissal which still exist today. [19]

20. *"And make no mistake about it: Confronting a teacher requires a great deal of backbone. Marching alone into battle against a teacher and his whole army of supporters is a terrifying prospect."* [20]

Strickland, G. (1998). p. 152.

Citation 21, 22, 23. CHAPTER 20

21. Dr. James John Unger ... had successfully coached Georgetown University's debate team to several winning seasons. [21]

22. With a beautiful Mediterranean Revival style of architecture, it was the oldest high school in Palm Beach County. [22]

23. *"You are the only person in the world who really cares whether your child learns anything, so you must take responsibility for your child's education."* [23]

Strickland, G. (1998). p. 304.

Citations 24, 25, 26, 27, 28. CHAPTER 21

24. *Gifted Characteristics Checklist.* [24] This checklist is one component of prime importance in identifying students for the gifted program in Palm Beach County. See below for more details.

[The state of Florida Department of Education and] The School District of Palm Beach County {have} defined procedures which guide each school's Child Study Team through the eligibility process for students who are potentially gifted. The process begins when the student's teacher, parent, or other qualified personnel observe outstanding academic abilities when compared with others of the same age group. The reporting of these observations initiates the process of collecting necessary data to determine eligibility. The eligibility requirements are defined in **State Rule 6A--6.03019.** This rule states that a student is eligible for gifted education if the student demonstrates **[ALL]** of the following:

Plan A Eligibility – [My students fell under Plan A.]

- The need for a special program

- A *majority of characteristics of gifted children* according to a standard scale or *checklist*

- Superior intellectual development indicated by an Intelligence Quotient (IQ) of two or more standard deviations above the mean on an individually administered standardized test of intelligence, [i.e. a **score of 130 or more**].

    Author's note: The checklist noted above originates with the district **ESE** headquarters. The form labeled **Gifted Characteristics Checklist Grades 6-12** is used in middle schools. Elementary schools have similar checklists designed according to grade levels, beginning with PreK and Kindergarten, Grade 1, Grades 2 and 3, Grades 4 and 5.

    To be successful on the screening **checklist** which provides **24 characteristics of gifted students**, a student must score greater than 50% with a rating of "3" or "4" on the line items.

    Author's advisory: If students obtain an acceptable rating on the checklist, they will be referred to the district psychologist for an **official IQ test as** described earlier. But the process will **STOP HERE** if students are not rated high enough on the checklists by their teachers.

Plan B Eligibility

To identify potentially gifted students from underrepresented populations: There is another checklist for this category, *Gifted Characteristics Checklist for Under Represented Populations.*

- English Language Learner **(ELL).**

- Students whose families are labeled as Low Socioeconomic status, receiving free or reduced lunch (Low **SES).**

For more information, refer to websites of the Florida Department of Education: http:/wwwfldoe.org and The School District of Palm Beach County: http: /www.palmbeachschools.org.

25. *"The identification process should be based on the use of multiple criteria . . . "*[25]

Parents, teachers, and school administrators can work collaboratively to identify gifted and talented students in **Connecticut.** Each group has valuable information that can be used to ensure that all children—those with demonstrated abilities or those with the *potential* to demonstrate such abilities are identified.

Bureau of Teaching and Learning - Connecticut State Department of Education.

26. *"Districts shall use multiple objective criteria for identifying student . . ."*[26]

Highly Capable Program in the **State of Washington** - Q & A on Legislation and Advocacy. This article is provided as a service of the Davidson Institute for Talent Development. http://www.davidsongifted.org/.

27. *"I view all of our work in this field as a war against the forces of mediocrity . . ."*[27]

Knobel, R. & Shaughnessy, M. (2002). Reflecting on a conversation with Joe Renzulli: About giftedness and gifted education. *Gifted Education International.* 16, 118-126.

28. *"The underachievement of gifted students is a perplexing phenomenon."*[28]

Reis, S. & McCoach, D. "The underachievement of gifted students: What do we know and where do we go?" *Gifted Child Quarterly.* National Association for Gifted Children (NAGC). Vol. 44, No. 3, 152-170. Summer 2000.

Citation 29, 30, 31. Chapter 22

29. Those legendary convoy ships sailed laboriously around occupied Norway . . .[29] *Wikipedia.*

30. Lend-Lease Act of 1941.[30]

31. *Ryans Building Jupiter Tradition.*[31]
Addis, N. *Jupiter Tequesta Journal.* March 27, 1980. p.14.

TIME TO FLIP BOOK !

TIME TO FLIP BOOK !

CPSIA information can be obtained
at www.ICGtesting.com
Printed in the USA
BVOW06s2149060218
507440BV00001B/41/P

9 781524 698829

Literacy & Love
Go Hand in Hand

To help your child experience
Confidence & Success
From Preschool through High School
Look Inside For

Twenty-Two Timeless Tips
To Trump The System

Flip Book Over For
Never Trust a Teacher
Susan Fay Ryan - Doctor of Education

authorHOUSE®

CONTENTS

Page

Literacy & Love Go Hand in Hand 1

Tip

1   Praise & name your child
    in a BEDTIME serenade 3

2   Talk it up! NURTURE your newborn
    with language & laughter................................ 5

3   Read for LOVE & learning........................... 7

4   Reap imaginative rewards
    through CREATIVE play 11

5   Sing, dance & play with a PRO:
    Preschooler Reading Often! 15

6   Infuse preschoolers with a
    LIFELONG, library habit 19

7   Emerge as an EXPERT on
    public school excellence 21

8   Crack the code! Adopt an
    INFALLIBLE reading recipe 23

9   Stash the cash!
    Seek EARLY evaluation 25

Tip		Page
10	Establish rapport with your child's teachers. Watch out for arrogant, volunteer CLIQUES!	29
11	SCRUTINIZE your children's homework with daily devotion	33
12	Become an ACE detective. Size up your child's competition	37
13	Keep a CLOSE EYE on your children's friends	39
14	Teach your children RIGHT from wrong	41
15	Rule wisely and well WITHOUT corporal punishment	43
16	Say "NO!" to thoughtless, negative labels	45
17	Monitor and inspire MIDDLE SCHOOL readers	49
18	Value the VERBAL. Dabble in dynamic debate	51
19	Connect with computers. Teachers and counselors, REACH OUT to caregivers in need	53

Tip		Page

20 Protect your child from
teacher mob mentality.
DIVIDE & CONQUER 57

21 Cultivate a climate for
higher education.
Explore TECHNICAL training 61

22 Let guidance counselors
guide you, but TAKE HEED! 67

Appendix A 71
Appendix B 77
Citations & Reference Notes................................ 85

Literacy & Love Go Hand in Hand
Prepare Your Children for a Happy,
Successful Life at School.

Before being critical of teachers, parents and guardians must prepare the children under their care to be ideal students when they arrive at school. Setting high standards sends a strong, healthy message to children. If they do their part from the outset and their children are equipped to learn, parents can then, in turn, find fault with teachers who may not be holding up their end of the bargain.

In this supplement to the larger book, I offer simple but fundamental guidelines for parents as they begin their childrearing years and gradually ease their children into the world of public school. On the topic of children with specific learning disabilities, please refer to **a)** *Preface* of *Never Trust a Teacher,* p. 3, **b)** *Tips #9.7, #9.8,* pp. 26 - 27, and to **c) Part 1 of APPENDIX B**, pp. 77 - 78.

Although these **Timeless Tips** may appear obvious to a great number of parents, there are many parents and caregivers who do not realize their importance, or how much of a difference these **TIPS** can make for their children as early as infancy.

I cannot over emphasize the vital need to prepare children academically, socially, and ethically so that all children can excel at learning. All children should feel not only *physically,* but *intellectually,* safe and secure in their school environment.

By the latter, I mean that students need to feel prepared and confident that they can and will succeed in school as *well* or *better* than their classmates. Parents, by default, are granted both the responsibility and the enjoyment of empowering their children to be lifelong learners. Happily,

Literacy and Love Go Hand in Hand.

TIP #1. PRAISE & NAME YOUR CHILD IN A BEDTIME SERENADE. Make your children the star attraction of a song that you compose especially for them. Include their full name. Become a subtle, but constant, cheerleader for your children.

1.1 Begin when they are infants. Sing directly to them—softly and soothingly—just before they fall asleep. At the end of the song, ask your children to say their entire name. This will happen sooner than you think. In the meantime, until your children are talking, you can respond on their behalf.

Children love *hearing* their own name, and they especially enjoy *reciting* their own name. Your child's nightly song offers a continual reassurance of admiration and respect. It gives the recipient comfort, confidence, and a strong sense of self. You will be amazed at what a simple song can do!

1.2 Soon, your children will request their song every night. After a long day, you may feel too tired to sing. But you will sing that song once again to please your child. After twelve years of singing to my oldest child, she diplomatically advised me one evening, "That's okay, Mom, you don't need to sing my song anymore."

She had probably been planning that message for months but didn't want to hurt my feelings. I was a bit wistful at this rite of passage, but I knew that the song had enjoyed a good long run.

1.3 Fortunately for me, I had four other children who still appreciated their song, and one child who continued listening to it past the age of twelve.

Note: I used the same song for all five of my children. I simply substituted their names. To this day, no one complained. In fact, the song became a beloved family ritual handed down to the next generation. One of my granddaughters requests

TIP #2. TALK IT UP! NURTURE YOUR NEWBORN WITH LANGUAGE & LAUGHTER. Talk and laugh with your baby often as you go about your caregiving routine.

2.1 If you are carrying your baby around, or when your infant is nearby, talk softly and animatedly, telling your baby everything that you are doing.

"Nicole, I will give you a lovely sponge bath. Is the water nice and warm?"

"Look, Mustafa, Daddy is feeding a biscuit to our doggie, Fido. Yes, he likes it!"

"I'm going to change your diaper now, Ananda. How does that feel?"

"Mommy is eating cereal with Elsa and Mary. It's delicious! Yum! Yum!"

"You are such a wonderful boy, Pierre. We are so lucky to be together. Yes, we are lucky!"

"Okay, Ricardo, now I will put you in your car seat. Let's go for a ride. Are you ready?"

2.2 Without this interaction, children may be disadvantaged when they start school. Your voice is a soothing and powerful tool for learning. An article in the New York Times explains,

"Another idea—is creeping into the policy debate: that the key to early learning is talking—specifically, a child's exposure to language spoken by parents and caretakers from birth to age 3, the more the better. It turns out, evidence is showing, that the much-ridiculed stream of parent-to-child baby talk—is very, very important." [1]

2.3 Congratulations, if you are one of those parents who knew instinctively that talking to newborns produces great

benefits for both mother and child, but even if you were not, let the experts guide you. *It's not too late!*

2.4 When your child is in the early stages of talking, it often seems that friends and relatives like to ask questions of your child to elicit a response. They mean well, but you sense that your child may feel bombarded with questions.

Your protective instinctive kicks in.

At times like this, you may be tempted to answer in place of your child, feeling pressure for your child to perform.

Looking at it from different angles:

a. Diplomatically advise those asking the questions to do so with moderation.

b. Relax and let your child respond *or not*.

c. Your child will learn naturally to become an independent talker without parent backup.

2.5 The use of handheld screens by babies and toddlers has become a topic of great interest to pediatricians. Researchers are studying the use of these devices as they relate to speech development. Many factors must be taken into consideration, and much more research is still needed.[2]

TIP #3. READ FOR LOVE & LEARNING. Read and tell stories to your children as soon as they are born or even earlier. Continue reading to them into their middle school years.

3.1 Reading to Infants.

a. Talking and reading to your children are overlapping **TIPS**. Reading is another way to become close with your baby and to facilitate language development. First, use those many sleepless nights with your newborn children as a time to bond with them and launch their informal education.

Cradle them, read to them, and tell them stories. Your child will be comforted by the sound of your voice, and you will remember those special moments for a lifetime. Many parents believe that their babies recognize the sound of their voices immediately after birth from hearing them when in their mother's womb. In a web article, the reviewer cites a study from **Acta Paediatrica** which confirms this belief,

"The main message for new moms is that their babies are listening and learning and remembering during the last stages of pregnancy. Their brains do not wait for birth to start absorbing information, says study author Patricia K. Kuhl, PhD. " [3]

b. In the same article, speech pathologist, Melissa Wexler Gurfein, states,

"This may suggest the importance of the mother not only to talk during the last trimester of pregnancy but to continue to talk to her newborn from the moment of birth to help facilitate language development." [4]

c. With continued daily and or nightly reading, not only are you instilling a love of reading in your child, but you are developing listening skills in your child and—ever so subtly— you are teaching your child how to follow a story line from beginning to end.

d. Later, when your children are talking, they will instinctively begin to *memorize* story books you have read to them. They will then, themselves, be able to *read* stories aloud to their family members.

A marvelous moment will have arrived in your household. Children believe that they are literally reading like grownups and feel great pride when they can entertain their families in this manner. All of this is important to the reading process.

e. As you read to your children after the age of three, always say the name of the book's *author* and *illustrator* after you have read the book's title. There are several reasons:

(1) Children need to learn at an early age that those who are responsible for the book deserve to receive credit for it by those who read it. A book's creators should never be taken for granted.

(2) Tell your children that they may write or illustrate a book someday. It is within their reach. Many young children want to be firefighters, doctors, or members of the police force, all noble service professions often depicted in picture books. Why not add writer or illustrator as a possible career? Your children may pursue *multiple* career tracks. Let them know that is an option.

(3) *Falling in love* with an author is one of the best ways toward becoming an avid reader. Emotion and logic come together when children are charmed by an author's style or subject matter, and as result, they want to read another book by that author. Conveniently, there are a number of children's book authors who have written several books.

f. Additionally, many authors have created a *series* of books that keep children spellbound. Children set goals to read each book in the series, and if the author is writing *currently,* children eagerly await the next volume. Adults do the same

with respect to authors, often as a result of their childhood reading habits. As children mature, they gradually expand their repertoire of authors.

3.2 Reading to Middle Schoolers (Refer to TIP #17). Even the best readers in my middle school classes enjoyed it when I read aloud to them. With your own children of middle school age, you can select books to read to them that they might not otherwise choose—books that will capture their attention, inspire them, and compellingly elevate their level of learning once they are exposed to them.

3.3 Reading to Communicate. Whatever the age of the children, parents or relatives can use the subject matter of books to engage them in worthwhile discussions, keep them abreast of current events, and develop their critical thinking skills. Don't miss this opportunity to stay close to your child, and as a bonus, learn what's happening in their world outside the home. Children often describe exploits of their friends and classmates in these types of discussions.

3.4 Reading to Pass on the Pleasure. Your good parenting patterns trickle down to future generations of your family. If your children become parents, you will witness your own children teaching your grandchildren to read, much as you taught them. You will see your grandchildren deriving pleasure from books. Auspiciously, the partnership of *Literacy and Love* cycles onward.

TIP #4. REAP IMAGINATIVE REWARDS THROUGH CREATIVE PLAY. Recognize the types of early play and the importance of play in your child's development.

Piaget wrote about three main types of play: [5]

4.1 Practice play. This can be recognized as imitation when babies imitate actions and sounds of others. One common example is when a child waves and says, *"Bye Bye,"* after mimicking a parent. Feel free to make goofy gestures and silly sounds in front of your children. You will be promoting healthy exercise in your children and encouraging them to talk and laugh. Not only is laughter good for the soul, it is a central component in developing a child's imagination.

4.2 Symbolic play or imitation. Actions of this type occur at approximately sixteen to eighteen months. Piaget wrote about his daughter using a walnut to represent a cat. As she moved the walnut along with her hand, she made cat sounds. My daughter Joy did something similar with a sneaker. To this day, I hold a distinct image in my mind of that event—although at the time, I did not realize that there was an official term for it.

She sat on the floor with an adult sneaker in her left hand. With the other hand, she took the long lacing of the sneaker and put it up close to her right ear. Then she began to talk to the lacing while keeping an eye on the sneaker. It was clear to see that for her the sneaker had become a telephone—the kind from another era with a long cord and a receiver. This is the beginning of pretending, an all important milestone in a child's development on the way to *higher order thinking.*

4.3 Games with rules. These types of games usually begin when children are between the ages of seven and eleven, but preschoolers can engage in simpler games of the same nature.

Hide & Seek is one example. Children develop more intricate rules as their games evolve. Adults play games with rules such as *Chess* and *Bridge* on a more complex level. Sports fall into this category. For inclusiveness, older players can partner with younger players in many games.

4.4 Other recognized experts in early childhood describe additional types of play:

a. Play as make-believe.[6] Pretending is one of the most delightful of childhood activities. Think back not so long ago to some of your own favorite, pretend activities.

b. Play as fantasizing.[7] When children are exercising their imaginative powers, they are inventing their own play which can entertain them for hours on end.

c. Solitary play.[8] It is important for children to be able to play alone. Creative thinking is the key to enjoyable solitary play. As you observe your children in safe, solitary play; you will notice contentment within themselves which helps them to become independent. Being able to occupy themselves in this manner goes a long way toward helping them become resourceful, self-reliant adults.

d. Cooperative play.[9] Active imaginations lead to compatible side-by-side play wherein children are able to get along well, enjoying each other's company without selfish disagreements. Ideally, at this stage, children can play in harmony without the need for adult interference.

e. Play as reading aloud.[10] You can provide the greatest of all play by reading aloud to children. Just look at their wide eyes, astonished looks, and innocent smiles. Behind those expressive faces, flights of fancy soar.

Every time you change your voice to imitate a character or make outlandish sounds to add excitement to a story, you are

role playing. Children love it. As you may have noticed, they are natural actors. Remember the words from Hamlet,

"The play's the thing!"

Above all, **enjoy playing** with your children without fear of indulging in guilty pleasures. You are helping them to become healthy and alert with lively imaginations.

TIP #5. SING, DANCE & PLAY WITH A PRO:
Preschooler Reading Often!
Let loose and have fun. To download this lively song and reading
warmup activity, visit our website www.nevertrustateacher.com.

5.1 For twelve years I was President of **the** Board of Directors
of a preschool in Jupiter, Florida.[11] I enlisted community
support to construct a lending library at the preschool where
preschoolers could regularly check out books. At that time, I
wrote the lyrics while introducing the following enduring and
endearing message to nurture literacy in preschoolers: [12]

****

Literacy and Love Go Hand in Hand
(Musical Score Written & Sung by Brett DuPuis)

Preschool is a Reading Wonderland
Where Literacy and Love go Hand in Hand.

We use PLAY to help me be a PRO
Let's read every day and have fun as I grow.

Chorus
I'm a PRO, I'm a PRO,
I'm a PRO, PRO, PRO!
Hey, Preschoolers, what's a PRO?
"Preschooler Reading Often!"
(voices of children)

Hey, Preschoolers, what's a PRO?
"Preschooler Reading Often!"
(voices of children)

I'm a PRO, I'm a PRO
I'm a PRO, PRO, PRO

****

All Right! Now Let's PLAY with the PRO's.

This intentionally repetitive song was designed for three and four-year olds who sang, danced, and clapped to the energizing rhythm until the music stopped. Each day, all children in that age group participated in this activity as a warmup to their story time. The three children singing the response, *"Preschooler Reading Often!"* were four years old when the recording was made. Their crystal clear voices project innocence and beauty. Many of our favorite, repetitive songs remain with us for a lifetime.

5.2 My doctoral research in early childhood emphasized the importance of *creative play* in the daily life of a young child **(TIP #4)**. It is well documented that *creative play* is a building block to higher order thinking. Accordingly, I devised the following acronym:

PLAY: Parents as Literacy Advocates for Youngsters

and provided parents with expert research on the topic. Parents and children were given bright yellow buttons with black lettering to reinforce the concept of early-age literacy. Parents enjoyed displaying their slogan:

We **PLAY** with the **PRO'S!**

5.3 One weekend afternoon, when I was grocery shopping, a student from the preschool bolted away from his mother, smiling from ear to ear, and ran up proudly to advise me,

"I'm a PRO!"

Naturally, I was thrilled to hear that he was internalizing the song's mantra displayed on the children's *literacy buttons* which they cheerfully wore each day. He intuitively knew that he would touch my heart with those words.

Research and experience have taught me that it is more important for children and adults to be **PROUD** of themselves rather than to hear external praise from others. True confidence and pride originate within ourselves. I am convinced that those **PRO's** of yesterday are strong, proud readers of today.

5.4 Parents and caregivers of preschoolers, in the interest of *early-age literacy*, this *Timeless Tip* will serve your children well. Now, as always, it is important to

SING, DANCE & PLAY with a PRO!

And remember, from one generation to another, that

Literacy and Love Go Hand in Hand.

TIP #6. INFUSE PRESCHOOLERS WITH A LIFELONG, LIBRARY HABIT. As your child moves from infancy to the preschool years, make frequent library visits.

6.1 If you are an avid reader, this will be easy for you to do. If not, you will become a devoted reader with your children through their amusing and imaginative books. While they are very young and before they enjoy the novelty of reading on tablets, take your children to the library at least every two weeks. Make each visit a big deal, much like an inviting field trip.

6.2 Children will be fascinated by the varied selection of uniquely illustrated, colorful books on display. As a bonus, there are story hours. Parents should select some of the books for their children, and children should be encouraged to select a number of books on their own. After the library visit, while driving home or to another activity, parents will be pleased to hear their young children reading or *pretending* to read from their new batch of books. This is how it all begins.

6.3 You may take your children to a bookstore to see customers browsing and buying books. At the same time, there might be an engaging book talk for the children. You could also read with them while drinking hot chocolate at the store's coffee bar.

No doubt, it is fun to buy books occasionally and to display them in a bookcase in your child's room. But, books are expensive and space is limited. Libraries will prevail in the long run.

6.4 After your visit to the bookstore, go to the library and point out to your children some of the same books you saw on the shelves of the bookstore. Not all of the new books at the bookstore are new publications. Many of them have been in print for several years and are already waiting for your

children to check them out at the library. Explain to your children how they can save money by choosing the library. Teach them a lesson in finance and an appreciation of books at the same time.

6.5 Libraries may permit patrons to check out from twenty-five to fifty books at one time. Check out as many books as you and your family can manage. Teach your children at an early age how to take care of books and help them learn how to return library books on time.

Parents can avoid paying fines by setting up two large bins of different colors in a convenient location. Label them accordingly—one for all of the library books that have been read, and the other for those that have not yet been read—or will be read over and over again.

This is a simple way to make certain that the books are accounted for and will be ready to return on the next visit. Younger children can keep track of the numbers and work on their counting skills with this exercise. Being in charge of this book collection will give your children a sense of *responsibility and pride.*

TIP #7. EMERGE AS AN EXPERT ON PUBLIC SCHOOL EXCELLENCE. Keep up to date with the outstanding public school programs available in your state, from preschool through high school. My grandchildren continue our family's journey in public schools.

7.1 Preschool programs can be crucial to early childhood development. Elementary and middle schools continue to develop their magnet programs, and many, ever-expanding high school magnet programs rival those of prestigious, private prep schools. It is imperative to become familiar with similar programs in *your school district* and in *your state* that can benefit your children. Please refer to **APPENDIX B** for a sampling of other public programs not listed here.

7.2 The School District of Palm Beach County has initiated and embraced innumerable innovations since my children entered Jupiter schools in 1974. Magnet schools have made a substantial improvement to the quality of education throughout the county and the state. Increasingly large numbers of students choose to apply to top tier, out-of-state universities in addition to Florida's highly-ranked state universities. This reach for excellence on the part of the county and the state has affected the next generation of my family.

7.3 Readers, **take note** of the educational journey that my oldest granddaughter and her classmates began fifteen years ago when they were three-years old. Your children can make a similar journey in the public schools of *your state.*

a. *Preschool:* Northboro Elementary School. West Palm Beach. **Montessori Magnet Program**. At this school, students began formal reading at three and one-half years of age with the books recommended in **TIP #8.** My oldest granddaughter had begun to read those books at home with her parents before she started school, and as it happened, the school used the same series in the classroom.

b. *Kindergarten - Grade One:* Palm Beach Gardens Elementary School. Palm Beach Gardens. **Full-time Gifted Program.**

c. *Grades Two - Five:* Palm Beach Public Elementary School. Palm Beach. **(1) Full-time Gifted Program. (2) Orchestral Strings Program.**

d. *Grades Six - Eight:* Bak Middle School of the Arts. **Performing Arts Magnet.** West Palm Beach. **(1) Full-time Gifted Program. (2) Orchestral Strings program.** In recent years, students in the orchestra traveled to New York with their teacher and their musician classmates to play at Carnegie Hall.

e. *Grades Nine - Twelve:* Suncoast Community High School. Riviera Beach. **International Baccalaureate Program (IBP).** Suncoast offers three additional magnet programs: **Computer Science (CS), Innovative Interactive Technology (IIT), and Math, Science & Engineering (MSE).** Several Suncoast students are accepted each year into Ivy League Schools or their equivalent like MIT.

7.4 As a preschooler, my youngest granddaughter, who is four years old, enjoys her world of exploration and will soon begin **VPK**. At every opportunity, she selects books for her parents to read to her. My six other grandchildren attend Florida public high schools, middle schools, and elementary schools in three different counties.

They, as their parents did at that age, devote their time to school work and other strenuous activities like baseball, basketball, dance, debate, gymnastics, music, soccer, swimming, volley ball, and water polo. Generally speaking, their parents have followed and are still following *Twenty-Two Timeless Tips to Trump the System.*

TIP #8. CRACK THE CODE! ADOPT AN INFALLIBLE READING RECIPE. Take the mystery out of the reading process. If your child is ready, you can begin teaching formal reading skills before your child attends kindergarten.

8.1 Take charge of your children's education early on. Don't wait until they start school. Remember, you as parents, are your children's first teachers. Some parents may want to begin teaching reading earlier, but I think age four, in general, is appropriate for formal reading. Although it is not critical that your child learn to read before kindergarten, many children can pick up the skill at that age, so why not give it a try? *Nothing ventured. Nothing gained.*

8.2 Here's a simple system that my family has used successfully for over *fifty years.* In fact, we have found it to be *infallible.* I used it with my children, and they have used it with their own children, all of whom have been reading above grade level since they began school. Begin with the alphabet.

Obtain several sets of colorful, three-dimensional letters about one to two inches high. Keep one set on the kitchen or dining room table. Keep one set in the car or minivan. Place another in the play area. First practice letter recognition, emphasizing the sounds of each letter. Make it a way of life. When your children are fluent with their sounds, you might form two and three-letter words with the block-like letters with which they can try to sound out a word.

8.3 Of prime importance are small, large-print picture books with stories comprised of three-letter words only. My favorite series comes from a company outside of Boston, Massachusetts, which has specialized in these books for over five decades **(TIP #7).** Each book covers a different vowel sound and several consonants, for example:

Book (1) *bag, man, sap;* **Book (2)** *bed, men, set;*

Book (3) *fit, rim, nip;*

Book (4) *lot, cob, hop;* **Book (5)** *fun, but, rub.*

8.4 Gradually your child will blend sounds and form words. **Voila!** Your child has learned to read. Proceed to books with four letter words, continuing on sequentially with degrees of difficulty. Teach your children two of the major rules for reading:

> *1. When two vowels go walking, the first one does the talking. Examples: beat & coat.*

> *2. Silent 'e' at the end of a word makes the vowel say its own name. Examples: cake & like.*

8.5 Older children can learn exceptions to these rules when they are more fluent. With continued, gentle practice of the above, your child will gain the skills and confidence needed to excel in reading. This system is straightforward, produces excellent results, and can be used before your child arrives in kindergarten. The key to this strategy, as with many, is **patience** and **consistency** of application.

8.6 In a nutshell, the formal reading process is the result of working with your children informally for several years: scribbling, singing, playing, pretending, talking and, above all, **reading aloud** with them. Teaching your children to read should be a relaxed experience that evolves gradually. If you sense that your child becomes tense in the process, by all means, put the activity on hold. In the end, children will learn to read when they are ready, but there is much to be said for proper encouragement all along the way.

TIP #9. STASH THE CASH! SEEK EARLY EVALUATION.

Invest in your children's future. In advance of kindergarten, prepare to hire a reputable, private psychologist to assess their cognitive abilities.

9.1 If your children appear unusually intelligent, curious, or talented beyond their age, you may believe that a psychological evaluation would be appropriate before they start school. First find out about the status of gifted programing in your school district and then learn how your school district identifies gifted children.

9.2 In some cases, children may be identified as gifted when they are preschoolers at **no cost** to parents. As an example, the New York City Department of Education offers a battery of tests to all resident preschoolers to determine their eligibility for gifted and talented programs before the children begin kindergarten—as referenced in **APPENDIX A.**

9.3 Many school districts operating under their state's guidelines have regulations in place to provide services for gifted children **once they are enrolled in the system**. Under these circumstances, children can be referred in two ways to the district's psychologist for a **no-cost evaluation:**

a. Parents can request an evaluation.

b. Teachers can refer the child for an evaluation.

In either case, the process will likely involve a long wait, taking up a large part of the academic year. School psychologists, who are few and far between, carry a full case load.[13]

9.4 If you are living in a school district as described immediately above, and you want your child to start kindergarten in a gifted class on **Day One**, you must take the initiative **on your own** to have your child evaluated by a private psychologist when your child is a preschooler. It is important to work with

25

a licensed psychologist well versed in the testing of gifted children, or the results can be skewed.

9.5 Once you receive the official documentation classifying your child as gifted, you will need to set up an appointment at your local school with your child's guidance counselor who would start a cumulative file for your child and put the appropriate machinery in motion.

Since many guidance counselors do not work during the summer as part of their contract, it is advisable to make the appointment in the spring before your child enters kindergarten. This would allow time to process all eligibility requirements so that your child would begin kindergarten in a gifted classroom at the *outset* of the school year.

9.6 Customarily, a gifted label will put your child on the fast track to academic excellence in the public schools. Still, all is not utopia with regard to the status of gifted classes or gifted students.

Accordingly then, in **APPENDIX A,** I have listed a number of advisories that relate to the topic of gifted child education, including a brief discussion of gifted children with learning disabilities **(Advisory 11).**

9.7 As mentioned earlier, my expertise does not extend to children with *special needs.* Pediatricians, however, and alert child care providers are knowledgeable in recognizing exceptionalities. If necessary, they can and should make referrals for special services so that parents will be informed early on regarding the best course of action for their children.

9.8 Included in **APPENDIX B, Part 1**, are *four programs* that were designed to assist with the early identification of and education of children with special needs:

  a) **Early Steps**
  b) **Child Find**
  c) **FDLRS**
  d) **VPKSIS.**

The entire list, while not exhaustive, is a *sampling* of programs that may also exist in your town, county, or state with the same or similar titles.

It is important to *reemphasize* here that if parents are not satisfied with what the public sector offers by way of an evaluation for their child, they may wish to consult a private psychologist for a second opinion as **TIP #9** suggests.

TIP #10. ESTABLISH RAPPORT WITH YOUR CHILD'S
TEACHERS. Volunteer if you have time. Watch out for arrogant
cliques. See Parent Letter to Teacher, next page.

10.1 If you can visit the school occasionally or volunteer in
some way, you will learn much about what goes on in your
child's class and around the school as a whole. I worked at
schools where loyal helpers came to the school almost daily
and took on a variety of nearly insurmountable tasks to keep
the school running smoothly. They dedicated much time to
fundraising and organized a teacher appreciation luncheon
each year.

10.2 On a negative but realistic note, many volunteers, as part
of an *arrogant clique*, ingratiate themselves with administrators
and derive real or imagined prestige from their position.
Skillfully, yet maliciously, they exclude other volunteers who,
they fear, may encroach on their territory, possibly by offering
new vision regarding school policies and procedures.

10.3 In another category are genuine, *guileless* volunteers who
work directly with teachers. They render faithful assistance
to students who need more attention than the teacher can
provide. Several conscientious parents and grandparents
worked regularly with my colleagues and me to help needy,
responsive students improve their reading skills. Teachers
drew up individual lessons for the children, and dependable
volunteers carried out their instructions with great patience
and attention to duty, ignoring the political games of the
unyielding inner circle.

10.4 If you cannot take time to volunteer, you will, nevertheless,
want to initiate close contact with the school, at the outset of
the academic year, before any problems may arise. A *sample
letter* follows for your convenience. This correspondence
would help to establish and maintain *good communication*
with the school in the best interests of your child.

Parent Letter to Teacher

Date _____

Full name of Child (below):

_____

Full name of Parent/Guardian (below):

_____

Relationship to Child (below):

_____

Dear

_____,

Name of Teacher (above)

I work outside of the home and am seldom able to visit the school. Please know, however, that I hope to maintain excellent communication with my child's teachers. I want to be kept fully informed as to my child's academic status and conduct in class. I expect my child to be an A student and maintain the highest standard of behavior.

I realize that a teacher's job is a most difficult one, and I would like you to be assured that I support your effort to teach my child in the best manner possible. If my child is remiss with regard to homework, class assignments, grades, attitude, or conduct, please contact me promptly at

email:_____ or phone: _____

Thanking you in advance for your assistance, I wish you and your students a most pleasant and productive year ahead.

Sincerely,

_____

Signature of parent (above)

In order to indicate receipt of this letter, please sign below and return this part to me via my child.

Cut here ....

I have received and read your letter.

_____   _____

Signature of teacher (above)   Date

_____

Name of teacher printed (above)   Name of subject printed (above)

TIP #11. SCRUTINIZE YOUR CHILDREN'S HOMEWORK WITH DAILY DEVOTION. Monitor all assignments consistently and carefully.

11.1 If you have followed the strategies previously outlined, your children should be in good shape to start school and compete with the best of them. Your job, however, will become even more difficult now. In the early years, you need to supervise your children's homework each week night and on weekends.

It is noble to trust your children, but when it comes to homework, that's a different matter. First, it is **not okay** to believe your children when they tell you that they have no homework. I made that mistake a few times. In other words, follow the advice of the old Russian proverb, **trust but verify.**

11.2 It's natural for children to try to get away with something if they think that they are not being supervised. Good teachers will post assignments online or send home weekly assignment sheets so that you will know what they expect. Keep up to date on assignments, due dates, and any possible changes to same.

Next make certain that your children have completed assignments correctly in accordance with instructions. If not, help them to do so. It is not unusual for children to finish their homework and lose it in their backpack. Develop a system of **loss prevention.** Assist them with organization.

11.3 A common homework assignment may involve **studying for a test** with no written work due. Many students consider this abstract exercise as having **no homework.** In such cases, you would need to review the material to be tested with your children, helping them to become fully prepared.

11.4 Some teachers put forth misleading instructions or make errors, so if you and your child are having trouble

understanding an assignment, you need to communicate with the teacher as soon as possible—at the latest by the next day.

Full comprehension and excellent grades should result. If they don't, you need to schedule a conference with one of the administrators or guidance counselors to arrive at a sound solution. Always act quickly to minimize damage.

11.5 If you prohibit your children from using electronics when they are doing their homework, they may feel rather isolated and a little lonely as they work. They will often enjoy having adult company nearby.

At some point, you may find that your children are truly conscientious students who need no supervision. My compliments are in order if you have been able to bring your children to that level of responsibility. That appears to be the exception, however, rather than the norm. Unending distractions lure students away from their schoolwork.

11.6 During my thirty-three years of teaching at middle schools, I attended many conferences with parents who had given up on their children by the time they entered sixth grade. They *shamelessly* shared their philosophy on child-rearing which I found abhorrent. In my presence, they told guidance counselors and other teachers that their children were old enough to be accountable for all of their school assignments on their own.

They made it clear that they had no intention of helping them. To sum up, they told their children to *grow up* and learn to accept the consequences of poor choices and resulting bad grades. They were proud of their *hands-off* approach which to me demonstrated nothing short of ignorance. In all of those cases, after such a conference as described, I observed even greater deterioration in the schoolwork of the neglected students—for lack of any parental initiative or inherent desire to provide assistance.

11.7 Middle school students are children—still in their *formative years.* Beyond question, they need mature, responsible parents to guide them or, when all else fails, a *wise, caring surrogate* who can pick up the pieces. If parents want to help their children but lack confidence in their ability to do so, they need to meet with capable counselors to seek an *alternative solution.*

TIP #12. BECOME AN ACE DETECTIVE. SIZE UP YOUR CHILD'S COMPETITION. My mother used this approach. I followed her lead.

12.1 Be certain that your children keep up with the top students in their classes—beginning with kindergarten, straight on through their senior year of high school. Make it a point to know who those high achieving students are at all times. Once your children go to college, they will be on their own. You can relax. By then, the habit of striving for excellence will be fully inculcated within them.

12.2 If your children are not among the highest ranking students, find out the reason for their deficiency and get them the immediate *remediation* they need. Prevent them from falling helplessly behind their classmates. Put your children on a path to success within a continuing cycle of excellence.

12.3 Create high expectations for your children and instill in them the confidence to achieve worthy goals. This strategy is not to be confused with calculating, cutthroat competition. I refer to healthy *rivalry* which can be carried out in an upbeat manner demonstrating openness, fairness, diplomacy, and *camaraderie*—with good friends bringing out the best in one another.

12.4 In the lower grades, I determined my children's class rankings by their reading levels. As to be expected, being advanced in reading was the result of our family's strong emphasis on *early-age literacy*. My children's grades in the other academic disciplines fell into place accordingly. *Always remember*, that there is room for more than one scholar in the honors ranks. Why shouldn't your children assume their *rightful place at the top?*

TIP #13. KEEP A CLOSE EYE ON YOUR CHILDREN'S FRIENDS. Love your children without suffocating them but guide them to choose friends wisely.

13.1 Ideally, a friendship should be that of equal partners with children of the same age enjoying **silly** and **safe** adventures. One friend should not dominate the relationship. Unhappily, some children want to manipulate others for their own selfish reasons. Being clever, these young **con artists** put pressure on your children to do their bidding. Naïve parents often place a measure of undeserved trust in these imposters because the latter understand how to impress parents with their smooth-talking ways.

13.2 Teach your children to realize their own self-worth and to stand up to these **so-called** friends. Fill your children with confidence so that no one takes advantage of them. Help them to try new activities and to conquer unfounded fears. Work with them continually so that they will have a solid sense of self and the courage to become leaders.

13.3 Some of these false friends may have inattentive parents who provide little supervision for their children. Their carelessness could spill over to interactions with your children. Observe the parents of your children's friends carefully. It is wise to associate with parents who teach their children to act responsibly and who place a high priority on their children's education.

13.4 If you notice that your children repeatedly act **out of character** after being with certain friends, you need to take swift action to exclude those relationships altogether. Explain your reasons, but don't be afraid to make **bold moves.** Your window of opportunity is small. Your children will be adults all too soon—with your power and authority over them **long gone.** Act in your children's best interest before it is too late. In time, with your guidance, and as your children mature, they will make better choices with regard to making friends.

TIP #14. TEACH YOUR CHILDREN RIGHT FROM WRONG .... whether or not you belong to an established religion.

14.1 This seems simple enough. My experience in the classroom has shown me that many children have not been taught these concepts in the home, or if parents tried to teach them, they failed.

Start by teaching children respect for their caregivers and their teachers. If you have disagreements with teachers, be careful to handle them in a way that your children are not left with lasting, unfavorable impressions regarding the teaching profession.

14.2 Teach your children about proper conduct in school, the importance of taking their assignments seriously, and the necessity of completing them on time. Teach them to take pride in all that they do. School work is their job.

During class, there will often be students craving attention who seek to disrupt the environment. They look for allies in their contrary behavior. Teach your children to resist these types of disturbances. They need to learn to maintain their focus on the task at hand and ignore or reject the bad behavior of classmates.

14.3 Teach your children the value of honesty. Many students take others' belongings, tell lies for any number of reasons, and cheat on tests if the opportunity arises. You must continually work with your children to uphold their self confidence **(TIP #13)**. When they are confident, they have the courage to resist the powerful forces of peer pressure.

14.4 Bullies are cowards who relish having accomplices. They would like to recruit your children to join them in acts of defiance. Today cyber bullying represents a significant problem. It may begin at home with name calling on the internet—and continue at school with a number of destructive consequences. Parents of bullies often profess to be shocked

at their children's aggressive behavior, when upon analysis, their own attitudes and behaviors may have contributed to their children's hostile actions—*in the first place.*

14.5 One effective manner of curtailing this problem is for parents to teach their children the appreciation of diversity when they are very young. Children customarily assimilate prejudices of their parents and sooner or later, they may wield them as weapons directed at classmates. Trouble later erupts in various forms.

14.6 Parents must teach their young children about the importance of ***doing the right thing*** *and* the avoidance of being physically or psychologically hurtful to others. They need to solidify that concept regularly through family discussions.

My generation grew up chanting out the phrase, ***"Sticks and stones will break my bones, but names will never hurt me."*** [14] In one sense that aphorism was intended to ward off violence and retaliation. But from another perspective, if parents reinforced it with their victimized children, it sent the wrong message, completely ignoring possible long term, harmful effects to a child's psyche. ***Names can and do hurt people.***

14.7 Some excellent resources for young children and teens on the topic of hurtful behavior are age-appropriate news magazines, newspaper articles, and television news stories. Using examples of people in the news, performing good or bad deeds, can be a ***compelling way*** to generate discussions on societal values and proper deportment, while promoting awareness of timely local, national, or international topics.

With an expanded frame of reference, your children will be able to think more objectively when making decisions. As a bonus, they may become super debaters able to argue both the ***affirmative*** and ***negative*** side of an issue.

TIP #15. RULE WISELY AND WELL WITHOUT CORPORAL PUNISHMENT. Avoid disciplining your child in anger. Set appropriate consequences and abide by them.

15.1 If you have evidence that your child did something wrong at home, school, or elsewhere, teach your child how to deal with the repercussions of an action and how to act more responsibly in the future.

Parents need to accept the fact that their child was at fault, and they must help that child learn from the experience. At times, parents find their child's misdeeds amusing, and they look the other way. This can easily lead to more unacceptable behavior.

15.2 If your child's friends are involved in the incident, explain to your child the importance of thinking for oneself and making independent choices. It is the duty of parents to remain keenly aware of their children's activities in order to prevent a transgression. Nevertheless, parents may at times be genuinely surprised and embarrassed by a child's misconduct.

15.3 Clearly, parents need to demonstrate that they are in charge. Above all, their disciplinary measures must be *rational* and *realistic*, and they must stand firmly behind them once imposed. If parents continually back off from an established consequence, their children will soon be running the show.

Indeed, it does *not* take long before indecisive parents lose almost all control. Through my students, I have observed many families burdened with this type of struggle each and every day, with parents *not knowing* where to turn. Often caring and well meaning, they never found a way to discipline their children effectively. In many instances, the children in such families ended up in repeated trouble at school or with the law—or with *both.*

15.4 It is wise for parents to seek counseling if they manage their children's behavior to extremes as follows:

- If they are weak and *wishy washy* with no decision-making skills

- If they resort to ineffective, angry shouting matches with their children

- If they inflict physical punishment on their children

Many parents **alternately** choose the above parenting styles depending on the occasion. With them, there is no middle ground. They and their children become equally frustrated and confused without a dependable system of discipline in place.

15.5 Common sense tells us that almost all parents will allow themselves to be manipulated by their children at one time or another. On the whole, however, parents must **rule the roost,** and figure out how to discipline in a level-headed manner, without the use of physical force.

TIP #16. SAY "NO!" TO THOUGHTLESS, NEGATIVE LABELS AFFIXED TO YOUR CHILD. Steer clear of inflexible, narrow-minded teachers.

16.1 Some classroom teachers jump to conclusions and label students unfairly as to their ability. This is a time-worn problem. Last year, one of my friends reported to me the following incident involving her son Zack who was attending a Florida middle school.

16.2 Identified as a gifted student before he entered kindergarten, Zack excelled in all of his classes since he started school. He continued to enjoy reading far above grade level each year.

A congenial, honor-roll student with many friends, he was conscientious about completing assignments. Then, a problem arose in his sixth-grade science class where Zack earned the following grades:

- A ... in the first major assignment of the academic year

- C ... in a chapter test

- D ... in a month-long project monitoring the solar system

16.3 Upon learning of these three grades and comparing the quality of his work from one assignment to another, Zack's parents realized that they had been *inexcusably negligent* in supervising his output. It happened that both of them had been extra busy with their jobs. Moreover, they had taken for granted that he would do well in all of his classes, as his previous work habits and grades had led them to expect.

16.4 When they analyzed the solar system assignment, Zack's parents observed that he had rushed through each day's work, had written sloppy notes, and had submitted an inferior product. After they discussed it with him, he was

sheepish and crestfallen. He realized that he had taken the easy way out, and he admitted that he had been spending way too much time on his new skateboard after school. When report cards were issued, Zack earned a C in science for the term and A's in all of his other classes. Zack was not pleased with the C on his report card. It spoiled his otherwise spotless record.

16.5 When Zack's mother spoke via telephone with the science teacher, he attempted to handle the problem right then and there. Instead, Mom asked for a meeting in person.

The teacher acted **annoyed** but reluctantly set up a time before school several days later. At the conference, my friend inquired as to how she could help her son bring up his grade. The teacher glanced for a moment at his gradebook and then told her with great conviction that there was nothing he could do to facilitate her request.

16.6 "Your son is a **C** student," he instructed her. "You should leave things as they are. Don't ask too much of him. My daughter is in the same grade, and she is also a **C** student. My wife and I don't pressure her with high expectations. She is just a kid, and we want her to be happy. That's what really matters."

16.7 Aghast and angry, my friend excused herself from the conference and walked straight to the guidance office where she arranged a schedule change for Zack. Realizing that her son's teacher held an **unwavering low opinion** about Zack's capabilities, she reported to the counselor that she and the teacher had **irreconcilable differences.**

16.8 As predicted by Zack's mother, her son did well in his new science class with a different teacher. At the end of the school year, he earned the honor of having the highest score in the sixth-grade, countywide science assessment. It

was obvious that Zack enjoyed doing his best, reaping the academic rewards that went along with hard work.

Ironically, when Zack received the award, his previous science teacher presented it to him in the auditorium, on stage, in front of his peers. Zack's mother was very glad that she had acted instinctively, in the best interest of her son, by removing him from a *negative environment.*

Zack's parents demonstrated no open hostility, but they held in lowest regard the insensitive, presumptuous teacher who had given up so easily on their son early in the year.

16.9 This incident shows how quickly teachers can become prejudiced against a student and how rapidly they may make *inaccurate, long-lasting judgments* about a student's ability to learn.

16.10 It also demonstrates the need for parents to exercise *consistent supervision* over their children's homework—no matter how dedicated their children may normally be.

A parent's role includes *oversight,* guidance, and encouragement **(TIP #11).** In this case, Zack demonstrated his intelligence and his maturity when he took a good, second look at the inadequate science project he had submitted. In the end, he was grateful for his parents' intervention. He even told them lovingly, *"That's what parents are for."*

TIP #17. MONITOR AND INSPIRE MIDDLE SCHOOL READERS. Make certain that your middle school children find time for valuable, recreational reading.

17.1 Prepare yourself for the fact that middle school libraries contain books which you and other parents might consider too *socially advanced* for your children. Although the maturation process is far from complete, sixth graders have made a significant leap to maturity by the time they arrive at eighth grade. But it is important to keep in mind that middle school students can run the gamut from *ten* to *fifteen* years of age.

You observe your children living in a *transitional state,* a veritable twilight zone. Along with it, in that zone, is the library media center with an *explosion* of reading material not available in elementary school. You may be hoping to preserve an idyllic, unsophisticated, middle school cocoon for your children until they proceed on to high school. It seldom works out that way.

17.2 There is no denying that your children's physical, social, and intellectual *metamorphosis* is in full swing. You can shield your children only partially from undesirable outside influences. Although you may not sanction some of the books your children will come across, if you have given your children an ethical background along with a strong foundation in critical thinking, they should be able to weather the forces of the Information Age.

17.3 Two organizations that create recommended book lists each year and give awards in the field of young adult literature are **School Library Journal (SLJ)** and **Young Adult Library Services Association (YALSA),** a division of the **American Library Association, (ALA).**

17.4 You may want to familiarize yourself with labels that deal with ages of the reading audience, although it is evident

that there is a considerable range in the young adult category. Librarians, authors, and readers have reached a somewhat fluctuating consensus [15] as follows:

- **Teen Fiction: Ages 10 – 15**

- **Young Adult Library Services Association (YALSA):
  Ages 12 – 18**

17.5 Book titles can be deceiving. Book reviews are subjective. You may *not share the same values* as those held by prominent book reviewers or even those held by your friends. The only way to know for certain if you approve of the content for *your* children is to read the books yourself. Of course, you could read a limited amount of books but obviously not an untold number of titles. Perhaps a parent's group could assist in the screening process.

17.6 The good news is that a *wealth of worthwhile* reading material is waiting for your children. Talk to librarians and other parents and take advantage of it. At some point, children will want to order books online and may show a preference for reading on tablets or listening to audio books. In my experience, children of this age enjoy reading in more than one modality, interchangeably reading traditional books and their electronic counterparts.

TIP #18. VALUE THE VERBAL. DABBLE IN DYNAMIC DEBATE. Engage in lively, provocative discussions with your children. Be leery of TV and electronics.

18.1 Make time for quality conversations. Your children will become highly verbal at an early age. Dinner table discussions are excellent, but realistically, dinner is often on the run. When my children were quite young, we spent a great deal of time in the car, doing errands, or driving to visit friends and relatives.

As they grew older, we drove to sporting events in which they regularly participated. In that era, cars were not equipped with video players, and children did not have cell phones for playing games or texting friends.

18.2 When my passengers were not reading their library books, we had serious and humorous chats expressing differences of opinion on a medley of topics. Those conversations were an integral and formative part of their early education.

Our dynamic exchanges prepared my children to be natural debaters as they learned to argue both sides of an argument with vehement certitude. Moreover, I used those opportunities to observe and correct my children's grammar when necessary. I did not let a grammatical mistake become a permanent, unchecked bad habit.

18.3 My children are parents now and drive wagons or minivans with DVD players. It goes without saying that having this technology is a big advantage for parents with tired, squirming children on a long trip, and it provides a wonderful distraction from sibling squabbles as parents pay close attention to the road.

Children are frequently lulled to sleep by such videos, and parents can thereby drive in peace and quiet. Nevertheless, parents often miss valuable opportunities to talk to their

children in the car especially on short, local trips. Indeed, parents need to take advantage of their **captive audiences**. Limiting cell phone use is a must.

18.4 Oversee your children's television viewing. Watch programs with them and use their themes as catalysts for discussion of newsworthy topics or values you want your children to learn. It is fairly common for children to imitate behaviors of characters they see on television.

They may even begin to act in a disrespectful manner toward their parents as do the actors in their prescribed roles. Parents must address this behavior before it gets out of hand.

18.5 Make it clear that in your family's world, children do **not** take their cues from imaginary characters on television. Explain that caring, responsible parents are obligated to protect their children from undesirable, outside influences, many of which may come from the entertainment media.

Provocative, invigorating talks will help maintain gratifying communication between you and your children at any age level—beginning with childhood and continuing on into the years when you can enjoy your children as adults.

18.6 Today with the **enticement of electronics,** some outstanding students have fallen into video game addiction with devastating consequences for their school work and general wellbeing.

Taking it to another level, students who become excessively involved with social media can become entangled in a host of problems that overflow from home to school. Up against constant competition for valuable *parent* and *child interaction,* parents need to **set a limit** on their children's electronic activity and **on their own.**

TIP #19. CONNECT WITH COMPUTERS. Your computer will serve as a vital link to the school. Teachers & counselors, reach out to caregivers and families in need.

19.1 Meet your children's teachers and keep in close contact with them. Make the most of your computer to facilitate awareness of your children's progress. Electronic grading programs enable teachers to keep you up to date with your child's grades. Depending on rules set by the school system, many elementary and middle school teachers will post grades at least twice per week. Some teachers will give students daily grades and post them before leaving school in the afternoon.

19.2 Along with your child, you can easily and expeditiously check grades by accessing the school's website. Make it part of your routine. Using this method, if your child receives a bad grade on any type of assignment, you can send word to the teacher in a timely manner to determine the reason. The teacher may have made a simple, mechanical error in posting the grade or a substantive error within the grading system itself. If the low grade is accurate, you can assist your child with obtaining prompt remediation.

19.3 Many high schools require teachers to update their grades every Friday. If families are away from their computers, they can access the school's website via their cell phones. Gone are the days when students could hide bad grades from parents by deleting teacher messages from land-line answering machines or by destroying regular mail delivered to the house. Technology has made it possible for parents to become instantly apprised of their children's academic progress or lack thereof.

19.4 To inquire about something that gives you pause in your child's class, it is more convenient to *email* teachers rather than attempt to talk by phone. Most likely, teachers will check their email each morning before the start of classes and again several times throughout the day. Scheduling a conference

with a teacher and your child may be needed to address a concern before it develops into a full-fledged problem.

19.5 Computers can be the vital link in promoting student success. Teachers often write weekly newsletters about classroom activities. They post homework, project descriptions, and important due dates. Those without access to the school's website must be certain to request a written printout of weekly assignments or a monthly syllabus of activities.

19.6 One of my friends is a hardworking grandmother without higher education. At various times, her grandson came without his parents to live with her for much of the school year. She had no computer and no computer skills.

She did not know how to help her grandchild with his homework, and she had no idea about accessing his grades electronically. She found out about his grades only when report cards were issued. The school offered her no outreach.

19.7 There are countless others like her—unprepared to offer academic assistance to children in their care, let alone connect up to the school via a computer. At best, they are concerned about feeding and clothing the children and keeping them drug free. Homework hotlines are common, but without guidance from a caregiver, students may not take advantage of them.

19.8 If you know caregivers who cannot afford the expense of a computer or a smart phone, advise them to speak to a school administrator or a counselor about their situation. There may be older computers at the school, still workable—but no longer in use—that could be assigned to them. All caregivers need to be made aware of the *major role* that computers play in delivering information to them from the school.

19.9 Caregivers without a computer—but knowing how to operate one—could use a computer at the public library or in

the school's library media center. Or, counselors may be able to locate a funding source to help with the purchase of a basic computer system for families in need—not only to facilitate better communication between home and school but to assist students with their homework, projects, and research.

19.10 Teachers, counselors, and administrators in all such instances must initiate the outreach and determine how best to provide assistance to the entire family. One way would be to offer caregivers fundamental computer training at the school. Technology teachers may take on this enterprise. Free email service can be arranged. Transportation to the school could be provided as needed for those caregivers who have no car or do not drive.

Grandparents and other caregivers in this category require a strong support system. If properly taught, they can learn new skills quickly and in the *nick of time* to help their families.

19.11 Not without controversy and complications involving privacy, many school districts across the United States assign take-home computers to each student. One advantage is that all families will have more of a level playing field for monitoring a child's progress.

19.12 One segment of a school's population may be *homeless,* even in middle to upper middle class neighborhoods. Some of these families conceal their living arrangements from the school. Two of my middle school students, a brother and sister, living in their car, kept their lifestyle *secret* for many months. The children were very smart and always clean. They needed services, but their mother was proud, and the children were ashamed to reveal their status to anyone. Teachers and counselors must be on the *lookout* for this scenario as well.

TIP #20. PROTECT YOUR CHILD FROM TEACHER MOB MENTALITY. Divide and conquer. Schedule individual conferences. Bring along a witness.

20.1 There is a tendency for a school's guidance department to schedule conferences with all of a student's teachers and their parents at the same time. There may be an occasion when you might choose this arrangement, but if you have one or more serious concerns to probe, I do not recommend it. It is generally advisable to be accompanied by a family member or friend, or **both**, who can take notes.

You have a right to meet with each teacher **individually.** Circumventing the system in this manner may take longer, but it will be well worth the extra time.

20.2 Group conferences are arranged primarily for the **convenience** of teachers, guidance counselors, and administrators. As a rule, they do not serve the best interests of your child and may result in a discouraging, demoralizing encounter for parents. I suggest avoiding them for some of the following reasons:

20.3 Meeting with several teachers at once can be **stressful** for two parents together—and even more so for **one parent alone**—a more commonplace occurrence. Often reminiscent of a stern tribunal, the group conference is a carefully crafted ritual taking place on the teachers' home territory where they feel completely at ease.

You, the parent, on the other hand, may be uncomfortable, no matter how many conferences you have attended previously. Choose a friend to join you who will likely be less emotional.

20.4 As one would anticipate, some teachers are courteous and respectful of you and your child, whereas others—**not so much**. Consider yourself fortunate if you have a rewarding experience. Other teachers are brusque, detached, and

annoyed, not hiding the fact that they are anxious to get on with additional assignments. They may need to meet a student for morning detention, show up for bus duty, or sit in on yet another conference.

Many schools hold multiple conferences on the same day of the week in the library media center before classes begin. Teachers and counselors may come and go throughout your meeting, table hopping from one conference to another. An elevated noise level can add to existing distractions where a parent is trying to maintain focus and arrive at solutions.

20.5 A familiar element of a group conference may include teachers' tending to *gang up* on your child. If one teacher makes a disparaging or highly critical comment about your child, other teachers often pile on, *cowardly,* going along with the crowd. In other words, they feel less visible lashing out at your child when others might be doing the same.

20.6 Furthermore, negative attitudes on the part of teachers can be contagious and linger *beyond the conference.* Teachers holding a high opinion of your child may be subtly persuaded to look at your child through another teacher's jaded lens.

Or, to put it a different way, one teacher's derogatory remark may subconsciously cause other teachers to lose their objectivity with respect to your child's attitude and effort in their classes.

20.7 Even if the overall conference is a positive one, parents generally feel rushed during these multi-teacher presentations. When several teachers are *bombarding* you with reports of your child's performance, there is an overload of material to absorb. You will want to make detailed notes on the information provided by all faculty members.

The limited duration of the conference leaves you little time to reflect on that exchange and ask pertinent, *follow-up questions* right there on the spot. You will want to have a

clear understanding as to the input of each teacher. You may have several **unasked** or **unanswered** questions still pending.

20.8 One teacher with seniority, with whom I often attended conferences, offered a ***one-size-fits-all*** remedy for each student. She arrived at the conference early and was always the first teacher to speak. With a pleasant, slick, demeanor, she took the parent by surprise, quickly offered her advice, and left the meeting before the parent could process the information or ask even one question.

Just like that, she was gone, and it was on to the next teacher's input. Guidance counselors were **shamefully intimidated** by her and offered no objections to her high-speed approach. I often wondered if parents tried to reach her subsequently for a more personal evaluation of their child.

20.9 Keep ***accurate records*** of your child's school work and bring to the conference whatever is needed to present your case. Prepare a list of questions and major concerns.

You will find that when convening in a quiet environment with one teacher, instead of a group, you and the teacher will get to know each other in a more relaxed manner and, in most cases, be able to arrive at an agreement on how to help your child.

Individual attention from one teacher is far superior to fleeting, superficial consideration from a group. In this setting, you can develop a rapport with the teacher that will stand you in good stead should there be any future concerns.

20.10 Together you and the teacher can set goals for your child and determine strategies for achieving them. A one-on-one meeting will undoubtedly result in more progressive outcomes for your child and pave the way for another congenial, follow-up conference at a later date, if one were to be necessary.

TIP #21. CULTIVATE A CLIMATE FOR HIGHER EDUCATION EARLY ON. Generate enthusiasm for college. Explore technical training opportunities. Beware of car culture. Keep outside jobs to a minimum. Advocate for college when there is no clear choice.

21.1 Generate enthusiasm for college. If you want your children to attend college, higher education should happen smoothly and seamlessly for your children. From the time your children are in kindergarten, initiate talks with them about **when** they go to college, not **if** they go to college.

Chat with them about cousins, friends, and baby sitters who attend college. As they grow older, point out high-profile persons who graduated from colleges that prepared them for an enjoyable and rewarding career. Later, your family might follow a college sports team and visit colleges to drum up interest.

Although many remarkably successful people did not receive any type of training beyond high school, they are the exceptions. Statistics sharply indicate that earning potential over a lifespan is greater for college graduates—or **graduates of accredited, specialized programs**—than for secondary school graduates with no additional schooling.

21.2 Explore technical training opportunities. It is advisable for parents of children with a technical aptitude, not inclined toward college, to keep abreast of programs that may coincide with their children's interests and be of great advantage to them. In his book, **The Industries of the Future,**[16] Ross (2016), has written about innovative, technical programs that can lead to financially sound careers.

For these positions, students will need **advanced training** but not a college degree. Completing prescribed courses of instruction and earning the required in-field certifications

will be sufficient to forge ahead with stable, remunerative employment.

21.3 Focus on lifelong learning. Your discussions about continuing education should not primarily be about earning more money. They should emphasize the intrinsic value of education and an appreciation for learning. Tell your children that learning will not end after high school or even after college. *Learning is infinite.* Learning endows us with the energy and exhilaration by which we lead our lives.[17]

21.4 Beware of car culture and its distractions.
Avoid the *Car is King* mentality with your children. Our family had little money, but we managed to provide a safe, previously owned vehicle for our children to share, and we covered the insurance ourselves. School work and sports took priority.

I have seen many teens work outside the home to save money for their fantasy car. Next they worked to pay car insurance. In so doing, they spent less time on their studies, and their grades dropped dramatically. Some of those high school students came to enjoy having money, more money than their student peers—who had next to nothing.

Ultimately, they were influenced by new friends who worked fulltime, and they began to devalue education. They wanted to have fun. They decided not to study beyond high school. They did not have a plan for their life. They went with the flow.

As time passed, life on their own became increasingly difficult with minimal earning power. They had slipped into a dismal rut and had difficulty extricating themselves from it. Their wrong turn had taken its toll. Years went by until they entered community college or an advanced training program. Some never got back on track.

21.5 Keep outside jobs to a minimum. In cases of economic hardship, I understand that high school students may be

required to enter the workforce. Kudos to them for their courage, stamina, and responsibility in sharing their family's financial burden.

Still, from what I have seen, unless they prove to be exceptional students with boundless energy, the majority of teenagers need a considerable amount of rest. It is difficult to take on challenging classes and participate in demanding, extracurricular activities while also holding down a job.

Summer employment can be acceptable as long as it does not interfere with other, more enlightening pursuits, like the study of *Great Books* via the **Socratic method** or taking an empowering computer class to learn **code.** With a few brief interludes, my children did not go out to work until after high-school graduation. Yet they have been on the job, **nonstop,** ever since. Parents, if possible, **postpone the inevitable.**

When they are toddlers, the work of children is playing and problem solving. For older, school-age children, on through their teens, their work is studying, learning, and more **problem solving.** They are preparing themselves for adulthood which should not arrive prematurely.

Allow your children to bask in the carefree moments of youth while they are able to do so. In due time, the endless demands of the workplace will be an everyday occurrence, year after year after year. But eventually that devotion to hard work can bring about a satisfying career, truly an accomplishment and a blessing.

21.6 Encourage students to move forward. Some students plan their careers with great conviction at an early age. There are those who choose to be lawyers, general contractors, photographers, or doctors, and they work for years to achieve those goals. My electrician, as an example, chose his profession when he was in his first year of high school. After graduation, he completed the necessary training, passed

exams, and earned the appropriate license required by the state of Florida.

Later, at the age of forty five, he earned a **patent** for creating a system of unique outdoor lighting which he went on to manufacture and sell with great success. Steadily and contentedly, he has worked at his dream job for many years and expanded it joyously with his inventiveness. People like him are fortunate in their decisiveness involving career choices.

21.7 Advocate for college enrollment when there is no clear choice. Other students, like my children when they were in high school, have no idea what career to pursue. They express no interest in medicine, the fine arts, engineering, or anything technical. For that reason, some students **never begin** college, while others **drop out** after a year or two.

Students not knowing what to study should be encouraged to enroll in college **in spite of their uncertainty** and remain there until they earn a degree. Liberal arts may be the answer for them. Advise them to choose one or two areas of concentration, even if they do not find them exciting.

In this way, before deciding on a career, they are, at a minimum, **moving forward,** instead of standing still. Such a choice is far better than the alternative. Life has many twists and turns. Passions and pastimes mutate with time and maturity.

Even when students have seemingly focused, **without a doubt,** on one career, they often change their minds and completely revise their plans. Numerous adjustments may be made before an evolving career becomes crystallized.

Accordingly, **earning a degree is what counts,** no matter the undergraduate area of specialization. To be sure, a record of academic excellence overall will enhance a student's resume.

21.8 Employers will value a degree. After college, a certain percentage of *liberal arts* graduates, like my children, will go on for advanced study, and others will go directly into the job market in search of non-technical work. By and large, their future employers will offer substantial wages along with adequate health care plans.

Employers look upon a degree as an age-old symbol of *discipline.* Beyond that, they will detect character traits in applicants that are particularly appealing to them. They will train and guide those *new hires* as they see fit, *regardless* of their undergraduate major.

In fact, many employers will pay for an employee's advanced degree. Otherwise known as the *foot-in-door strategy*, it is reassuring to know that if students manage their future well, when they are young, they can avoid playing *catchup* later in life.

TIP #22. LET GUIDANCE COUNSELORS GUIDE YOU, BUT TAKE HEED! Bond with high school counselors and initiate a search for colleges and scholarships.

22.1 As soon as your children enter high school, meet with their guidance counselors. Advise them that you would like to become a *partner* in finding the right school for your children after graduation—along with at least a partial scholarship. Ask the counselors for advice on how and where to begin your search. Learn the ropes and remain persistent. Those next four years will fly by!

22.2 Be mindful of application deadlines for both colleges and scholarships. This is the time to start inquiring about financial aid at four-year universities or at technical schools. A competent guidance counselor will surely be of valuable assistance to you.

Many counselors, however, are *apathetic or ill informed.* In that case, you must take up the gauntlet yourself to ensure that you have the essential data at your disposal. Locate and follow all of the pathways necessary to arrive at your goal.

22.3 You will have several years in which to become well versed in this endeavor. Compare notes periodically with the counselor. I understand that the majority of guidance counselors are overworked. All the more reason, it is incumbent upon them to set up a system of checks and balances to prevent students' applications from falling through the cracks.

As time progresses, you will determine the caliber of the counselor. With regard to scholarships, it will likely be necessary to perform *due diligence* on your own. In addition to suggestions from counselors, you will have the benefit of websites, scholarship applications for your mobile phone, resources through the public library, and conversations with other like-minded parents.

22.4 Follow to the letter of the law all application instructions. Here is an intriguing partial scholarship I found after a 30-second search:

Tall Clubs International Student Scholarships

Are you under 21 years of age and about to start college in the fall? If so, you may be in luck! TCI annually awards student scholarship(s) of up to $1,000 each to tall students who are under 21 years of age and attending their first year of college in the following fall. [18]

22.5 As noted earlier, helpful guidance counselors are to be commended, but on the opposite end of the spectrum, there have been many disconcerting stories pointing to unconcerned counselors not doing their jobs. My daughter Joy was privileged to have a guidance counselor, who later became the principal of the school. He encouraged her to apply to Brown University. He followed through with all facets of the application.

My son Nick was not as fortunate. After applying to a certain university out of state, he never heard back from that university one way or another as to his acceptance. After calling the admissions office to determine what had transpired, I learned that Nick's high school references had not been received at the university, and no further action was taken on his application.

Luckily, Boston College had been Nick's first choice. Parents must make certain that each section of their children's application has been duly received by the colleges to which they have applied. ***Take nothing for granted.*** Obtain receipts for all materials submitted. Applications can be misplaced, even in this computer-assisted age.

22.6 An incident involving a colleague emphasizes the need for continuing parental awareness in locating scholarships for their children. My friend, a gifted musician, reported to

me that when he was preparing to graduate from high school thirty-three years ago, he had been eligible to receive a four-year music scholarship to a Florida university. Unfortunately, he was unaware of it until many years later when it was too late.

He was not sophisticated enough to search for this award on his own. Additional impediments were the *inertia* and *ignorance* on the part of his parents and advisors. All persons in authority were impotent on how to assist him.

22.7 This regrettable *sin of omission* serves as a harsh reminder that parents and guidance counselors must remain ever vigilant when helping students prepare for college. Today, with our easy access to information, there is no excuse for being uninformed.

It's imperative to make the most of our rich reservoir of research tools. The concise motto of my alma mater, Milton High School, expressed it well, *Knowledge is power.*[19] Remember to wield it strategically for the betterment of your children and their future.

APPENDIX A

Gifted Programs – Availability & Reflections

Advisory #1. The New York City Department of Education currently uses two nationally recognized tests to identify gifted and talented students who will enter **kindergarten** at the beginning of the academic year. There is no charge for these tests. One is the Otis Lennon School Ability Test – 8th Edition (OLSAT- 8). The other is the Naglieri Nonverbal Ability Test (NNAT2). Children who score between 90% and 96% on these tests will be placed in schools with gifted classrooms. Children scoring 97% or above are placed in one of several **elite public schools** where the **entire** student body is recognized as gifted and talented. Parents are notified of the results in April of the year when their child will enter school.

As to be expected, there is **intense competition** for these public school slots. Internet websites list test preparation guides. Some parents act as tutors for their own children. Other parents enroll their **preschoolers** in a **test preparation program.** Students are reevaluated after third grade with math and reading tests in order to continue in the high level programs for fourth and fifth grade. It seems that middle school programs for gifted and talented are largely nonexistent. Parents seek alternatives.

Advisory #2. By way of contrast, the School District of Palm Beach County, Florida offers fulltime gifted programs to children in kindergarten through eighth grade. Once children are identified as gifted, they are eligible to retain their placement in the program throughout middle school without being reevaluated. Not all Florida counties offer fulltime programs.

Advisory #3. Some school districts *across the country* have no funding for gifted programs. In others, their gifted programs offer only part-time access with little substance.

Advisory #4. Parents of gifted students in some school districts may be entitled to choose which school they deem best for their children instead of sending them to the school officially assigned to their neighborhood.

Advisory #5. Because gifted students grasp concepts quickly, they can work at a rapid pace rather than wait for lengthy explanations given to other students who require more time in processing the information. Ideally, gifted classes offer opportunities for higher order thinking where topics can be studied in depth. Teachers who are themselves gifted may easily understand their gifted students along with their occasional idiosyncratic methods of approaching a topic.

Advisory #6. In a number of situations, however, teachers of gifted classes lack proper training or fall short in their own intellectual abilities. Students may be brighter than their teachers who fail to present appropriate challenges in the classroom. Gifted students may become discouraged for lack of quality instruction. It is advisable for their parents to talk to other parents whose children have taken classes in previous years with such teachers. They may be helpful in pursuing realistic options before making drastic schedule changes.

Advisory #7. Teachers are sometimes concerned that gifted students who have attended the same classes together from elementary school through middle school tend to stay within their own gifted clique to the exclusion of other students. Parents need to make certain that their children have diversified experiences with children outside of the gifted program so that they will have a balanced social life and that they do not belong to a *coterie of intellectual snobs.* Bearing this in mind, some parents of gifted students prefer not to

place their children in gifted programs but opt instead for heterogeneity.

Advisory #8. Wearing the label of gifted does **not** guarantee success in the classroom. There are many gifted *underachievers* who perform poorly in school. In observing those students carefully, their teachers recognize that they have the natural ability to achieve academic success. But, in fact, they put forth no effort and earn bad grades. They are *mysteriously* challenging to parents and teachers. When I was teaching classes of gifted students, I met concerned parents of underachieving gifted students. They knew only too well that their other children, classified as *average* or *above average,* were achieving more success in school and seemed better adjusted than their gifted child.

In that same vein, I have talked with several teachers of the gifted who confessed to me that they would unquestionably choose to work with a student who had been placed in a *regular* or *advanced* class rather than work with a *nonperforming gifted* student. Their job in those situations could be daunting. It is a matter of continually striving to determine what works for those students without giving up.

Sometimes emotional problems are at the root of nonperformance. With the proper blend of teachers, counselors, and a stimulating curriculum something may click to spark student interest and promote a change of course. The secret is to find that *right combination.* For some students, it may not be found within the classroom.

Schools officials hope to prevent gifted students from dropping out of school. Yet, it cannot be denied that there are those nonperforming gifted students who have achieved phenomenal success *outside* of the academic arena at another time and place.

Advisory #9. In another category of students officially identified as gifted, there are students who try to keep up with their classmates but are unable to do so. When I first encountered students of this type in my middle school gifted classes, I checked out their IQ scores and then spoke to the coordinator of the gifted program. She explained to me that it was not uncommon for students to meet the gifted criteria when they were four years of age because, at that time, they were highly verbal youngsters. Verbal ability was *heavily weighted* in their early evaluations. It seems, however, that the IQ score can at times be a misidentification, not an accurate measure of their ability, rather something akin to a *false positive.*

As time wears on, the performance of these students consistently levels off at the average range. This incongruity presents problems. Parents, in denial, often blame teachers for their children's inability to maintain the rapid pace of their gifted classmates.

The *good news* for persistent Florida parents, however, is that once a child is labeled as gifted, the child cannot be forced to exit the program for nonperformance. The *bad news,* for the children in this category, is experiencing the frustration of lagging behind their *whizz-kid classmates,* no matter how much effort they expend.

Advisory #10. When two or more children in the same family are tested for gifted, and one of the children fails to achieve the qualifying placement score, that child can feel dejected and diminished in stature. A parent must consider this possibility and decide if it is worth going forward with the test in case of such a result.

No matter how much a parent attempts to sugar coat the rejection, sensitive children may carry with them a lingering feeling of inferiority in comparison to their siblings. Parental wisdom, as always, is needed in deciding what is best for each child.

Advisory #11. It is important to realize that a child may be classified as gifted but also have a learning disability. These categories are not mutually exclusive. Both types of students fall under the umbrella of Exceptional Student Education **(ESE)** and as such are legally entitled to a number of academic protections. In 1973, when I worked as a teaching intern in Cohasset, Massachusetts, there was one student in my class who was classified as a gifted student with *dyslexic dysgraphia.* Along with his high **IQ,** he had extreme difficulty with handwriting—so much so, that it was classified as a learning disability. Accommodations were made for him. Whereas other students wrote research papers by hand or typed them, he had permission to dictate his work into a tape recorder.

Advisory #12. The School District of Palm Beach County addresses *acceleration* in its Gifted Education Handbook,

"The goals of acceleration are to adjust the pace of instruction to the student's performance capability, to provide an appropriate challenge, and to reduce the amount of time in classes/subjects in which the student has achieved mastery." [20]

Like Palm Beach County high schools, the majority of high schools across the country do not offer classes geared solely for gifted students. Gifted and advanced students alike can take Advanced Placement **(AP)** classes which may serve them well. If those classes are not sufficiently challenging, students can find *alternative* routes to advanced study via many *nationwide magnet programs* such as those offered through the School District of Palm Beach County **(APPENDIX B).**

If those classes are still not demanding enough, students can make arrangements to be dually enrolled in both high school and college at the same time, depending on where they live and what programs are available near their home.

As an example, the **Florida Atlantic University High School (FAU HS)** offers such a program to students in ninth through twelfth grades. Although located in Palm Beach County, the program does not fall under the School District of Palm Beach County.

The school is part of the state university system. Students enter the program in ninth grade and can begin taking college level classes in tenth grade. By the end of the four years, some students have earned their college degree. Almost all of the students complete three years of college within that time frame, and they will need one more year to earn a baccalaureate degree. That fifth year is considered to be outside of the official **FAU HS** program.

One of my friend's daughters graduated from this program. She earned a four-year college degree when she was eighteen years old. After waiting three years, she applied to law school and was accepted at two of the *nation's top schools.*

As one can readily see, there are *pros* and *cons* with respect to such rapid advancement. Some students would be emotionally and socially immature for this type of acceleration. Correspondingly, parents may simply want their children to have a more traditional college experience in keeping with their long held views.

Others students thrive in this kind of environment and don't want to waste time with extended study schedules. Moreover, in this case, the fast lane can drastically reduce the financial burden that an undergraduate education imposes. For its program, **FAU** charges no fees for tuition or books. At this time, there is a *minimal* activity fee and a *nominal* parking fee.

APPENDIX B

Public School Programs – Palm Beach County, Florida

The following list is a **sampling** of public school programs offered in Palm Beach County, Florida, that may exist in other Florida counties and in many other counties throughout the United States with the same or similar titles. Details can be reviewed on their respective websites. Where applicable, I have included at least one representative school for each program listed. **Parents** need to do their **homework** to find the right program for their child.

1. PRE-KINDERGARTEN PROGRAMS

a. **Early Headstart** (Birth - Age 3).

b. **Pre-school Headstart** (Ages 3 - 5).

Both of these Pre-K programs are available for low income families. Make certain that in whatever type of daycare you place your child, the caregivers offer reading preparatory activities. For the good of your child, it is best that you supplement those activities as needed with the suggestions offered in **TIP #3.**

Early childhood education experts refer to pre-reading activities as emerging literacy. Before enrolling your child in a daycare, **observe** the caregivers closely to determine how they interact with the preschoolers. You may find that they are merely biding their time until the end of the day and show no genuine interest in the children.

c. **Early Steps** (Birth - Age 3). This program is part of Florida's Early Intervention Program funded by the **Individuals with**

Disabilities Education Act **(IDEA)** and administered by Children's Medical Services, Department of Health. Referrals for the following services are often made by pediatricians: Physical Therapy **(PT)**, Occupational Therapy **(OT)**, Speech and Language Therapy **(SLT)** or Special Instruction **(SI)** which addresses behavioral problems.

d. Child Find (Birth - Age 21). The **IDEA** requires all schools both public and private to identify and evaluate all children with disabilities.

e. Florida Diagnostic & Learning Resources System (FDLRS). This program provides support services for exceptional students. It works in conjunction with **Child Find**.

f. Voluntary Pre-Kindergarten (VPK). This free program, *not based on family income,* is available in Florida and certain other states. It is generally required that the child be at least four years old on or before the first of September.

g. Voluntary Pre-Kindergarten Specialized Instructional Services Education Program (VPKSIS).

This program is designed for children with *special needs*. For eligibility, children need an Individual Education Plan **(IEP)** from their local school district. **Child Find** may assist in this identification process.

h. Pre-school Montessori Magnet Program (Ages 3 - 5). Northboro Elementary School. West Palm Beach. This program follows the educational philosophy of Maria Montessori.

2. ELEMENTARY SCHOOL PROGRAMS

a. Dual Language - English/Spanish. Liberty Park Elementary School. Greenacres. Palm Beach County offers its preferred model of this program in a number of schools. Several states

have other models offering partial to full immersion in the foreign language. These programs nurture bilingualism, as they teach literacy and content in two languages.

b. International Baccalaureate Primary Years Programme (IBPYP). Morikami Park Elementary School. Delray Beach.

c. Math/Science Magnet. Pine Jog Elementary School. West Palm Beach.

d. Montessori Magnet. S.D. Spady Elementary School. Delray Beach.

e. Orchestral Strings. Palm Beach Public Elementary School. Palm Beach.

f. Science/Math Magnet. Poinciana Elementary School. Boynton Beach.

g. Technology Magnet. Boca Raton Elementary School. Boca Raton.

h. The Conservatory School @ North Palm Beach (TCS). El Sistema Music Model. Formerly North Palm Beach Elementary School, this facility planned at the outset to house *Kindergarten - Grade Eight* for students in the **Choice** music program by the academic year 2016 - 2017.

3. MIDDLE SCHOOL PROGRAMS

a. Biomedical Sciences. Lake Worth Middle School. Lake Worth.

b. 1) Communication Arts. 2) Music-Vocal. 3) Theatre. 4) Visual Arts. Palm Springs Middle School. Palm Springs.

c. Dual Language Program - English/Spanish. Conniston Middle School. West Palm Beach.

d. International Baccalaureate Middle Years Programme (IBMYP). John F. Kennedy Middle School. Riviera Beach, *Grades Six - Eight,* extending into **High Schools** for *Grades Nine - Ten* until the full IB Program takes over in *Grades Eleven - Twelve.*

e. International Spanish Academy. Okeeheelee Middle School. Green Acres.

f. Leadership Academy for Young Men (African American/ Afro Centric Studies). Roosevelt Middle School. West Palm Beach.

g. Literary and Fine Arts—Writing & Literature. Watson B. Duncan Middle School. Palm Beach Gardens.

h. Pre-Biotechnology. Bear Lakes Middle School. West Palm Beach.

i. Pre-Culinary Arts. Eagles Landing Middle School. Boca Raton.

j. Pre-Engineering. Congress Middle School. Boynton Beach.

k. Pre-Medical Sciences Magnet. Western Pines Community Middle School. West Palm Beach.

l. 1) Pre-Teacher Education. 2) Band. 3) Dance. Lantana Middle School. Lantana.

m. Science/Math Magnet. Howell L. Watkins Middle School. Palm Beach Gardens.

n. Technology. Jupiter Middle School. Jupiter.

4. HIGH SCHOOL PROGRAMS

a. 1) Center for Pre-Law. 2) Medical Magnet. 3) Teacher's Academy. Palm Beach Lakes Community High School. West Palm Beach.

b. 1) Environmental Research & Field Studies Academy. 2) Medical Magnet. 3) Multimedia Magnet. 4) Technology Magnet. Jupiter High School. Jupiter.

c. Equine/Pre-Veterinarian Academy. Wellington Community High School. Wellington.

d. International Baccalaureate Program (IBP). Suncoast Community High School. Riviera Beach. In addition to the standard diploma, students can earn an **Advanced Placement International Diploma (APID)** or an **International Baccalaureate Diploma (IBD).**

The **IBP** is found in schools throughout the country and worldwide. Other schools in Palm Beach County offering the **IBD** are Atlantic High School, Forest Hill High School, William T. Dwyer High School, and Pahokee Middle-Senior High School.

As referenced in **TIP #7.3e,** Suncoast Community High School offers three additional magnet programs: **1) Computer Science (CS), 2) Innovative Interactive Technology (IIT), and 3) Math, Science & Engineering (MSE).**

e. Medical Magnet. John I Leonard High School. West Palm Beach.

f. Performing Arts Magnet. Alexander W. Dreyfoos School of the Arts. West Palm Beach.

g. Science & Math Magnet. Spanish River Community High School. Boca Raton.

h. Technology Magnet. Don Estridge High Tech Middle School. Boca Raton.

i. Additional high school programs include but are not limited to **Aerospace, Animation, Auto Collision and Mechanics, Biomedical, Construction, Engineering, Fashion Design, International Spanish, Robotics, and Sports Management.**

j. Schools offer instruction in a number of languages to include **American Sign Language, Chinese, French, Haitian Creole, Italian, Latin, Spanish.**

5. UNIVERSITY EARLY ENROLLMENT PROGRAM

Florida Atlantic University High School (FAU HS). Boca Raton. [Referenced in **APPENDIX A, Advisory #12**]. This program is part of the state university system. Students start participating in the program in *Grade Nine* and begin taking college level classes in *Grade Ten.* Some students graduate with a baccalaureate degree after four years. A majority of the students complete three full years of college at the end of *Grade Twelve.* A fifth year, not part of the official program, is needed to earn the degree.

6. OTHER PROGRAMS, CERTIFICATES, EXAMINATIONS

a. Advanced International Certificate of Education (AICE). Wellington Community High School. Wellington.

Many other states in addition to Florida participate in the **AICE** program. It offers an international diploma administered by a non-profit department of the **University of Cambridge** in England, entitled **Cambridge International Examinations (CIE).** Students choosing to earn this diploma usually begin in the ninth grade. According to current information posted on the **Cambridge AICE Diploma** website, more than 500 universities

accept **Cambridge** qualifications, including all Ivy League universities as well as Stanford University and Massachusetts Institute of Technology.

On that same website, Stuart Schmill, Dean of Admissions at MIT, has stated that,

> *"One of the things we find with students who have studied Cambridge International AS and A Levels is that they have a real depth of understanding on the subject matter that they have had classes in, and a real engagement with it."* [21]

b. Advancement Via Individual Determination (AVID). This program, offered in seventeen schools in Palm Beach County, is described as follows on the website of the School District of Palm Beach County:

"AVID targets students in the academic middle — B, C, and even D students — who have the desire to go to college along with the willingness to work hard. Potential AVID students are capable of completing a rigorous curriculum but are falling short of their potential. AVID pulls these students out of their unchallenging courses and puts them on the college track: acceleration instead of remediation." [22]

c. Take Stock in Children (TSIC). West Palm Beach. This successful venture is a statewide program that begins at the middle school level and is designed to help low-income, at-risk students get to college:

"Incorporated in 1995 and maintaining a 94 percent high school graduation rate, TSIC is Florida's flagship and most successful mentoring and scholarship program. In every Florida county, TSIC scholars in middle and high school pledge to meet regularly with their mentor, maintain academic standards, and remain drug and crime-free on the way to achieving a high school diploma. The reward for fulfilling these commitments is a four-year scholarship to a Florida state college, university or vocational school." [23]

Well organized, the program does what it purports to do. One of my friend's children participated in this project and was awarded a four-year college scholarship after high school

as part of the Florida Prepaid College Foundation. With its meritorious goals & continuing accomplishments, this program is inspirational. **TSIC** deserves high praise.

In summation, the preceding compendium offers a partial list of outstanding **choice programs** within The School District of Palm Beach County. For a comprehensive review, refer to the district's website: www.palmbeachschools.org. Your state will offer similar public programs promoting excellence for your children.

Citations & Reference Notes

1. Rosenberg, T. (2013, April 14). The power of talking to your baby. *The New York Times; New York edition, SR8.*

2. Handheld screen time linked with speech delays in young children. Web article. *AAP News.* American Academy of Pediatrics. May 4, 2017.

3. Mann, D. [Martin L., M.D reviewer]. (2013, January 3). Babies listen and learn while in the womb. *WebMD Health News.*

4. Gurfein, M. W. Ibid.

5. Singer, D. G. and Revensen, T. A. (1996). *A Piaget primer: How a child thinks.* A PLUME BOOK. Published by the Penguin Group. New York, NY, 41 – 52.

6. Isenberg & Jacobs (1982). *Playthings as learning tools.* John Wiley & Sons, Incorporated: New York, NY.

7. Wolfgang, C. H. & Sanders, T. S. (1981). Defending young children's play as the ladder to literacy. *Theory Into Practice, 20 (2) 116-120.*

8. Isenberg & Jacobs (1982). Ibid.

9. Adcock & Segal. (1983). *Play together grow together.* Mailman Family Press: White Plains, NY.

Note: In academic dissertations, it is customary to offer research with recent publication dates, but for this book, I chose to include References #4 - #8 above because their content is universal, timeless, and essential for understanding the world of young children. *Similarly,* the following series on *Play* by Marilyn Segal, Ph.D, published in 1999, by Newmarket

Press, New York, NY., is considered a classic in the field of early childhood development.

Dr. Segal, now deceased, was the mother of **nine** children, a distinguished developmental psychologist, a dynamic child advocate, and my *first teacher* in my doctoral program at Nova Southeastern University.

Your child at play: *Birth to one year - discovering the senses and learning about the world.*

Your child at play: *One to two years - exploring learning, making friends and pretending.*

Your child at play: *Two to three years - growing up, language, and the imagination.*

Your child at play: *Three to five years - conversation, creativity, and learning letters, words, and numbers.*

10. Trelease, J. (2013). ***The read-aloud hand book.*** Penguin Books; Seventh Edition. New York, NY.

11. Thelma B. Pittman Jupiter Preschool, named after its late founder, took shape in the 1960s. Its beloved founder was a visionary. She brought out the best in all of the children and their families who came from diverse racial and economic backgrounds. As part of my doctoral program, I installed a lending library in the preschool. I solicited community groups for funding and wrote grants to earn money for books.

Volunteers built book shelves and a large checkout counter complete with a drop slot for books. All preschoolers had a personalized library card in the form of a book with a photo of themselves reading in the library.

With my initiative, the director created a scholarship for college-bound high school graduates who had also been

TBP Preschool graduates. The preschool and its traditions continue today under the strong leadership of Ruth Lawson, daughter of its founder, along with a dedicated Board of Directors.

12. Dupuis B. and Ryan S. (1991). *I'm a Pro! Preschooler reading often.* Riviera Beach, FL.

13. The School District of Palm Beach County through its Office of Public Relations Management released these figures as of 10-8-15: Number of students: 183,000; Number of Psychologists: ninety-four full time; four half time.

14. Cupples, Mrs. G. (1872). *Tappy's chicks and other links between nature and human nature.* Strahan & Co. Publishers. Ludgate Hill, London.

15. The Young Adult Library Services Association **(YALSA)** of the American Library Association **(ALA)** defines a young adult as someone between the ages of twelve and eighteen, while **Teen Fiction** is written for the ages of ten to fifteen; *WIKIPEDIA*.

16. Ross, A. (2016). *The industries of the future.* New York, NY: Simon & Schuster.

17. An ongoing desire for learning may be seen among retirees who enthusiastically attend lifelong learning seminars in great numbers. One example of such a program is *The Lifelong Learning Society* of Florida Atlantic University where experts in a variety of fields offer a series of invigorating lectures at both the Jupiter and Boca Raton locations.

18. Website: Tall Clubs International. tall.org/tci-cts/scholarships-2/.

19. *Knowledge is power* - The English version of this phrase is credited to Thomas Jefferson in 1817 and 1820, in the *Thomas Jefferson Encyclopedia* available at the *Thomas Jefferson Website,* www.

monticello.org/site/jefferson. Prior to that, Francis Bacon wrote similar sentiments in Latin in 1597, in *Meditaciones Sacrae* as did Thomas Hobbes in his *Leviathan* in 1651.

20. *Gifted Education Handbook.* School District of Palm Beach County, p. 31.

21. Website: **Cambridge Advanced International Certificate of Education (AICE) Diploma.** www.cie.org.uk/programmes-qualifications-advanced/cambridge-aice-diploma/.

[There are two levels of study: (a) Advanced—Subsidiary, (b) Advanced—More difficult.]

22. Website: **Advancement Via Individual Determination (AVID).** School District of Palm Beach County, Florida. www.palmbeachschools.org.

23. Website: **Take Stock in Children (TSIC)** www.takestockinchildren.org.